# KAMCHACHA
## Rhodesian Game Ranger

Bryan Orford

Copyright © Text and Pictures, Bryan Orford

All rights reserved

No part of this publication may be reproduced, or stored in a retrieval system, or transmitted, in any form by any means, whether electronic, mechanical, photocopying, recording, or otherwise, without written permission from the author.

ISBN 0-7974-3122-5

E-mail bush@netconnect.co.zw

First printed in Bulawayo, Zimbabwe 2008

## INTRODUCTION & ACKNOWLEDGMENTS

Thomas Patrick Orford was a true conservationist, who protected and preserved African wildlife throughout his years. Tom like many bush folk had an unusual life and it is worth putting on record. He may not have been the greatest hunter or conservationist, but he has left his mark and few could deny he had character. The main daily newspaper in Zimbabwe, the Herald, showed his picture at least 5 times and he is pictured in LIFE magazine. He has been mentioned in over ten books to date and the number is growing. Kamchacha as he was called by the black tribesman, mixed with prime ministers, politicians, game rangers, scientists, pioneers, ranchers, housewives, tribesmen, poachers, all and sundry. These colourful people have added extra drama to his story, giving us a taste of the character and life of those times.

Many of the stories are anecdotes from Tom and his contemporaries and recorded as I heard them. Some of the stories may have been told in more detail elsewhere and may be slightly different. I have tried to keep it as historical and chronological as possible and hopefully the stories are error free and the contributors made no mistakes. Some spellings of places may have old names in the text and I apologise if there is any name of any person which might be incorrect. I have tried to protect certain people and some words or phrases in quotation marks indicate a possible exaggeration. I take no responsibility for omissions, additions, exaggerations, poor English or mistakes that may have crept in from the many contributors. I am simply a youngster listening to old timers and am really no expert about what happened before I was even thought about! I just hope you enjoy the book, learn something and have a good laugh.

This biography of collected anecdotes and stories could not have been done without the help of those mentioned in this book. I would like to thank all who contributed, some reluctantly and some enthusiastically. Thanks to Dawn Field (Orford) and Colin Harrison for the many hours they toiled over the text, correcting so many mistakes.

I would like to thank Adrian Reed, Albert Chauke, Alan Elliot, Alan Jones, Alan Shaw, Alan Savory, Alex Inggs, Annabelle Hill, Arthur Wood, Ashley Lay, Barry Duckworth, Barry & Mary Ball, Basil Stein, Bengani Nyambe, Ben Kaschula, Bill Taylor, Bob Truman, Bobby & Keith Young, Bobby Thomson, Bob Cole, Bob Gawler, Brian and Shirley Mitchell, Brian Hughes, Brian Sherry, Bruce Couper, Buck de Vries, Charley Davey, Charlie Mackie, Chris Foggin, Chris van Wyk, Christine Fothergill, Clem Coetsee, Clive Lennox, Clive Stockill, Colin Bickle, Colin Saunders, Crawford Nish, Dan & Joss Landrey, Dave Blake, Dave Rushworth, Dave Scott-Donelan, Derick Sibanda, Dick Nash, Dion Bolt, Don Broadley, Don Price, Don Stott, Douglas Khumalo, Dudley Rogers, Elaine Bosman, Elf Gifford, Ernie Van Staden, Fiona Wilmot, Frank & Jean Junor, Fred Agree, Gary Hopkins, Gail Amyot, G.K Atkinson, George Enslin, George Style, Gil Orr, Glen Tatham, Gordan Cormack, Gordon Haines, Graham Child, Graham Hall, Graham Jardine, Graham Paxton, Hannes Wessels, Hans van der Heiden, Heron Gonde, Hienie & Mary Stanger, Hilary Drysdale (Fothergill), Hoffman van Zyl, Howard Shackleton, Ian Henderson, Ian King, Ian Lennox, Ian Nyschens, Ian Player, Ian Salt, Ian van Heerden, Ian van der Lingen, Jackie Pringle (Myberg), Jackson Masuku, James

Lapinsky, Jan Savory, Jeremy Anderson, Jeremy Winch, Jerry Rubenstein, Jerry Wilding, John & Rusty Hatton, John Gifford, John Herbert, John Osborne, John Stevens, Johnny van der Meulen, John White, Johnny Johnson, Jordie Jordaan, Joyce Bristow, Kate Reese, Ken Drummond, Ken Orford, Ken Mcdonald, Kerry Kay, Kevin Heasman, Kevin Thomas, Kevin White, Keith Meadows, Kobus du Toit, Kwanele, Louis Myberg, Mac Gloss, Malcolm King, Maluti, Margaret Peach (Haslam), Mark Brightman, Mark Butcher, Martin Fothergill, Martin Nel, Mike Bromwich, Mike Bunce, Mike Clark, Mike & Jenny Fynn, Mike Scott, Mitch Drummond, Mike Le Grange, Moses Magavadhera, Mr. Oosthuizen, Nick Marsberg, Noel Swart, Owen Shaw, Paddy Curtis, Paddy Orford, Pat Austen, Paul Coetsee, Paul Connelly, Paul McKay, Pebbles Williamson, Peter Abbot, Peter Johnstone, Peter & Pat Wright, Peter Thomson, Phil Nel, Pierce Taylor, Ralph Ferreira, Ray Sparrow, Richard Amyot, Richard Aylward, Richard de Angelo, Richard Peek, Richard Smith, Rob Austen, Robert Matanodza, Rob & Paddy Francis, Rob Gee, Rob Hopkins, Rod Evans, Roger Greef, Roger Savory, Roger Whittal, Ronnie van Heerden, Ron Thomson, Roy Killick, Sam the tracker, Samson Ndhlovu, Sandie Cox, Sandy Innes, Scott Bailie, Shielagh Van Reenen (Orford), Sir Roy Welenksy, Stan Elliot, Sue Thomas, Terry Fenn, Tim Braybrooke, Toney Davey, Toney de Boyce, Tony Ferrar, Tony Osborne, Tony Seward, Tora Balance, Trevor Edwards, Trish Tomlinson, Van Vuurens, Vernon Booth, Viv Wilson, Wally Herbst, Wayne Grant, Wally Lacey, Willie de Beer, Jeff Calvert, Wilson Zano, Yunnie Karessolos

Others helped in various ways and I would like to thank them for their contributions. The photographs with no credits showed in this book, are from the Orford collection. I have purposely placed many of them in the book, as a 'picture is worth a thousand words'. Tom took most of these. I took some, while others were probably taken with his camera, although he may have collected a few.

The book cover has a picture of Natal Parks catching white rhino in 1962 to translocate to Rhodesia. Ian Player is behind, bending down (squatting) appears to be Nick Steele tying the rope and the game scout looks like Magqubu Ntombela. The lower picture shows Tom bathing in a water trough while in the Game Department. The back page shows Johnny Folomani with the pack of hunting dogs Ketch, Bingo, Neffies, Tiger, Joe and Buster on Nuanetsi Ranch. The lower picture is of Rupert Fothergill releasing an antelope on Operation

Noah. The last picture is by Ronald Hadden for the Ministry of Information.

Also references:
- Animal Dunkirk - Eric Robins & Ronald Legge (especially 1959).
- Rhodesian Farmer 4th Jan 1963, 1st July 1961, 28th Oct 1960, 28th Nov 1958
- Parks Reports
- Population status, sexual behaviour, and daily activity pattern of the white rhino in Kyle NP - P.R Condy
- Sunday Mail May 14 1978
- Margaret Peach (Haslam) - My place in the Sun & personal discussion
- Graham Child – Behaviour of large mammals during the formation of lake Kariba & personal discussion
- Operation Dragon Rouge - Randy Moorehead
- Operation white rhino – Ken Rochat and Nick Steele
- Fort Victoria News 2/3/62, 7/9/62, 23/11/62, 16/11/62, 9/2/61 & 19/11/71
- Chronicle 7 Aug 1962
- Natures Paradise – Jen and Des Bartlett
- The Far Interior – Edward C Tabler
- Randy Moorehead From Simbas to Ninjas: Congo's Magic Warriors (2003)- Richard Petraitis
- The Herald 18/7/65, 14/8/65 and 22/6/73 Colin Neilson
- The Lowdown - Article by Mike Roscoe
- A Population crash of the reedbuck Redunca Arundinum in Kyle National Park Rhodesia by Antony Ferrar and Michael Kerr.

One of the great callings in life is to preserve the wonders of God's creation around us. I would like to dedicate this book to the men and women of the Rhodesian Game Department and Rhodesia's National Parks who have played their part. They did a great pioneering role in game capture, the scientific management of wildlife and game farming. They helped save people and animals, dealt with marauding elephants, killed man-eaters, crop and livestock destroyers and arrested criminals. They started many of our great parks and hunting areas that now cover a large part of Zimbabwe. Through their heroism on Operation Noah, they made it a noble act to save wild animals and stimulated conservation in Africa. Without saying too much now, I suggest you read on and follow the story of Tom's life.

# CONTENTS

| | | |
|---|---|---|
| 1. | YOUNG AT HEART 1934-1953 | 6 |
| 2. | NUANETSI 1953-1955 | 19 |
| 3. | THE GAME DEPARTMENT 1955-1960 | 33 |
| 4. | ELEPHANTS 1955-1963 | 50 |
| 5. | WANKIE EARLY DAYS 1958-1963 | 59 |
| 6. | OPERATION NOAH 1959-1963 | 72 |
| 7. | KYLE 1960-1966 | 90 |
| 8. | RHINO 1959-1968 | 107 |
| 9. | GONA RE ZHOU 1957-1964 | 122 |
| 10. | BIRCHENOUGH 1964-1965 | 135 |
| 11. | WANKIE CULLING AND CAPTURE 1966-1968 | 147 |
| 12. | WANKIE & GWAAI 1966-1968 | 162 |
| 13. | ROVING WARDEN 1965-1972 | 178 |
| 14. | MABALAUTA 1972-1976 | 194 |
| 15. | COMBAT 1961-1979 | 213 |
| 16. | THE WHEELS FALL OFF 1976-1978 | 235 |
| 17. | ADRENALINE TIMES 1978-1982 | 246 |
| 18. | THE QUIET YEARS 1982-1986 | 261 |
| 19. | WATERFORD 1987-1994 | 275 |
| 20. | THE OLD DAGA BOY 1995-2004 | 292 |

*Birchenough Bridge 1933, the bridge almost finished, PHOTO Stanger family*

## CHAPTER 1
# YOUNG AT HEART 1934-1953

### *His Grandparents*
Tom would often joke that his Irish grandfather was a sheep thief. The story went that he was either unceremoniously expelled to darkest Africa, or decided it was a good idea to come out to Africa to avoid arrest. In fact, Thomas Patrick Orford (Dominic) did quite well in South Africa. He married an Afrikaans girl named Gertrude. Gertrude was either the sister or niece of Catherina (Cato) Petronella Smuts, who was the mother of the South African Prime Minister Jan Christian Smuts. Dominic lived in Petrusville, Seymour and Kimberly. At one time he owned some racing stables, but then proceeded to gamble his wealth away. Thomas Patrick Orford (Pat) was born to the couple in 1904. Things took at a turn for the worse one day, when Pat was 12 and his father Dominic came to him and said, "Patrick get dressed; your mother has died." She had a rheumatic heart and passed away at the young age of 33. Later on Dominic died, when he was run over by an ox wagon in the Karoo.

### *His Parents*
Pat and his sister Eileen lived at Petrusville in the Cape Province

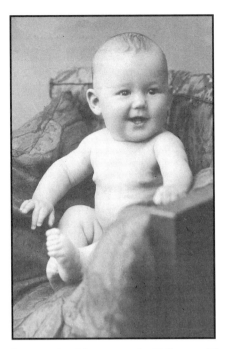

*At 9 months Tom wins 1st prize in baby competition!*

before moving to Bloemfontein. It was there that, with their cousin Lily Fourie, Pat and Eileen were taken under the wing of an aunt, whilst still in their early teens. Lily became a 'sister' to them and they remained 'family' for the rest of their lives. Lily's brother John held a senior position on the South African Railways and while stationed at Bloemfontein he helped Pat join the clerical staff there. Circa 1930 Pat met Olive who lived in a reasonably large; double story building with her parents, who utilized the premises as a boarding house. Eventually, Pat married Olive, while Eileen married a sheep farmer named Samie de Jager. Unfortunately Eileen could not have children.

## *The Stangers*

Lily married Edmund Stanger, who loved shooting springbok for biltong on Samie's farm. Edmund was an Austrian German by birth who happened to be in South Africa at the outbreak of World War One. Being German, he was interned at Fort Napier. He loved South Africa and decided to stay on after the war ended. He was a multi talented man who spoke German, Afrikaans, English, was good with Latin and knew some of the local languages. In addition, he was a brilliant craftsman as well as a good oil painter. He may even have painted at Fort Napier while he was imprisoned there. While in the German army, Edmund acquired a love for guns and later he had a good selection of 'very' German guns. He hunted in the North East Transvaal using the traditional ox wagon and horses and it was this idyllic hobby that he continued later, when he eventually settled in Rhodesia. The Stangers moved their family up to Rhodesia in the

1930's and after having a good look around in different parts of Mashonaland, they decided on a farm at Rusape. The farm Chimbi Source reminded Edmund of home and it was a beautiful bit of country. He didn't know too much about farming, but he did know a lot about cheese and his expertise was soon put to work developing a successful dairy.

### *Enter Tom*
Pat and Olive produced three children: Tommy (another Thomas Patrick), Ken and Sheilagh. Tommy was born in 1934 in Bloemfontein. He was brought to his mom black and blue and in a very sorry shape. Some damage was done to him with the instruments, which caused a nervous twitch on the one side of his face. Tom was to spend his childhood in Johannesburg. He grew into a good-looking baby and when 9 months old won first prize in a baby competition.

### *The Brothers*
Tom was really a very gentle person, much like his father and being a good boy rarely got into a serious argument, let alone a fistfight or brawl. When he and Ken were at a kids' party in Johannesburg, he accidentally pushed Ken over a rockery and broke his arm. While Ken was very proud of his newly plastered arm, Tommy could not accept that it was an accident and cried for three days. On another occasion the young brothers were in their Sunday best of white shorts, white socks and white shirts with little red bows. They were on their way back from Sunday school, when they came to a shop selling ladies underwear. In the window display was some not so dainty ladies wear, of a "grotty" pink and mostly ugly form. Ken pointed to a large bra and laughed saying, "Ha, ha, ha, look at those titty bags!" Tommy wanted to clout him. One word led to another and the two boys climbed into each other and their Sunday best soon ended up a dirty white.

### *Joburg*
Some of their childhood was spent in Johannesburg where Tommy attended Kensington Ridge Junior School before going to Jeppe Boys High. Tommy's young sister was very proud of him when he once had the main part in the school play and showed his great acting talent as Sherlock Holmes. He had his deer-hunting cap, dressing gown and

*Crossing the Sabi River at Birchenough Bridge using oxen, PHOTO Stanger family*

strode around saying, "Elementary, my dear Watson." He also had some aptitude for poetry and this remained a passion for the rest of his life. School wasn't easy for Tommy, being English among so many tough Afrikaner boys. At one time the other kids got their hands on him and gave him a good hiding. Ken had the same problem and also had his share of fistfights and on one occasion turned the tables on his bully. Ken, who was younger than the bully, who had started the fight, managed to get on top of the boy and was beating his head with a brick before Tom stepped in to stop the fight.

### *Rusape Interlude*

From a very early age the Orfords went up to Rhodesia to stay with the Stangers on their holidays. When Tom was about 5-6 years old he lived on the farm at Rusape for about a year. Here Lily Stanger, who was a teacher, taught him through correspondence school. Edmund Stanger (known to Tommy as Oupa) was vitally interested in wildlife and the bush. He soon realized that Tommy was also very interested in all things wild. This was the beginning of Tom's education by Edmund who was one of the greatest influences on his life. Tom would watch Edmund shoot guinea fowl, baboons, springhares and dassies, which were then used to make karosses. Tom was not yet allowed to shoot a weapon, but he desperately wanted to hunt springhares. He saw older folk going after the springhares and he longed to join in, but was told he was too small to hold a gun. His response was simply, "No you hold and I'll shoot." Despite this, he was told it would take a long time before he could hold a .22 rifle or an air gun and shoot his first springhare. So he devised his own scheme to catch these bouncing rodents. He would go to a springhare hole, wait for one to leave and ambush it when it returned. He asked Edmund if he could do this and with Edmund and Lily's permission he was allowed to carry out his plan, but only if the garden boy Zimbayi went with him. Tom did not like this at all, because he felt that Zimbayi was too big and the springhare would not come out of the hole. Two weeks later Tom went about building a hide with grass. The new plan was that when the springhare came out he was going rush up and close the hole and then chase the springhare with the dogs. Zimbayi was instructed to sit in a tree and quietly observe the scene. After about two hours they both came back home without a springhare. Tom felt the springhare had 'sensed a rat' because Zimbayi, who was perched in the tree, had moved around too much.

### *Hard times*
During World War 2 Tom had a rough childhood in Johannesburg and it was tough for the whole family. All his Dad's friends were called up for military service, while Pat continued to work for the railways. Many of Pat's friends never came back and Pat became a loner. Pat had been frail and after getting pneumonia went into hospital and subsequently had a reduced income. When he came out of hospital he was broken hearted and the stress nearly killed him. There were financial problems at the time from trying to bring up and educate three children on the lowly salaries of railway clerical staff, compounded by difficult general problems in the country during the war and post-war years. Semi poverty in the country was common at the time and many people were struggling. There was little food on the table and winters were cold. Pat used to put his great coat over the kids to keep them warm. It was a time when top sheets were a luxury and were used only when the doctor came. Even parents would dress well for the doctor's visit. Pat's efforts speak for themselves as Olive never had to go out to work despite all the family tribulations.

### *Socks*
There were lighter times when the boys also got up to mischief. Once, an old man who was a family friend, came to visit their father. As

they were short of a place for him to sleep, they let him have one of the two beds in the boys' room. This meant Ken and Tom had to sleep in the same bed. When darkness shrouded the night, the bed next to theirs began to snore badly. Tom said to Ken, "We can't sleep, because this man is making a noise." After much deliberation, Tom grabbed his school sock and put it in the old man's mouth. Suddenly, the choking man jumped out of the bed. Tom and Ken immediately covered their heads with the blankets and pretended to be asleep. Peeping out cautiously, they noticed the old man's eyes were now wide open. Tom emitted a small laugh and the man asked who had done it. Tom didn't answer. He was too busy chuckling.

### *Sheep Poacher*
The boys often spent their holidays with Aunt Eileen on the Karoo sheep farm and in 1947; Tom and Ken left Johannesburg and stayed there for a considerable period of time. While Tom was here, he went at night and stole a sheep from the nearby farmer. With his friends, both white and coloured boys, they took the sheep into the hills to skin and then braaied the juicy meat. Tom took some of the meat and left portions hanging outside the houses of poor people with a nice message 'written by the farmer!' On Sunday everyone went to church and the poor folk came across and thanked the unknowing rich farmer for his generous gift. Later, when Tom grew up, he went to apologize to this farmer. The man's reply was, "You never killed a sheep here." Tom was then warned, "If you come back, I will hit you with this stick." The two boys went to a little Afrikaans medium boarding school in Petrusville and during the brief time they went there they learnt to speak good Afrikaans.

### *Dassies*
The boys spent some of the time hunting on their uncle's farm in the Karoo. Dassies, at that time, were declared vermin by the state, who paid you 6d (5c) for each full dassie skin produced. Only the head skin was retained by the state – the remainder given back to the hunters for disposal or the making of karosses. Needless to say Tom and Ken were avid hunters of dassies, what with the 'vast' fortunes to be made. At this time, Tom was about 12, Ken about 9 and Sheilagh about 7 years old. All three of them one day set out on a dassie hunt accompanied by their trusty dogs and carrying their clubs. They had decided on a range of kopjes about three miles from the farm. The

*In Joburg 1937, Tom with his mother Olive*

hunt was extremely successful and they caught 7 dassies that would net them the magnificent sum of 35c. The hike back to the farm was exhausting to say the least, particularly as Tom was playing the big White Hunter part to the T. The other two were treated as mere savage bearers and had to do all the carrying. The three miles felt like a hundred to them at the time. For their pains the bearers earned 5c each and the White Hunter earned 25c.

## *Cape Town*
As Pat rose up the ladder, he was continually transferred in the railways and was to eventually end up in Cape Town in 1948, where Tom went to Observatory High. Tom's Mom didn't want them to go there, as she was concerned about the climate affecting Pat's health. But it was Tom who got sick in Cape Town and he was rushed to a Catholic hospital for an operation. The surgeon who worked on Tom was drunk as he took Tom's appendix out. In the operation, part of Tom's spleen was sliced away and to top it all, the surgeon left the swab inside the boy's body. Olive found him very sick and badly infected. Finally, a mother superior, who was also a qualified surgeon, had to do another operation to remove the swab and save Tom. This was one reason why Tom didn't like drunkenness. It took him a while to recover from this operation and he had some stomach problems. Tom never really did like Cape Town.

## *To Rhodesia*
In 1949 Pat decided to move the family to Southern Rhodesia and to seek work on the railways, but the job on the railways did not

*Tom kills a turkey killing eagle at Chimbi Source PHOTO Stanger family*

materialize. When Pat first arrived he needed work and Edmund Stanger offered him work at the Chimbi Source dairy. Later Pat took up a lecturing job at the Salisbury polytechnic. Tommy had always wanted to go to school in Rhodesia and so was delighted to be able to finally attend Prince Edward, a well-known and respected high school in Salisbury. So he finished his schooling at P.E and came to Rusape for the holidays.

### Chimbi

Life at Chimbi was great for the kids. For many years there were no boreholes there and the Stangers could not find underground water, so they used a wagon to bring water to the house. They used a hand pump and a donkey cart with two 44-gallon drums to collect the water. The kids used to help out with this and other farm chores. Even though water was short, aunt Lily made sure everyone was shaven, had clean clothes and clean hands and elbows definitely had to be off the table at dinner. In the evenings Edmund, being a good musician, kept the family amused with the violin and clarinet and the family also learned to entertain themselves with board games such as 'blow football.' It was at Chimbi that all three kids learnt to ride bicycles and here they trundled full speed down to the gum trees, where they fell off and learnt to master wheels.

### Edmund

Edmund Stanger used to go on hunting trips with friends and family by an ox wagon to the Lowveld areas down from Rusape. These trips may well have fuelled Tom's enthusiasm for wild places. Edmund encouraged the love of nature in Tom, with his great stories, details on how to prepare your rifle and aiming techniques, tracking, wind directions and the rest. Like many men of that time, he had shot the odd leopard, small cats, jackals and antelope, but he shot mainly for the pot. Edmund did not shoot for the pleasure of killing. To test his accuracy, he would put up an empty tin, some cardboard on a tree or use a mark on a rock, so earning him the African nickname 'Chibayi matombo'. Tom used to sit and listen to Edmund for hours with his eyes wide open and his ears as well. There were always plenty of questions and in later years, long discussions would take place on which rifle to use, the size of the bullet and other details. Tom would talk enthusiastically and he learnt a great deal about good cameras and guns. If you go to Chimbi Source today, you are most likely to still find the family chasing springhares. Edmund used to shoot troublesome springhares on the run with the help of fox terriers.

## *Farm Life*
Beautiful Chimbi Source was a farm boy's paradise and Tom walked everywhere, either off with his friends or on his own. He used to explore and enjoy the bush, kopjes, ruins, caves and bushman paintings. Edmund was trying to build up his game population, therefore no indiscriminate shooting was allowed and certain places were no go areas. It was only after careful training with the .22 rifle that Tom was allowed to shoot the odd bird and guinea fowl. At this stage Tom was no academic and devoted all his reading to books on cavemen and their hunting methods, big game hunting, early Rhodesia and paradoxically wild life conservation. During his High School days and throughout his life he was totally absorbed in these sorts of subjects. He was an avid reader of such books and while he enjoyed fictional works, he certainly preferred the factual works. Oh yes, he also read a great deal on cowboys. Tom was something of a non-conformist, not necessarily a loner, but with little interest in the normal pursuits of childhood, such as pop-music, soccer, rugby, cricket, marbles, tops, kites or ganging up with friends. He rarely enjoyed boyhood games or pranks and considered Ken and Ken's many friends to be hoodlums or at very least juvenile delinquents. Generally, his tastes in music ran more towards light classic and classic, but never pop-music, which was for 'hoodlums, vagrants, layabouts and juvenile delinquents'. One of Ken's friends here was Tinkey Haslam who was

*Sheilagh, Tom and Ken*

to later join Tom in the Game Department, where they spent many years working together. Tom would sometimes, as a young man, go across on the bicycle to visit the next-door farms. One farm in particular had four girls and was definitely worth a visit.

## Pets

As for pets, well, Ken acquired a pet dassie at Chimbi. He bottle-fed this dassie until it was almost fully grown and it used to follow him around like a dog. His name was 'Das Vuilbaard' (Das Filthy Beard) and he used to sleep with Ken, tucked under Ken's chin. The only problem was that when he felt the call of nature, he would hop off Ken's bed onto Tom's bed, do his business and then hop back onto Ken's bed. Needless to say this was one animal that Tom did not cherish very much. Much to Ken's regret and Tom's delight the house dogs finished him off one day, for no apparent reason. Edmund at one time liked snakes and must have passed the interest on to Tom. Tom kept a pet vine snake for a while, which used to enjoy the warmth of his body and clothes. It was only later that Tom found out it was deadly poisonous. Tom also brought duiker fawns to the family house in Eastlea Salisbury, but they didn't do too well.

## Prince Edward

Tom was no scholar at school and did nothing special. He was an intelligent but lazy member of Form 4C at Prince Edward. He sat Cambridge at the end of 1950 and scraped through his History, Geography and Afrikaans. Tom was described by the headmaster as keen, attentive, hard working, well mannered, well conducted, with good intelligence, pleasant manner and he was a conscientious boy. The headmaster said, "His interests lie in the country rather than in the town, he is keen on riding and shooting." It is interesting that Tom applied for a job in the Forestry department while only 16 and still at school. This is the department that National Parks came under and showed where his heart was. As he did not do well at school his parents underrated him, however, as at an early age he was very well read in his own fields. He didn't like boarding school much and was totally disinterested in sport and other academic subjects. Prince Edward was modelled after the English public schools. It had its traditions and discipline. They were smartly dressed with their typical P.E maroon sun hats. When visitors arrived at the school, they were to be greeted courteously by boys topping their hats. This was drilled into the kids. They had their routine and lessons that grinded on for what seemed forever. The classrooms were chilly in winter and on cold days the boys would get warm by sitting in the concrete storm water gutters, around the quadrangle. At break time every foot of gutter that had been warmed by the sun was occupied. School had some advantages. On Wednesday afternoons, a 'crocodile' of about 30 older Girl High School girls arrived at the Beit Hall for Mrs. Hood's ballroom dance class. Those old enough and tall enough could enrol for these classes…and meet girls! Tommy was remembered as a good chap, with a cocky nature, but not at all in the unpleasant sense. He always seemed full of bounce. He was in Selous house and once played in an inter-house rugby match against Jameson house. The opposing fly half, Ian King, was meant to be sticking to the less harmful game of tennis. And Tom came zipping around the scrum and tackled him, fracturing Ian's ankle and landing Ian in trouble with the tennis master (the dreaded Fussy Wootton).

### *First Work*
After leaving school at the end of 1950, Tom worked for Old Mutual Insurance in Salisbury for about six months, but hated every minute of this frustrating job. He then worked at Barclays doing a typical office job. But he spent all his spare money on guns. At Old Mutual he earned the princely sum of 20 pounds a month, most of which went to his mother for rent.

### *Girlfriends*
Tommy had various girlfriends and once Sheilagh caught him snogging (kissing) a girl called Margie. She was the girl from next door and Tommy being embarrassed and not wanting to get into trouble with his folks, bought off his sister. He spent his hard earned salary on a nice second hand bicycle, which he gave to his sister to

*Pat Orford with croc on Lundi River 1944*

shut her up. On one occasion Tom went to the movies with a girl he wanted to break up with. He coated some impala droppings with chocolate and during the movie passed them to her. After tasting this delicacy, she was soon off looking for someone else. Ken, his wild brother, joined the bank, was promoted steadily and ended up in a senior executive position. As a party animal he often clashed with Tom. The family thought Ken would come back one day with a really shoddy wife, but instead he ended up with a charming and beautiful girl named Verity. Sheilagh was to eventually marry a farmer, Boet Van Reenen and later she briefly became a member of parliament.

## *Sheep farming*

By this stage Tom was already keen on joining either National Parks or the Game Department. He tried again in 1951 for a job as a learner game warden of National Parks, but was turned down. Rich Uncle Samie wanted Tom to come down to the Cape and take over the sheep farm in the Karoo. Uncle Samie had switched from wool farming to German Merino sheep stud farming. He had imported some of the best bloodlines in the country. Having no children of his own, it was his idea that Tom would learn the ropes with a view to taking over the lucrative business from him. Ken was a favourite with Eileen and her husband, but Tom was the older. On receiving a telegram telling him to come down immediately, Tom took the train down to Petrusville. His uncle was waiting for him and as he got off the train, uncle Samie gave him the keys to a brand new Blue Streak, Pontiac convertible. It was white with red leather seats. "This is for you," said his uncle. Tom was whisked off to the farm and they parked in the garage next to a brand new sedan of the same make. "That is also for you my boy," Uncle Samie piped up. In the bank was more than a 'million' pounds, the ranch was full of sheep and the barns were full of all the necessary equipment to run such a farm. There was little social life there in the barren Karoo and Tom found much of it revolved around the bottle. Vice wise Tom tried smoking a pipe for a while, but was never known by his sister to have got drunk in his youth. Tom knew that he had to go home, as he had had enough. So after about 6 months he went to his uncle, thanked him for the offer and then packed his bags, taking the train back to Rhodesia. "I was a 'millionaire' for a month and it was one of the unhappiest months of my life," claimed Tom. He had just turned down the chance of being a wealthy sheep farmer in the Karoo. His view was that sheep were not only too tame, but were surely the most stupid animals in the whole world. Tommy always used to say that when sheep were putting their heads together in the morning, they were making up their minds as to who would die next! – But he sure liked eating them. Later on in life he did inherit a fair sum of money from Aunt Eileen. On Tom's arrival back across the border in Rhodesia, it was spring with the mopane trees in bloom and the cicadas in full cry. Tom taking this all in was full of emotion and started to cry. A lady came across and asked him why he was crying. Tom full of feeling replied, "This is a holy place!"

*Tom at Mutual dinner, Grand Hotel 1951*

*Tom with his first lion 1953*

## CHAPTER 2
# NUANETSI 1953-1955

### *To Nuanetsi*

Tom was still not interested in town life. When he began to pester Archie Fraser and asked him for a job (who was in charge of the Rhodesian Game department), Archie told him he was too young. Archie insisted that if he wanted to join his staff, he had to be 21 and he needed more experience. Using a reference from Eddie and Lilly Stanger, detailing his bush skills, he replied to an advert for a vacancy on Nuanetsi Ranch, 'for a young man prepared to track lion and wild dog etc.', that were causing a great deal of livestock losses. He got his dream job and was off to Nuanetsi Ranch in the South East of Rhodesia. Nuanetsi Ranch had at one time been the largest, surveyed cattle ranch in the world, being about 3.5 million acres in extent. Once, this huge piece of land had belonged to the British South Africa Company. The B.S.A. Company used to walk their cattle to Beitbridge in earlier days to sell their livestock on the South African market. The 1930's foot and mouth disease outbreak and the resulting financial difficulties, caused them to sell it to the Imperial Cold Storage Company.

*Nuanetsi 'cowboy' ca1954*

***African cowboy***
Tom was now an African cowboy, with the added responsibility of vermin/problem animal control. He worked as a very young section manager on the ranch and this enabled him to obtain a wealth of experience. He worked on Nuanetsi Ranch for about two and a half years, becoming a good horseman. Although cars were replacing horses, horses were still the main mode of transport on the Ranch, as they were needed to round up the cattle. Cattle work involved dipping, herding, training and using large spans of oxen. Tommy once herded cattle from the Tuli block all the way to the Nuanetsi. Here horses, holstered revolvers, rifle scabbards and cattle with plenty of wildlife were the norm. Tommy was in his element and because there was a large amount of predators, he started to learn about big game hunting. The cattle had to be corralled at night, due to the numerous lions.

***Freedom***
The Ranch gave Tom the opportunity to work in some interesting places; particularly the Tokwe and Mtilikwe sections and he spent some time at headquarters. Gordon Haines once saw Tom at the Ngundu section. Tom proudly showed him his garden where Tom was successfully growing green beans. Tom regarded himself as an 'agriculturalist!' Tom fell in love with the Lowveld, with its freedom and wide-open spaces. To explore the wonderful countryside, Tom would be off with his camera, thinking on his beloved Perciful Gibbons, Kipling and other poets that he had taken to heart. During his spare time, as he was not really into hunting and fishing, he would spend many happy hours in the bush walking and exploring. The Mtilikwe where Tom used to roam is now mostly covered with sugar cane and human settlement. Nearby Tom remembered sitting on

*Dosing cattle on Nuanetsi ca1954*

Chitsanga Hill (now in the middle of Chiredzi town) and looking down on a herd of buffalo in a sea of bush. There was not a human being in sight. There were many interesting ruins on Nuanetsi Ranch and Tom often spoke of the line of ruins going down from Great Zimbabwe towards the South East, this being part of the Arab gold trade network, of a thousand years ago.

## Wildlife

Poachers had to be dealt with and snares were a major problem. Antelopes would be seen walking around with snares on their heads. On one occasion, Tom and Noel Swart had to carry several truckloads of snares, having collected about 4000. Tom was to spend some time based with Noel and his many foxies and the two became good friends. Noel did not think that Tom would ever marry; mind you there weren't too many women down at Nuanetsi! Herds of up to 300 zebra roamed Nuanetsi, along with hartebeest, lots of sable and a wide variety of other creatures. There was so much game that one had to be extremely careful driving at night. A tame eland grazed around the homesteads while Tommy was there. Then there was a giraffe called Tiny, which used to steal cigarettes out of people's mouths. Shooting for the pot was part of the job and it was probably at this time that Tommy nearly came unstuck while hunting wildebeest. He went out with only 3 bullets and after shooting and using up these bullets; he

*Nuanetsi cheetah caught in trap and killed*

found himself a target of some vicious horns. The wounded wildebeest charged and hooked him in the belt. It was a good lesson and he always carried lots of ammo when hunting later on in life. During these early cattle days he saw a mamba kill at least 7 young cattle along a fence line. Whilst running past a termite mound towards their mothers they disturbed the snake, which rapidly bit each one in succession and they all died.

### *Folomani*
By this stage Tom had a way of tongue-lashing poorly performing staff. However, from others he was working with, he was learning a great deal. He build up a great friendship with an old Ndebele mentor named Johnny Folomani. This Black Nimrod was the 'foreman', hence the name 'Folomani'. Folomani had a Lee Medford .303 that he used to kill over a hundred lions before Tommy came along. Johnny was experienced in the art of lion hunting and killed about one hundred and twenty lion during the two and a half years he was teaching Tommy. As Nuanetsi Ranch was a cattle ranch, the lions had to be exterminated and so it was that Folomani and Tommy became famous in the area, for their dogs and for their lion hunting. Tom recalls on one occasion, however, when a bull did their work for them by killing a lion that broke into one of the cattle pens. Tom regarded Johnny as a humorous man and an African gentleman. This is what he

*Tom on Nuanetsi with others on a lion hunt. Central black person behind the hunters is Johnny Folomani, a well known black hunter at Nuanetsi*

had to say about him, "Now Johnny was a father to me and I revere his memory and always will. I worked on Nuanetsi ranch with Johnny, or rather, he was working there and I arrived later. Johnny Folomani was employed to control or help control, stock eating or stock mauling animals, in the shape of lions, hyenas, leopards, crocodiles, cheetahs, snakes etc. Now in those days Nuanetsi Ranch, under Arthur Wainright Colin, who was the general manager... we were losing from 800 to 1000 head of cattle a year to predators over the whole area of the ranch, which stretched from beyond the top reaches of the Mtilikwe, Ngundu, Tokwe, Mjena, Mkumi, M'papa...and right down to the south of the Bubye. Johnny Folomani took me under his wing ... and guided and protected and helped and trained me."

## *Christmas*
Tom's cook here was called Christmas and was the brother of Johnny. The brothers went lion hunting and wounded a lion. When the wounded lion charged them, Christmas took refuge in a tree, while down below the lion mauled Johnny. As Johnny desperately fought off the lion, Christmas refused to come down and help his brother.

Eventually the badly injured Johnny killed the lion, but was furious and did not want to know his brother after this. He regarded his brother as a coward and as one of the lowest of the low.

## *Predator Control*

The section managers would repeatedly get a phone call from headquarters asking what they were doing. Then requests would be made to sort out some problem animals. The culprits were usually lions, although hyenas and leopards also caused problems. Tom was evasive when asked about how many lions he thought he had shot. "What is numbers?" he once said. "Numbers mean nothing." He then let slip that he had killed an average of a hundred lion a year. This meant that he was harassing, shooting and poisoning lion on a regular basis, with most of the hunting taking place during the day. Tom did not like hunting cats at night, but had to spend many a night out dealing with them. August and September was said to be the worst months for lions, as they came up from Kruger Park in the South, moving through the Mateke hills onto the ranch. Tom worked in the areas most frequented by the lions and so had plenty of lion hunting to do. This area had produced great lion hunters in the past, such as Yank Allen, an American gunslinger, who had shot over 50 lion. Yank was once mocked as he used a revolver. He soon silenced his critics, however, by shooting the heads off 5 chickens and after that everyone was trying to buy revolvers. Tom liked revolvers and may have acquired this fondness for them, after hearing about Yanks Allen's exploits.

## *Deaf Hunter*

Not all hunters were successful in their attempts on lion. One of the white employees at Nuanetsi decided to take on the lions, even though he was deaf. He loaded his truck with some meat and headed off into the bush with his 'boy'. He fell asleep in the car while his 'boy' kept his eyes open for lions. Later on, the truck began to shake and the surprised 'boy' looked behind to see a lion in the back of the truck feeding happily on the meat. He tried to wake up his deaf boss with lots of shouting and the lion decided the noise was too much and cleared off.

## *Lion Hunting*

When Tom shot his first lion, he donated the treated skin to Eddie and

*The Lundi Bridge with the Rhino hotel on the other side 1953*

Lilly for having had such patience with him as a child. The skin was to hang at Chimbi Source for decades. Tom invited Eddie and his son Hienie to visit him at Nuanetsi, to show them how to hunt in the mopane bush, with all the 'steekgrass'. They were told to wear leggings and comfortable boots, in order to walk/track for miles through the Lowveld bush and thorn country. However, the Stangers were only able to make one visit and this was at a time when a wounded lion that had been caught in a gin trap was being followed. For a few hours they tracked with him during the afternoon, but had no luck in coming across the wounded lion. Gordon Haines met Tom and a friend on their way down to Nuanetsi when they were off on one of these lion hunts. The river was flooded and the two were waiting for the waters to subside, as they could not cross the bridge with their vehicle. Tom was quiet and his mate did the talking, saying to Gordon, "we are going hunting". Gordon said, "I hope you have taken enough food with you, as with this flooding, it's going to take you some time to get home". Gordon then opened the back of their bakkie (truck) to find that Tom's accomplice had it loaded full of beer and there was no food whatsoever.

## Dogs

Dogs were normally used for hunting lion. They were obtained from the Bulawayo S.P.C.A, where hunters could collect up to 20 dogs at a time. Tom commenting on this said, "We had a wide variety of dogs. At one time, we had 14 dogs. We always used to buy dogs or get dogs from the S.P.C.A, bring them down and we used to hunt lions or follow up lions, with this motley pack of hounds, who were introduced first of all to lions, by having their bodies rubbed with lion fat." With these dogs on the spoor, the lions were soon cornered and

*Tom with Whitey as a cowboy*

Tom would then finish them off with a rifle. Tom was really attached to his dogs and this caused him once to have a clash with a rich South African businessman, who came up to hunt on the Ranch. The two men were hunting lion mounted on their horses, when Tom noticed the haphazard way the man used his firearm. Tom warned him about it and mentioned the danger it could pose to the hunting dogs. However, the man refused to listen and in the melee of a lion hunt, he shot wildly, killing one of Tom's dogs. Tom was furious. He lifted his firearm and aimed it at the man. Tom demanded an apology, saying if he did not, he would also be killed in an accident. The visibly shaken man took a more sober attitude and apologized.

### *Ting-Ting*

Tom had one special lion dog that was superior to the others. This dog would run up to wounded animals and grab them by the ears and was great with lions. Tom had this to say, "I had a dog down there, which was a Scotch terrier by origin and given to me by a man named Jongwe Smith, who was the Hunters Association rep., living on Nuanetsi ranch, when I arrived there." This famous dog was named Ting-Ting and he had such a reputation that the trackers used to vie, as to who was going to carry him. His legs were so short that he had to be carried on horseback or by a carrier, to where the lions were found. Only then would he be put on the ground. He had his own platform of rawhide and this set in a backpack, accompanied by a

*Ting-Ting the lion hunting dog*

V.I.P water dish and his own water bottle. When it came to blood spoor, he was better than all the other dogs. However, if a rabbit, squirrel or rat ran across the blood spoor, he would take off after it. To solve this problem, Tom rigged up a fishing rod and reel, with a heavy line attached to Ting-Ting. He was kept on the line until the lion was spotted.

### Ting-Ting Strikes
One day Tommy and his gang of hunters were called in to track a lion that had been wounded by one of the directors of the ranch. They followed the lion with the dogs to its hiding place in a Buffalo Thorn bush. Tom approached this thick overhanging bush, which hid, what Tom used to call a 'Felix Malignis'. All the dogs knew that the lion was in there, but no cur was willing to go in. While the barking was going on; Ting-Ting crept through the grass and thorny branches around to the back of the lion. Suddenly the lion ejected out of the bush and up into the air towards Tom in an uncomfortable manner, its paws outstretched and making a big roar. Tommy shot the lion with his double-barrelled shotgun and as it fell, Ting-Ting ran out of the undergrowth and stood on the lion's head. Ting-Ting would not allow any other dogs near the carcass and the trackers scanned the ground, trying to figure out what had happened. From the tiny foot prints, they saw that Ting-Ting had grabbed the lion by the tail, had hung on and was dragged for a couple of feet before he let go. He had also chased the demoralized lion from the bush. Johnny Folomani held Ting-Ting aloft and cried for the benefit of his brother and the rest of the trackers, "This dog is more of a man than all of you."

### Lion Again
The Nel family lived at the Tokwe section of Nuanetsi Ranch. Here

*Johnny Folomani with a leopard on Nuanetsi ranch*

one day, an American man and his wife were hunting lion. This couple used to come out every year and had wounded a lion, which went into the reeds on the Nuanetsi River. Mr. Nel was asked to go in and finish off the lion, but was reluctant to go into the reeds. He was trying to figure out the best way to deal with this dangerous problem, when Tom appeared riding on his horse, with Ting-Ting on the saddle in front of him. Flip Nel said to Tom, "come on you are an up and coming young game ranger – go in and shoot that thing for me," and Tom said, "fine". He jumped off his horse, placed Ting-Ting on the ground and said, "Right let's go." The two of them followed the blood spoor into the reeds. Soon there was some yapping by Ting-Ting, the lion roared and a gun was fired. Tom walked out and said, "Hey flip there's your lion - go and fetch it". Ting-Ting's hunting days were sadly ended when a crocodile caught him.

### *Embarrassed*
Then there was a memorable Saturday when an impala was shot in the riverbed about a hundred metres in front of Tom's house, gutted and quartered and the meat placed on some reeds on the edge of the river. After sorting out the impala, Tommy and Folomani took off all their clothes and had a good wash in the river. Tommy had his 9.3 Mannlicher and Johnny had his double-barrelled shotgun. Tom was not aware that some guests had arrived at his house, which was also

used by visiting hunters. Tommy's room was at the back of the house. Tommy put on his 'veld-schoens' (home-made shoes) and hat wrapped with a lions tail and in this naked state, he and Johnny walked upriver a bit. They came to a high bank and at the base of the bank were a stand of reeds. As they looked into the reeds, they saw lion cubs and then heard a growl from their place on top of the bank. Tom saw what seemed to be a lion coming up to them and without a second's hesitation, the two naked men ran for dear life. Every time they looked over their shoulder, they caught a glimpse of something tawny and it was right behind them. Tommy did not even bother to open the wire mesh door, but burst straight through it. A lady was offering someone a plate of cakes and happened to be in his path of escape. He grabbed the plate continuing his flight, bleeding profusely until he got to his bedroom, where he removed the thorns from his legs. He got dressed and sheepishly exited his room and introduced himself to the visitors. None of the guests said a thing. Johnny stood outside and was wearing a red blanket, like a toga, which he had taken off the ironing board. He moaned, "Oh, baas! We are in great trouble." "Why is that, Johnny?" "Oh baas. That wasn't the lion chasing us. It was your two dogs," and no one dared talk about the incident. Years later when Tom went down to Pretoria, he was walking down the street, when a gentleman stopped him. "I know you. The last time I saw you; you were racing through the lounge naked and taking all our cakes and scones with you."

## *Shooting Blocks*

Civilization was coming to parts of the Lowveld. The Malvernia/Bannockburn railway line was being forged towards Lourenco Marques and the route of the line was cleared by bulldozers through the Gona re Zhou. There was a lot of game in this wild area and as things opened up, so the game was being slaughtered. Hunters had free reign, shooting elephants and buffalo in the tsetse fly areas and would load trucks up with meat. Ranchers were also turning their land into shooting blocks, as game competed with cattle. George Enslin was a teenager at the time and on school holidays was given the go ahead by Bob Van der Sande to shoot game down in the Nuanetsi area. Bob gave him a short wheelbase (a truck with a smaller back/box) and said, "Go for it." He was asked to shoot as many zebra, wildebeest and buffalo, he could find on the ranch. They were to hunt intermittently on Nuanetsi Ranch. Most of their meat was turned into biltong and a lot was probably sold in the Van der Sande butchery at Rutenga Junction. Nuanetsi ranch had been larger at one time with 100 000 cattle when it was owned by the B.S.A.C. Over many years parts of the giant ranch was sold off leaving smaller ranches and the smaller Nuanetsi ranch we have today. The Mateke hills section was cut up into 2000 acre shooting blocks. The land was advertised in South Africa and Afrikaners took up most of the ranches. That is why so many of the Lowveld farming communities spoke Afrikaans.

## *Dyker*

When Tom was at Nuanetsi they had advertised overseas for a surveyor to do this mammoth job. Edward Dyker a Norwegian who only drank one type of beer, lion ale, was contracted to do the work. Here are Tommy's recollections of this gentleman and his adventures, "Now this is the true story of what happened. Edward Dyker who in the second world war, was a major in the Norwegian intelligence, came out and was given the job of doing the survey, of the cut up of all the land that Nuanetsi ranch had decided to sell on the open market, at 2 and 6 an acre. Edward Dyker was among other things, a highly qualified surveyor, who had been previously (among other things) been in the Norwegian corps of military engineers; hence, his qualifications to do the survey of Nuanetsi ranch. One day while Edward was working on a blue ford pickup truck. In those days there were no 4 wheel drives there. The only other truck there was an international pickup. I walked into the garage and he was working on the springs of this truck, with his right hand assistant and driver called Simon. On the front seat of his truck, he had a .375 pre 64 Winchester, with an Alaskan scope on it. The scope on this particular weapon was loose. I asked Edward if he shouldn't do something about it, if he was continuing to hunt buffalo and he laughed and said he believed that wildebeest and zebra were far more dangerous than buffalo. A couple of days later while out with him on a fence line, he shot and wounded a buffalo bull. I have often wondered to this day, if he didn't do it deliberately, but then having seen the loose scope on the weapon, which I had forgotten about. We then followed this buffalo for a distance of about 5 kilometres. This bull never turned to fight and at the end of it, he said to me, 'you see they always run away,' …and the rest of it. I believe that this complacency was what ultimately killed him. Edward Dyker had three weapons with him at that particular period in time and a .44 colt Norwegian model, a Crag Jorgensen, the calibre I can't remember and the .375. He used to swim across the Lundi onto islands and things like that on the Nuanetsi, with this colt .45 hanging around his neck on a piece of rope. When I spoke about the crocodiles, he just laughed about them as well. A short time after these incidents I was sent down to South Africa to Onderstepoort, to qualify on the first time artificial insemination was to be introduced into the then Rhodesia. It was during this period of time, sometime during July of 54 that Edward Dyker was killed somewhere in the Muchena, Nkumi area. According to Simon, they set off one morning early, going up to check on work gangs that were working somewhere in the area. They came across a lone buffalo bull. Edward got out of the vehicle, shot the buffalo, which ran off for a short distance and then dropped on its knees. Edward then walked up closer to the buffalo to make sure of his shot, because .375 full patched ammunition or any ammunition was in short supply in those early years after the war. Edward got fairly close to the buffalo. The buffalo jumped up, hooked Edward in the abdomen and threw him up in the tree. His shorts were found later 12 to 15 foot up in a tree. Edward then fell on the ground. The buffalo glared at him. Edward, according to Simon again, (who was hiding behind a tree) then crawled backwards, using his elbows to go against the tree. He then sat up against the tree, told Simon, to take the truck please to headquarters, to inform Arthur Colin he was dead. The buffalo meantime stood and watched him all the time. Many hours later Jack Berry of the B.S.A.P Nuanetsi and I believe Brian Hughes was also there, although I am not sure of this, arrived in the late afternoon and it took them 14 shots with the .303 service weapon to kill the buffalo. Edward Dyker was a great man." The horns of this buffalo went to the local police station pub, although there is a possibility Tom may have switched the horns at some stage and taken them to Salisbury. Tom appears to have his dates wrong as Dyker was badly gored in January 1955 from just below his knees up to his chest. Simon could not drive, but managed to drive in first gear to go and get help. When they came the next day, a whole lot of men turned up with all sorts of weapons. Noel Swart thinks they opened up with amongst other things a 9mm, .404 and the heavy .375, but Noel was away at the time chasing wounded buffalo. Nuanetsi Ranch built the Lion and Elephant motel for Dyker's wife, so she would have an income, but Dyker's widow did not stay long. When the foundations were being laid, Johnny Folomani killed a lion and an elephant and Ivor Wentzel who was one of the managers,

*Zebra foal at Nuanetsi police camp 1953*

decided as a result, to call it the Lion and Elephant. The Lion and Elephant was and still is at this time, one of the few places of entertainment and accommodation in this district.

## *Salisbury*

Every time Tom went to Salisbury, he would stay with his family in the suburb of Eastlea. A 'dude' on a motorbike who had a ducktail hairstyle, what they used to call a 'teddy boy', was dating Sheilagh his sister here. This dude was trying to court Sheilagh and was an awful type. Sheilagh being rebellious at the time was dating what her parents did not want her to meet. Tom did not approve of the dude trying to get off with his sister and came out of the house with a stock whip – and after a few words told him to push off and the intruder was driven away. Another potential suitor was driven off by one of Tom's biting foxies, when the dog thought the boyfriend was attacking her.

## *Guns*

Salisbury was a great place to source guns and from the time Tom left school, he was probably the best customer of a firearms shop in the centre of Salisbury. The owner appears to be a Mr. Wantenaar. He probably rubbed his hands in glee every time he spied Tommy striding up the pavement. While other young men of his age were spending their money on cars, motorbikes, wine, women and song, Tom spent his money on rifles, shot guns and side arms. At one time or another Tom owned most of the well-known brands, such as Colt, Remington, Winchester, Benion and Purdey, Westley Richards, Mauser, Bruno, Mannlicher and a host of others. On Nuanetsi Tom used an old Martini-Henry .577 that fired a soft-nosed five hundred grain chunk of lead. Throughout his working life his great loves, family aside, were his weapons, dogs and his vehicles.

*Rupert Fothergill, Sir Robert Tredgold, Southern Rhodesia Prime Minister R.S.Garfield Todd, Archie Fraser, Ian Nyschens PHOTO Game dept. Annual report, 1956*

## CHAPTER 3
# THE GAME DEPARTMENT 1955-1960

*Archie Fraser*
Archie Fraser's initial responsibility in Government was to settle farmers on unoccupied land and deal with various game issues throughout the country. Over a period of time he was instrumental in bringing huge parts of Rhodesia under wildlife protection. He acquired most of the Zambezi valley, Chete, Chizarira, Matusadona, Kyle, Urungwe, Mana, Chewore, Gona re Zhou, Tuli and parts of the Deka. The Urungwe at this time was regarded by many as the finest wildlife sanctuary in Africa, outside of a National park. In 1952 he was appointed the first game officer in what was to become the Game Department. Over the years this department was to be known by several names and came under different government departments. To avoid confusion to the reader I will call it, simply, The Game Department or the Department. The Department of National Parks and Wildlife, which also had various titles during the early years, I will refer to as National Parks or Parks. Archie gradually took on more and more responsibility and began to build a fine organization. The main

*Rupert with his pet genet*

purposes of the newly formed Game Department were Vermin Control and the management of wildlife outside of the National Parks, i.e. hunting licenses, population surveys and the monitoring of other departments such as Tsetse and National Parks. This included regulating the sale of rhino horn and ivory plus the management of animal populations on privately owned land.

## *Game Ranger*
Tom loved wildlife more than cattle and when he had turned 21 he was finally eligible to join the Game Department as a ranger. Within a few days after his 21st birthday, he had visited Archie Fraser in his office and told him that he now had the required hunting experience and wanted a job in the Department. Archie was sick and tired of the youngster pestering him and so he put him on the payroll. One of Archie's good bits of advice to Graham Child (a later director of National Parks), was that "You should employ the best people you can. They will give you a headache, but then you will not have to worry. They will do the job." In many ways, this referred to employing people with strong personalities who could do the job, and Tom was one. The first game ranger was a strapping hunter of elephants named Ian Nyschens. The second was Rupert Fothergill, who became a legend in his own lifetime. Archie asked Rupert Fothergill to take Tom on as an apprentice and Tommy probably

*Rupert Fothergill bathing at water point*

started his work up at Kariba. Tom had thoroughly enjoyed his time at Nuanetsi but now he was realizing his dream, becoming the third Game Ranger in the new Game Department team. He joined officially at the beginning of October, but a compass he kept until he died was inscribed: 'Game Department September 1955'. He also treasured a plastic mug with the writing 'Kariba 1955'. He used this mug to feed wild animals and it was left imbedded with teeth marks. One of his first postings was up at Kariba at the Nyaodsa Game Department camp, roughly 13 kilometres from Kariba. Here they rangers hunted elephants, buffalo and other animals as the authorities were attempting to eliminate the tsetse fly from the Kessesse valley by killing the host animals. Black rhinos were also a threat to the expanding civilization here. One had to be killed after it interfered with a swing fog machine used to kill tsetse flies. This noisy machine was a good target for a rhino and it ended up in a tree. Tom may have been called 'Kamchacha' for the first time when he came to the Zambezi valley. Kamchacha was a word used by one of the Valley tribes and it meant the 'dancer'. In Malawi, the word comes from the Chewa language and means, 'unsteady and always moving'.

## *Tsetse*
From his headquarters in Salisbury Archie controlled his growing team and sent men like Tom out to remote corners of the country.

Even though the Game Department was involved in killing many of the problem elephants at this time, they had little on the Tsetse Department's wholesale massacre of wild animals. 41 886 animals were killed by Tsetse Department officials during the year ending 30 September 1955. This was their highest yearly figure ever, although they had killed a total of 592 483 animals by this time and the hunting had gone on for decades. The reason for this was the war on tsetse fly, which was necessary to prevent the spread of the fly into cattle areas. They also needed to eliminate tsetse flies in large uninhabited areas, which were being prepared for settlement by both white and black farmers. The flies used the wild animals as hosts and the only way to remove the tsetse fly in those days was by removing the host animals. It is interesting to note that within this figure 370 Rhino, 5 132 Roan, 35 261 Sable, 1 101 Hartebeest, 2 968 Oribi, 146 Suni, 38 Cheetah and 7 Nyala had been killed.

## *Fothergill*

Rupert Fothergill was once a precision engineer in Salisbury and took up the more interesting job of a game ranger. He was described as salt of the earth, straight down the line, nothing fancy, a rugged bushman, loved fishing and more physical than intellectual. Rupert Fothergill's African name was 'Katasora', which meant, 'the one who shoots in the eye'. Tommy liked and admired Rupert and many years later had this to say about him: "There were others in life who came along later, to wit Mac Matshlavasha, Hunyani Musengi and a wide variety of game scouts, who guided my feet as I stumbled around and turned me into something that I ultimately became fairly proud of. I also had as mentors Rupert Fothergill, Ian Nyschens, who was always at loggerheads with Rupert. Rupert being one of the world's greatest gentleman, who was cultured, a brilliant rifle shot and who could train young men and never asked anybody to do anything that he couldn't, or wouldn't do himself. His motto, his favourite motto in life, was that every man no matter whether you were dying or whatever you were, had to have a shit, shave and shampoo. In the Indian army of the 1930's if you read John Masters book 'Bugles and a tiger' and the other one 'The road to Mandalay', he pontificates on the qualities of having shits in the morning. Now the words 'sparrow fart' came actually from I believe Hindu or Pushta or some of those languages over there, which was originally barafata. This indicated a man who did his daily ablutions before sunrise. There were other names of those that were intermittent all over the day and those that you know had it at the night time. Anyway this was the history of the past." Tom used to talk a lot about Rupert, his philosophy and his discipline, from which he benefited from tremendously. Rupert set great standards by being as smart as possible whatever the circumstances and one of the things Tommy remembered was that they always had to start the day with shiny shoes.

## *Rocks*

Rupert's main hobby in life was prospecting, and he had many good claims around the countryside. If it had not been for the civil war that made it impossible to go into many areas, his family probably would have become rich. His father mined for most of his life and Rupert, like his father, loved collecting stones. Before Kariba Dam came into being, Tom and Rupert used to wander in the Zambezi Valley whilst doing fieldwork and it was here that Rupert found some rubies. The site now lies under the waters of Lake Kariba in the Sanyati area near Matusadona. Tom called Rupert a 'rock hound', saying he was very knowledgeable about rocks. Tom being the junior often had the unpleasant task of lugging all the specimens back to base. On the occasion when Rupert found the rubies, he placed the rubies in his pocket. On arrival back at camp, Rupert checked his pockets only to find that the rocks had fallen out because the pockets had holes in them!

## *Barry Ball*

Tommy, the apprentice game ranger, found himself fully occupied most of the time. By the end of 1955 Archie was to find himself still short of staff, with all his rangers out doing problem animal control in remote parts of Rhodesia. In 1956 the game section spent 945 mandays in the field and travelled 57 000 miles in the year on their duties. They now had Barry Ball, an ex policeman helping them. Barry had an African name that had something to do with biltong (strips of salted, spiced dried meat). He normally operated alone in the Beit Bridge-Gwanda area doing roving animal control. For Barry this was a marvellous time and using his .460 Rigby he ambushed poachers, shot hundreds of roaming stray dogs and handled aggressive elephants. Like Ian Nyschens and others, Barry lost count of how many elephant he shot. Barry's tracker Sanduridzai had an excellent photographic memory that was useful in recognizing individual spoors of animals on the ground. Barry, like Tom, also hunted with a man called Kadiki who was a short man and a good tracker and hunter. He was once there for Barry, saving the day when Barry had a misfire at a critical point in a hunt by passing a loaded double rifle to him.

## *Buffalo Hunting*

Tom and Rupert went down to the Sabi-Tanganda junction to deal with some cantankerous and dangerous buffalo. These buffalo had made their home in the extensive reed beds of the river near where the two rangers were camped. They were human wary, because many of them had been wounded by boastful hunters who claimed that a .303 rifle was a big enough gun for buffalo hunting. All attempts to dislodge the buffalo from the reeds had failed dismally with some folk being panelled (worked over) by the beasts. As Tom was a greenhorn, Rupert told him to stay out of the reed beds, as that was the buffalo hideout. Tom was left in camp one morning as Rupert went off to look for a wounded buffalo shot by a hunter. Being bored and full of bravado, Tom disregarded this warning and went off to investigate what was to be found in this swampy area. Off he went with his tracker and crawling along, he quietly parted the tall, thick, reeds. Then as he pushed the next reeds gently aside, he froze, for there in front of his nose, were some black hooves of what seemed to be some buffalo. Excited and hardly able to breathe, Tom remained on all fours and immobilized every muscle, preparing to zone in for the kill. Suddenly he felt an almighty thump from behind and his life flashed before his eyes, as he thought "what a way to die, nailed by a buffalo". He landed on his face and turned to try and see if it was a buffalo or some other nasty thing. Instead, he found Rupert smoking his pipe and there was a deep bellow from Rupert, "I told you to stay out of the reeds". He was told he should hunt buffalo like a man on his feet and not on his stomach. It had been Rupert's boot that had contacted Tommy's behind and not a buffalo's boss. Rupert then showed Tom that the hooves belonged to some cows that he had been stalking. Rupert and Tom also failed to persuade the buffalo causing trouble here, to vacate the very thick, reed bed cover.

## *Bush Camp*

Home in the bush was generally a tent but they often slept in the open, and this always had its risks and led to some interesting incidents. A pair of game scouts out on patrol had been sleeping peacefully under

*Mkwasine Game Dept. camp 1957*

the stars. However, early in the morning a horrified and totally paralyzed game scout watched while an elephant whipped the blanket off his sleeping companion and flung it up a tree - his comrade did not even wake up! Another amusing episode that could have turned out badly, but did not, was when Tommy and Rupert Fothergill were in the Bubye district dealing with some problem elephants, It was extremely hot and they. were sleeping under mosquito nets on the sand in the Bubye River. The previous night, a lion had come along and eaten some shoes, because they had blood on them. Tom was most upset about this and prepared himself for the return of the thief. During the night he was woken up by something scuffling at the foot of his bed. Lying on his back, Tommy quietly took out his .357 revolver and fired between his bare feet through the net. Immediately a large beast smothered him, spurting with blood. He yelled, "Lion, lion!" Torches were brought out cautiously by the others to investigate and, lo and behold, there was a dead donkey lying on top of Tommy. In dealing with lions killing stock in the Nuanetsi, Bubye district, Rupert and Tom would spend nights around cattle enclosures with hunting lamps trying to get the cats. Farmers used to hunt at night with 'Bulala' lamps, which were strapped on to their heads. Tom had many other interesting experiences in these early years. Once, when sleeping out in the open in the Lowveld he woke up to hear elephant dung thumping down all around his head - he was very grateful that nothing actually landed on him. Another night he woke to feel light rain on his face and on opening his eyes he found it was a lion standing over his bed. On another, even more extraordinary occasion, he was sleeping under a mosquito net attached to a branch of a tree when an elephant ambled along. The bull proceeded to feed around his bedroll and yanked the branch on which the net was attached. When the branch flicked up, the white net landed on the elephant's head. The elephant panicked and with much trumpeting and terror disappeared into the depths of the night, festooned with white netting. The following morning Tom found a trail of shredded netting in the bushes through which the elephant had made its escape. Some guys in those days would pee on the ground near the camp and hang up clothing to deter wild intruders as the smell of urine discouraged them.

## *Kit*

Initially their equipment was very basic and they used a one-ton truck for transport. There was not much in the way of a uniform in the Game dept. and they wore whatever was most suitable for the occasion. A South African V.I.P came down to the valley with Archie one day and they came across Ian Nyschens in a loincloth. There were some uncomplimentary remarks in Afrikaans by the V.I.P about 'a white k*****'. Ian understood perfectly what had been said! At first Tom's dress was a bit exotic, but he soon tidied up. He didn't have many clothes when he first joined the Game Department and would place his 2 pairs of shorts and 2 shirts under his pillow at night to get 'ironed' for the next day. When they came to a small town, Tom and Rupert would sit down together and enjoy civilized food, like ice cream and rice pudding. After weeks in the bush without luxuries, the few visits to head office in Salisbury were always a welcome break. At the end of the year the Game department staff could also enjoy a great Christmas break together in Salisbury, and once all came together for a party at the Fothergills. This was a fine bunch of men, very dedicated to their jobs, loving their work with animals and not concerned about material possessions or personal gain. No matter the hardships, long hours, heat, dirt, sleeping on the hard ground, mosquitoes galore, they always did their work. They worked hard and played hard and nothing got them down. Sitting around bushfires and relishing the wilds of Africa, they would chat away, while hyenas and nightjars sang their nightly cries.

## *Urungwe*

The Urungwe Non-hunting Reserve was established in 1955, but had been a protected area since the beginning of the century. It was situated in the Zambezi Valley between the Rekomitje River and the Portuguese East African border (Mozambique). It was later broken up and part of it became the famous Mana Pools National Park. A building programme took place in which buildings and other equipment were set up, while permanent staff were stationed in the reserve. Tom was busy here and remembers a hair-raising trip in which they used dugout canoes to transport equipment down the Zambezi rapids and they nearly all ended up in the river. The reserve was privileged to get a boat from Kariba named Tess, which made life a bit easier afterwards. Determined and aggressive poachers from Northern Rhodesia used to cross the Zambezi River to hunt. They would shoot game, load the meat on their makoros and then paddle back to safety across the river. Tom was now a 22 year old when he came across four poachers already in midstream on their way home. The poachers shot at him with a muzzleloader as they paddled hard towards the other side. Tom retaliated and one of his shots holed the canoe, which sank leaving the occupants floundering in the river and unfortunately two of them drowned.

*Sleeping Sickness*
In May-June 1957 while Tom was working in the Zambezi valley and travelling between Kariba and Mana, he contracted sleeping sickness. He stayed at his parent's house in Salisbury as the fatigue and malaise continued to worsen. Tom suspected that it was sleeping sickness and approached a doctor with his theory. This was dismissed and it was assumed by everyone that he had malaria. Tom then went to a local hospital where he got permission to go to the laboratory. Here he managed to get his hands on a syringe, microscope and slides. He drew his own blood, prepared the specimen and was able to identify trypanosomiasis under the microscope. On presenting his findings to the medical authorities, he was immediately admitted to Salisbury general hospital where he was fortunate to come under the care of Professor Gelfand, a very well known and respected specialist. Fluid was drawn from Tom's spinal cord and Professor Gelfand began experimental treatments that led to a full recovery. While in hospital Tom recalls being looked after by a big, big nurse who was very intimidating. Tom was reputedly the first human to have survived a full-blown dose of sleeping sickness. He was told to stay out of Tsetse areas after this and to do everything possible to prevent fevers of any kind. He did contract malaria later on in life and against medical advice was to frequent tsetse fly areas. Because he survived this ordeal, it became a newsworthy event and was mentioned in government annual reports and the public press. By the beginning of

*Rupert with zebra in distress during Mkwasine crisis*

September, Tom was back at work.

## Alan Savory

Tom met Alan Savory in 1959, and both these men were to have a huge and lasting influence on each other's lives. Alan having come down from the Northern Rhodesia Game department was working as a quelea control officer. He was based at Dott's Drift on the Sabi River. One day a short wheel base land rover arrived in his camp and out jumped Tom. He walked up to Alan and said, "Hi I'm Tom Orford and I've brought you some bread". Tom proceeded to give Alan 8 loaves of bread. A surprised Alan did not know what to do with all this bread and they became good friends. This was typical of Tom, always smiling and all heart - it was easy for him to make friends. Tom was very generous and loved giving things away - 40 years later Alan was still using a metal comb Tom gave him (bought in a Johannesburg pawnshop). If you admired or showed an interest in his camera or some other piece of equipment, he would often insist on giving it to you. If you said, "that's a nice camera you've got Tommy". "Well have it", he would reply. You would then have to say no. Tom was probably on vermin and elephant control at this time and his Sabi West camp was under some albizia trees and upstream from Alan's. Another lifelong friendship developed down there was with Burte Milne of the Tsetse department. Burte had worked with the submarines in the Royal Navy. Both Alan and Burte were to join the old Game Dept.

## *Mkwasini*

A doctor named Hornby from Kenya was working on the tsetse fly problem. As a result of his work a tsetse fence was put up from the Eastern border below Chipinga, through the Lowveld and Lone Star ranch, down into the Gona re Zhou. A problem with this new fencing was that it was not barbwire and was therefore ideal for making the snares that were popping up at waterholes. The fence was meant to stop the movement of wildlife, as they were the host of the deadly tsetse fly, which was harmful to both man and domestic livestock. However, when a drought year struck, the animals began to be trapped against the fences and died - especially buffalo and zebra. Vast herds of game were cut off from water on both sides of the fence. Ray Sparrow was ranching on Lone Star and contacted the newspapers, which then exposed the deaths on the fences. The newspapers reported 'thousands' of animals dying along the game fence. Tom was in Salisbury taking some days off. Rupert was having difficulty in the Mkwasini area trying to manage this new wildlife problem and needed some help, so he put a Mopane tree leaf into an envelope and sent it to Tom. Tom understood the message and immediately went to Rupert's assistance to help with the water supplies and poaching problems.

## *Rescue*

A vehicle arrived outside the Nuanetsi B.S.A.P charge office in 1957. Tom strode in with a wide brimmed hat, khaki shirt and shorts, hunting boots and wearing a colt .38 Smith and Wesson revolver in a low-slung holster. He certainly made an impression. Archie also joined Rupert to help him try to sort out the wildlife crisis. To cope with the shortage of water, they started pumping on the Mkwasini River, establishing pumps and temporary artificial dams close to the river at Chikwarakwara. They worked day and night to help the emaciated animals, using picks and shovels. The Game Department staff did their best to drive the game towards the few water points available, and were helped by the Sparrow and Style families and other ranchers in keeping the waterholes clear of sand. Elephants were a hindrance as they dug up water troughs and dirtied water, and on one occasion broke a dam wall. Some animals took to breaking fences to get access to these water points and this led to many serious injuries among them. There was one very brave zebra stallion who, on his third attempt, took a 100-yard run up and broke through the fence with the support of two stallions on either side of him. Having snapped through the fence, the herd plummeted through behind their saviour, but he fell on the ground badly injured and the Game staff had to put him down. Eland and kudu were more fortunate in that they could jump the fence. Tom and Archie visited a ranch where the present Mkwasine estate is now. While visiting the farmhouse, a kudu appeared in front of the building and collapsed from thirst. Tom ran into the house and grabbed some water, which he then took out to the animal and he tried to revive it. By the end of September, there were an estimated 1000 head of game pushing up against the fence. It was eventually breached by the Tsetse and Game Departments with gaps of up to 400 yards being cleared. The Game Department tried to drive the animals through with beaters and land rovers. Buffalo, on reaching the fence, would break back through the beaters causing considerable confusion. There was a great deal of shooting in the air, which didn't seem to distract the buffalo who normally put the beaters up in the trees; as you can imagine the beaters were far from enthusiastic after being treed by these enraged animals. As the waterholes in the Lowveld dried up, bush fires could be seen sweeping the horizon. Everyone was very worried about the plight of the game. When the rains came Tom was elated, the drought was broken. Later on in life he would dance and walk around in the rain, as soon as the first rains of the season arrived.

### *Game Ranching*
Ranchers on the Lowveld ranches were also slaughtering game and 2 282 zebra skins and 5 535 crocodile skins were exported from the country in one year. Initially, the concept of game ranching was not popular, even within the Game Department. Many people thought wild animals would be incompatible with farming and little was known about the animals themselves beyond species distribution. On the subject of game farming, Archie was heard to say, "This will never happen - over my dead body". The reply was, "you haven't got long to live my friend". Game ranching was pioneered in Rhodesia on the Hendersons' Doddieburn ranch, where the Americans Dasman and Mossman proved it could be done successfully. Alan Savory, Peter Johnson and others were part of this move in the late 50's and early 60's. Savory helped at Doddieburn at one time with the game management experiments and data processing. The Game Department took notice and soon began to encourage ranchers to take up game ranching. While moving around the Lowveld ranches on his duties, Tom encouraged this new type of farming. One of the pioneers was George Style who was about to introduce sheep on to his ranch when Tom arrived one day in 1961 and suggested George utilize the already plentiful impala instead. George went into game farming successfully

on Buffalo Range ranch and he was the second game rancher in the country. Others took up the challenge and Wildlife Utilization Services, which was a game cropping company, was formed by Dave Higgins, Alan Savory and Robinson to assist the ranchers. They employed professional game hunters to crop the game on behalf of the ranchers and kept two refrigerated containers to store the meat. One of their best hunters was Mike Bunce, who was paid per animal shot.

## *George Style*

There was plenty of elephant and vermin control and the game rangers spent a good deal of time staying with farmers and ranchers as they dealt with vermin. Tom often went off doing vermin control on his own. After Operation Noah started, George Style wrote Tom a letter and it is worth quoting, as George was a famous Lowveld rancher.

'Dear Tommy.

I have brought back after Rodney's wedding my typewriter, which has just had its annual overhaul, so here goes. Many thanks indeed for sending us "Animal Dunkirk" which is being much enjoyed by the family, Clive having been the first to grab it and take it to the seclusion of his room, and emerging a few minutes later to quote. - "Next to join the "front line" was twenty-five-year-old Tom Orford, who has been with the Game Department since he was 21" etc. Am very pleased to have the book, Tommy, and the photographs of yourself and Rupert are excellent. Many thanks, too, for all your assistance down here, which was much appreciated. Trust the 'tummy' has given no more trouble. Some people have extraordinary luck, and the day you left, at 11 p.m. that night, Ainslie and Lloyd-Roberts walked into five lions outside one of the kraals, as they were about to stampede the cattle. They delayed shooting I think but eventually Ainslie had a shot resting his rifle on Lloyd's shoulder, and must have wounded one as it grunted three times apparently. The bullet had gone through two twigs, no blood left and no lion found. Trapped a large female with 4 small cubs about 5" long inside her, last Tuesday night. Have built two stampede-proof kraals in the area and moved all the other cattle out, so have great hopes of getting on top of them now. Rodney's wedding went off very well and I wish you could have been there. We expect them back on Wednesday. Rain badly needed, though we were lucky to get .82 while away for the wedding last weekend. Have du Pont and a niece here for a few days and they leave on Tuesday. Wish you were here to meet Jennifer, aged 22. Just been to the States and Canada, and very attractive. Am sure you would fall, and all old wounds be healed. Wish I was 30 years younger! Must take them round the Ranch after tea. Clive has his Elizabeth down for the weekend, so not interested. Very best wishes to you from us all for Xmas and the New Year, and my regards to the "Boss" and Rupert when you see them next. Hope to see you down here again one of these days. Once again my sincere thanks for all your help'.

### *The Boss*
Throughout Tom's life, he abhorred violence of any nature other than hunting. Confrontations in his life revolved around the preservation of his beloved wildlife and the environment. He was uncompromising in this regard and was certainly not backward in coming forward when it came to crossing swords with bureaucracy or the rich and powerful. He enjoyed immensely the corresponding, sometimes vitriocally, with the powers that be. He also had a way of winding up and irritating his superiors. Archie Fraser had a way of moving his eyebrows in a threatening manner and would say to his subordinates, "don't you try that my lad". Tom got Archie so mad and frustrated once that Archie stated that he 'never' wanted to see Tommy ever again. Tommy recorded the conversation and promptly left Salisbury for the Lowveld. For months, messages came for Tommy to go to town, which he ignored! It was only after a frustrating long search that he was eventually found. Finally, Archie was able to get him on the phone and Tom had to listen to a tirade of words. Archie wanted to know why Tom had disappeared. After listening Tom said, "Do you recognize this conversation sir?" and played him back the tape of the conversation where Archie had said that he didn't want to see Tommy again. Archie was stumped and had to recant.

### *Poison*
The staff were involved with experiments in killing baboons and other vermin in the Chitomborgwizi Native Purchase area and the Magondi Native Reserve. First of all they used traps with falling doors of bush timber and wire netting. These traps caught some baboon, but were not really successful, as the baboons soon caught on. Monkeys,

however, were more easily caught. Because the falling log traps were a failure, they turned to poison and tried various types such as arsenide of soda, arsenic, strychnine and cyanide. It seemed to work as the populations began to thin out. Strange baits such as sweets, puddings and other exotic offerings were not attractive to the Magondi baboons. Pumpkins and sweet potatoes were the baits most often taken. Shooting at night with light calibre rifles also proved fairly effective. Another tactic was to use dogs and a large number of beaters to chase the baboons towards the gunmen. Failure to position the beaters and guns properly led to chaos, escapes and some beaters nearly getting shot. By 1964, Parks was using thallium sulphate for baboons, which was a tasteless poison and the baboons died about 5 days later. Tom's interest in poisons probably started at Nuanetsi Ranch and during his life he was always into pills, poisons and medicines. Somewhere there would be some cyanide or some other poison hidden away and he liked experimenting with plants, such as Strophanthus and Abrus. During one of these baboon experiments, Barry Ball was relaxing and having a good smoke on his camp bed. The other men were highly amused when his cigarette caused the mosquito net over his bed to go up in flames. Ben Kaschula was a District Commissioner at Sinoia. The District Commissioners often phoned the Game Department for help when there were game problems. Ben remembers Tom being sent out to do antipoaching and baboon control work in the Mtoko, Doma and Zambezi valley areas. Here there were many baboon problems and Tom was to liaise with the Ministry of Internal Affairs. Strychnine was being used to poison the baboons and Tom was meticulous in his handling of this very dangerous substance. Maize cobs were soaked in a strychnine solution and then laid out on the ground around the growing maize fields. Tom was very concerned that people might pick them up and eat them, so he made sure the local people were properly informed as to how the poison would affect them and were thereby protected.

### *Mtoko*

Mtoko was another very wild area and the Game Department staff often had to go up there to shoot elephant. Tom and his game scouts were called out to kill a lion that was indiscriminatingly slaughtering cattle in the area. They tried to track it by following the spoor away from the kills but the spoor always disappeared and they were failing dismally. Then they found out that the local people thought this lion was bewitched. One of the game scouts said, "talk to the villagers and find out what they think". So they went to the people to ask what they should do. The local witchdoctor said that the game scouts must do a sacrifice and if they didn't one of the game scouts would end up dying. They were told by the witchdoctor to get a chicken, a white cloth and a black cloth. All the game scouts except one participated in this ritual and the next morning they found and dealt with the lion. The game scout who did not take part in the sacrifice was run over by a bus when he went back to Salisbury.

## *Quelea*

The Game Department was involved with quelea control for the first time in 1959. A particularly large nesting site, occupied by an estimated 9 million birds and covering some 100 acres, was discovered in the vicinity of the Chipangayi River. A spraying unit was brought in from South Africa to deal with the problem and it appears Tom was drafted in to assist. Quelea control became one of Tom's frequent assignments. These tiny birds are often called the feathered locust, as they fly around in their millions, devastating croplands that are ready for harvest and bankrupting farmers. Most quelea colonies in Southern Rhodesia were located in the Lowveld. Although Alan Savory was qualified in the use of poisons on a large scale, he decided it would be more eco-friendly to use explosives on quelea, so he did another course in explosives. The change in tactics meant that scavengers such as storks would not get killed and the quelea carcasses would be available to the local people as food. This method proved very efficient and many quelea colonies were soon being blown up, with millions of birds dying, often falling ankle deep. The explosions could be huge and on one occasion, Alan rattled the windows in Gwanda, nine miles away. The birds were put into sacks by the local villagers and weighed before being eaten. Alan, who knew the average weight of a single bird, could then work out how many birds had been killed, for recording purposes. Later on a poison called Queleatox was used and this was effective in spraying both nesting and roosting sites. National Parks pilots would fly over the quelea colonies at night and spray the colony with this poison. Game scouts and rangers on the ground had to hold strategically placed lamps to guide the aircraft - this could be a horrible and potentially lethal job as the spray spread over a wide area.

## *Chipinga*

Hyena and Wild Dogs were rampaging through farms in the Chipinga and Chikora Mission districts of the beautiful Eastern Highlands. The attacks were frequent and on a very large scale with one farmer losing 127 head of cattle. The hyenas were very intelligent and were regarded with great superstition by the local people. Tommy talked of one notable hyena which travelled great distances and which, he reckoned, had a degree in avoiding traps. The poisoned bait would be carefully set and then the trick was to try and avoid leaving any human scent behind. So Tom carefully hopped from rock to rock until he was out of the trapping area. If the occasion warranted, Tom was also not averse to using animal dung on himself to disguise his own smell. This shrewd hyena certainly avoided Tom's persistent and determined efforts and I do not know if Tom ever got him. Due to all the predator problems in the Chipinga area, it was thought that a game reserve might help. In the 1960's they did create a hunting area and Tom was instrumental in setting it up.

## *Inyanga*

When Tommy was working in the mountainous Inyanga area further up the Eastern Border on vermin control, he visited a farmer called Colonel Wyrley-Birch in the course of his duties. Tom was young and still very shy amongst people he did not know well. Battling to make conversion while drinking a cup of tea, he looked around and noticed in the lounge a nice looking, reddish animal skin, hanging over the back of the sofa. Knowing that the colonel had been in India and trying to appear educated, Tom asked if the skin was from a dhole. (Dholes are fierce red wild dogs found in the mountains of India, which hunt in a pack and are remarkable in tackling large animals such as water buffalo and even tigers). The response from the colonel was "Oh no, that was Rover - damn good dog he was too."

*Rupert supervising digging during the Mkwasine crisis 1957*

*Tom with one of his first elephants 1956*

## CHAPTER 4
# ELEPHANTS 1955-1963

### First Elephant

The main task for the team of game rangers in the early days was the control of marauding elephants. In fact, elephant raids on crops were reported from all the districts of the colony and hundreds were shot annually for several years. Migrating pachyderms invaded the country from Bechuanaland and Portuguese East Africa. When an elephant strolled into the Borrowdale suburb of Salisbury, some residents feared the city was under siege! With the amount of time and energy spent on the large beasts it was fitting that the Department logo was an elephant. 1956 was the year in which Tom shot his first elephants. He hunted them in the Bubye, Gwanda areas and on Rhodesville Estate, which was situated between Gatooma and Que Que. The elephants at the latter place had been interfering with the new farms that were being opened up. One day near Que Que, Tom shot an elephant and climbed onto the animal. Using his binoculars, he could see the town in the distance and a businessman walking on the street. Sadly, areas where elephant could roam freely were fast disappearing. At Rhodesdale 38 elephant were killed, bringing the total killed here since 1952 to 93. The elephant soon moved on and headed for the

Umniati and Nyodoma river areas. Ian Nyschens stated that the Game Department shot more elephants than stated in official reports. This, he said, was because Archie did not want to get bad publicity. Black hunters were to be used by the Game Department, but were still on a temporary basis and mainly in a tracking capacity. Apart from the elephants, the men had to deal with buffalo, leopard, lion, zebra and hippo. In many cases when called out to deal with vermin, the reports were without substance and staff performed long journeys to no purpose. The game section killed 129 elephant during 1956. This was only a percentage of the number killed throughout the country. Tsetse fly rangers killed 90, game wardens of National Parks 33, native commissioners 35, amateur hunters (as deputies) 102, and royal game licensees on private land an estimated 40.

## *Weapons*

Before Brian Hughes joined the Game Dept. in 1958, some rifles were ordered by Ian Nyschens from Westley Richards, Birmingham and Ian did not realize the danger they posed to the staff. These weapons were the .425 Westley Richards bolt action magazine rifles and about three .500 calibre, box lock, ejector, double rifles. These were all of a standard, possibly 'game ranger' grade. Both types of weapons were ordered primarily for elephant control, some of this being in thickets and they failed miserably. The .500 rifles had 22 inch barrels and short stocks and were pigs to fire. They lacked length and weight in the barrels (25 inches would have been better) and they had the short stock. The barrels threw high and Brian Hughes was once hit in the face. The first time he fired one he was hit on the nose by his right thumb and literally saw two stars. These rifles gave some trouble to other staff, possibly ejector problems. The .425s were unwieldy, lumpy weapons with unsuitable stocks. On one of his weapons, Nyschens extended the recoil pad with a spacer, so that he could use it. The .425 was not a good weapon as it did not eject properly and was dangerous. People quite rightly did not want to use them and Tom lacked confidence after bad experiences with them, having had like others, close shaves when rifles jammed. While hunting crop raiding elephant in the South West of the country, Tom and Rupert had some bad experiences with their .425's. Later second hand, good double rifles were bought for those rangers needing them. Brian used a .470 non-ejector with 25 inch barrels by Army and Navy. This was a superb, plain but accurate and reliable weapon liked by Game Dept.

*Game dept. land rover crossing a Lowveld river late 1950's*

staff. Brian also used at one time a .404 Jeffrey bolt action and Rupert had his .375 magnum model 70 Winchester. Tom as result of early elephant hunting with unreliable weapons became a fan of big calibres, becoming very knowledgeable about weapons and was unrelenting on safety. In National Parks, weapons appear to have been better. Jordie Jordaan who worked with Tom at Wankie was issued with a .500 double Army Navy. Jordie took it down to near Kennedy pan and fired rounds through the two barrels until it was red hot. He found it suitable and he used that weapon for the rest of his career.

### *Greenhorns*

Ian Nyschens met Tom for the first time on the Umfuli River where Tom was doing quelea bird control. He also hunted a bit with Tom in the jesse bush of the Zambezi valley. Tom did not take elephant hunting as seriously as Ian and was in his element just being in the bush. Ian could not understand why Archie had not employed men with lots of elephant hunting experience, for what he regarded as being a mainly elephant control job. However, Archie knew there was a great deal more involved and Rupert and Tom managed to perform well in all the varied and dangerous tasks undertaken by the Game Department. Ian was not impressed with either Rupert or Tom, as they were novices at elephant hunting and he had some scathing remarks to make about their lack of experience. He found it easier to hunt elephant on his own than with the two greenhorns. He was also motivated differently, as he was hunting for profit. He took a particular dislike to Rupert, probably because Rupert once fired a rifle near Ian's head and caused him to go deaf in one ear. Tom respected Ian as a hunter, but was critical of Ian's choice of firearms for the

Dept., which nearly led to Tom's death a few times. Rupert regarded Ian as a poacher and was also unhappy with the firearm situation.

## *Ian Nyschens*

Ian Nyschens might go down in history as one of the better elephant hunters. He was ruthless, athletic and professional. He had already shot plenty of elephant in the wilder parts of Africa before becoming a game ranger in Southern Rhodesia. He hunted for ivory in the Congo, Sudan, Tanganyika and in the northern region of Portuguese East Africa, where he shot an elephant with 149 and 151 pound tusks. Most of the ivory he acquired was cut up into pieces and sold. 100 pounders were common in some of those wild places (a hundred pounder is an elephant with a tusk weighing 100 or more pounds). From his base in Northern Rhodesia, he used to cross the Zambezi River and poach elephants in Southern Rhodesia and the police hated him, as he would repeatedly outmanoeuvre them. Then Archie Fraser was given the responsibility of issuing hunting permits for big game in the tsetse fly belts. The Magochas (black hunters) were not allowed to shoot elephant, so Archie sold £1 licenses to farmers specifically for the tsetse areas. The farmers would go and shoot the elephants, then get their tractors and bring the meat home. However, they were not always successful at this job and at least one hunter was killed in the process. Ian bought a tsetse area permit that he used to hunt legally, with some poaching on the side, before he joined the Game Department. By employing Ian in the Department, Archie had the ideal man for dealing with problem elephants and Ian was allowed to keep whatever ivory he obtained during his official duties. Ian was given the African name 'Magora', which meant vulture. He would do some intelligent research when entering into an area to find out where the elephants were, using the tracks, verbal reports etc. He was so good at his job that the blacks thought he would dream where the meat was at night. They believed vultures did the same, hence the nickname. Ian used to approach a herd to about 15 paces and after shooting, would back off a bit. It was normally planned that there was a clear view of fire. He would also use a dead elephant as a shield when being attacked by a herd of elephant, or he would shoot from on top of it.

## *Kariba*

These were the years when the massive Kariba dam wall was being built. The area was wild and rugged with lots of game in the surrounding countryside. The Game Department was called in to shoot some elephant in the vicinity. The plan was to try to scare the elephants away from the dam wall and if killed, provide meat for the large labour force. The elephants soon learnt that this was a dangerous area and stayed away. Because of the poor road system, the few elephants that were shot could not be accessed properly and the meat unfortunately had to be left to scavengers. During this exercise, one of the rangers had to shoot 11 elephants in self-defence to protect himself and his trackers (this was probably Ian Nyschens).

### *Gongs Poort*
The Game Department was involved in a campaign to control about 1000 elephants that moved back and forth between Bechuanaland and the Gwanda/Beitbridge area. These and other elephants in the South West of the country were to keep the rangers very busy for years. Gongs Poort was once the site of a police station and is 15 miles west of the Beitbridge-Fort Victoria road (Lemco ranch area). The Gongs Poort elephant were destructive, pulling up many trees and were cheeky and aggressive. They were accused of killing a few honey hunters and no white hunters wanted to tackle them. As soon as you shot one, several of them came running to where the shot was fired and you found yourselves in a war. Archie, Rupert, Tom and Ian had numerous bad experiences with these animals and spent months trying to deal with them. There were many different herds and they varied in size. One day whilst hunting some of these problem elephants, the rangers wounded one that then ran off with a herd of about 40. The rangers took up the chase, with Rupert and Tom showing their fitness at this time. Ian with his .425 heard another herd of elephant behind them. This newly arrived herd zeroed in and began to chase the Game Department staff. The trackers ran away with the spare weapons, but were soon back, pursued by yet more elephants. Soon the men were turning around, finding themselves in a shootout. The elephants came in a determined rush and charged all over and weapons jammed. Ian says it was frightening even for him. When you consider he had shot possibly thousands of elephants in all sorts of circumstances, you can imagine how bad it was. Ian ordered the men to turn around and fire and they shot for their lives. Tom had been told by Archie to observe and learn to shoot elephants from the master and he was unarmed as a result. Ian not knowing this, turned around for support to see Tom

*Tom as a wandering young game ranger 1950's, notice lack of formal uniform*

armed with just a revolver, his compass, a water bottle, 2 different knives and a box camera, waiting in the Game Department's last stand. Ian said, "Tommy what are you doing man?" It was only because of Ian's experience that they got out of the situation alive and Ian was said to have shot 18 elephants on this occasion. Rupert, Barry Ball and Tom all gained valuable experience from hunting with Ian. Of all the bad incidents Tom had in these early days with elephant, this one really shook him badly. After this Archie contacted Ted Davison of National Parks saying, "I have this young lad, his nerve has gone and will you take him on". So, Tom was sent to Wankie to go hunting elephant with Ted Davison in the Gwaai valley. Ted suggested that Tom go on baboon, jackal and lion hunts and eventually back to elephant. Tom was an experienced lion and predator hunter and he gradually got his confidence and nerve back and eventually became a good elephant hunter.

## With Parks

The Game Dept. often worked with the Wankie National Parks staff with elephant control. Harry Cantle, Braybrooke, Ted Davison and other Parks staff shot a large number of elephant around Wankie. In 1960, they combined with the Game department staff to drive some 300 elephants out of the Mlibizi valley before the new tsetse fly fence was finally closed. This particular operation was delayed due to the need to cut land rover tracks through rugged country in which deep gorges made work difficult. The fall of rain helped move animals out of the area, as they were then not so reliant on the water at Mlibizi. By the end of the operation, most had gone either to the Kariba lakeshore or into the Kavira forest area. At least 43 elephants were killed and 2 wounded, with the Game Department continuing after the Parks staff left. Sheilagh and her husband Boete went to look for Tom somewhere up near Binga, intending to pay him a surprise visit. However, when they found Tom he did not give them a great reception, as he was too busy working. They found Tom in the middle of nowhere doing elephant control work. The work was hard and the salaries were not very salubrious. Tom would often be sent off fat and shiny by his mom and come back looking like a scarecrow and in an awful condition. Tom's Mum kept a close watch on where and what her young son was doing when he first joined the Department. One could tell if she had called into head office to enquire about him, because she always brought a chocolate cake for the staff. She was quite resourceful in getting chocolate cakes delivered to Tom in even the most out of the way places. It was while Tom was up near Wankie at this time that Archie decided to teach him more about elephant hunting. It was on a combined operation that Archie took Tom to Kamativi where the elephants were giving trouble. Here Archie shot an elephant at close range and failed to do a good job. The elephant then proceeded to do a reverse charge and Tom was nearly squashed as he was knocked over. This showed Tom that elephants could do both front and reverse charges. They returned to Main Camp saying the hunt was not a notable success. Tom had several bad experiences with elephant at this early stage leading to a high respect for the animals.

## *The Railway*

It was tragic that so many elephants were shot to make way for progress. Many of the troublesome elephants were simply bad due to human persecution and encroachment on their home ranges. Tom and most other rangers disliked this wholesale slaughter. With the building of the railway line going through the Gona-re-Zhou area, down to Lourenco Marques, elephant were shot along the line of rail, as they were molesting work gangs and raided nearby crops. One annoying elephant would walk down the line, pick up markers used by the construction workers and then throw them away. Tom and Rupert were there once when the elephants were stuck on one side of the new railway because they were afraid to cross. There was a drought and they needed to access water on the other side of the railway line or die of thirst. To convince the elephants to cross, the men came up with the scheme of putting elephant dung across the rails. When the elephants observed this, they got the courage to move over the line at that point. Tom also helped supply meat to some of the workers building the Bannockburn line.

## *Valley Mishaps*
In Tom's dealings with elephant, he spent much time in the Zambezi valley, Binga, Gokwe and Wankie. Tom loved the wild and beautiful Zambezi Valley, which was filled with an abundance of game, particularly in the Mana Pools area, where great herds of buffalo and eland roamed freely. National Parks, Tsetse and the Game Department combined their resources in campaigns to control the elephant in the Valley and so Tom found himself spending a lot of time in this wilderness paradise. Tom had a scary experience there once when he wounded an elephant and had to give chase. He was rushing to catch up when his binoculars, which were strapped around his neck, jerked up and hit him on the head. He fell down momentarily stunned. As soon as he was able, he jumped up and continued to chase the elephant. He sprinted through the thick jesse bush, with little visibility ahead of him, until suddenly he ran slap bang into the hidden elephant, which had stopped to rest. Tom fell over again, whilst the terrified elephant got a fright and took off again. When the game scouts came running up, they found a very dazed Tom lying on the ground. Tom, a bit defeated, told them to go and finish it off saying, "follow that elephant". It was while Tom was in the valley that he had another interesting elephant experience. He was

trying to shoot an impala, possibly for rations. He was carefully aiming through what looked like two Leadwood tree trunks in the distance through which he could see the impala beyond. When he fired, he found the two tree trunks were elephant legs and they departed rapidly one way and he the other.

*Some of the Game Department staff The man on left may be Phineas*

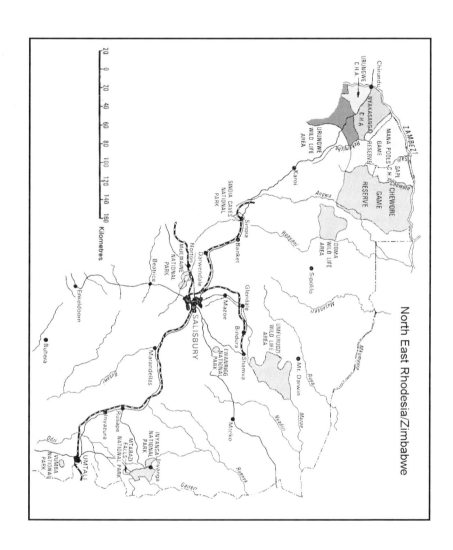

*Ron Thomson's pet Koni the gnu with Robert Smith at Main Camp.
PHOTO Min. of information by Cloete Breytenbach 1962*

## *Chapter 5*
# WANKIE EARLY DAYS 1958-1963

### Wankie Duties
Tom was often up at Wankie doing elephant control, game capture work and miscellaneous duties. The Game Department was examining a proposal to set aside an area adjoining Wankie National Park on the north and east with the idea of putting up hunting camps for paying customers. Not only would this provide a buffer zone between the farmers and the National Park, but it would also be another way of utilizing the wild life. The plan was accepted and the Wankie Controlled Hunting Area came into being. Game capture was also done here to restock Kyle and there were game counts in Wankie National Park in which the Game Dept. helped count 3500 elephant in the park and about 30 lions.

## *Main Camp*

When Tom came to Wankie National Park, he would stay at the single quarter huts at Main Camp. Ted Davison was the 'king' of Wankie, having looked after it since the 1920's. Ted's African name was Shakwanki and he was named after a pan called of the same name, which he had come across while following an old elephant path. After visiting this pan, his staff had given him this bushman name. Ted's wife Connie had a heart of gold and she did a good service in looking after the sick rangers. Some of the rangers were a bit nervous of Connie, who was called Sibamba. This nickname referred to her habit of grabbing you to get your attention while she spoke to you. Bruce Austen, who was one of Ted's staff, was called Malindela. Bruce was very patient and waited for his scouts at appointed places and this nickname may have derived from this. Then there was Tim Braybrooke called Mashilela or Khwehlela, which means he who coughs. Tim was another great character and got this name when he was about 22 for his smoking habit. Harry Cantle was called Ndebele (a local tribe), while Ron Thomson was named Mahobo. Mahobo was said to refer to Ron's shooting many elephant 'all in a pile'.

## *Game Capture*

Most game capture was done in the dry months and the Ngamo flats were the favourite catching ground. Here animals moved across the sandy open ground to get a drink and two stripped down land rovers would chase them at maximum speed. As they closed up on the animal, a Rhodesian pole and loop lasso was slipped over a rear hoof and pulled tight. After capture the eland, sable, roan, wildebeest, kudu and young buffalo were lifted into a land rover and driven to holding pens. Animals from the same herd were often put together to help them settle in the pens, which were built in advance. After dragging giraffes to a halt, a long stick was used to put a blanket over the head. Once blindfolded it would stand still and allow a special harness to be buckled around its body, on which ropes were attached. When the blanket was removed, the giraffe would try to run forward and the men holding the ropes in the front and both sides would guide it to the pens. The whole operation took less than half an hour. After about a week the required number would be collected, put on 5 ton Bedford trucks and taken away to their new homes. Transporting giraffes posed a hazard to telephone wires, which had to be lifted as they passed.

*Geri Tulley in a tourist promotion hunting elephant with Bruce Austen in the Wankie Controlled Hunting Area 1966, PHOTO Roy Creeth for Rhodesia Calls*

## Bushmen

Ted Davison made a verbal agreement with the bushmen to supply them with meat as long as they never poached in the park. This led to a permanent settlement of meat hungry Bushmen at Main Camp. In general, they were not regarded as being particularly reliable workers. Many though were exceptional in the bush and were to become valuable Parks' staff. They were great storytellers and often had a good sense of humour and were excellent trackers. Tim Braybrooke and others often had to deal with wily Bushmen poachers in the park and some were extremely dangerous.

## Patrols

When Tim Braybrooke arrived at Wankie he was issued on his first day with a horse, 2 pack mules and six pack-donkeys. Like other rangers, he had to sign a receipt for all this 'equipment'. Ted Davison told his staff that if they lost a horse or one of the mules they would be fired within 24 hours. If you lost a donkey the threatened punishment was a transfer to Lobuti in the middle of nowhere (south of park) for 6 months on your own. Tim had two pack mules called Whisky and Bob and his lead donkey called Mabaleka. When they went into the wild bush, there were no roads and Tim would follow elephant paths and blade mark trees on the route. Many of Wankie National Park's roads were made along his blade marks and he must have done some 600 miles of roads. Normally each ranger had a horse and Tim would take along his tracker called Japan. The men led the mules, which were often so good that they could walk with big pack

*Using land rover to catch giraffe
PHOTO Ministry of Information*

boxes through teak forests without walking the boxes into trees. Tim was armed in front with an armed man at the back of the group of about 5-6 men. On their trips they would check on water pumps and look for poachers. Junior rangers were told "goodbye" and would go on patrols for months at a stretch. It was tough being without white company for so long and sometimes rangers would jump on the train to Bulawayo, pretending to be on patrol.

## *Bruce*

Bruce Austen was a good horseman and once did a mounted patrol using two of his own horses. On his arrival from patrol back at Main Camp, he rode his horses on ahead. After arriving, he gave his horses injections for horse sickness, which meant they could not be ridden for a while. When the donkeys and mules began to arrive, Ted Davison wandered up and said, "You're back". "Ja" said Bruce. Ted continued with, "Don't unpack your kit; I want you to go to Robins." Bruce said, "I can't, I have just inoculated the horses, I can't ride them." Ted said, "That's fine, you'll walk." The donkeys were given a day's rest, while Bruce went to Dett to get supplies. Bruce went off on the patrol to Robins to pay the wages a good 100 miles away. All the way up there, the weather was stinking hot and oppressive. It was a hard patrol and Bruce spent the walk composing his resignation. However, on his way back the rains broke, the air was fresh, the skies blue and all the pans filled with water lilies. The bush took on its beautiful summer hue and everything sparkled. Bruce was overwhelmed and he forgot all about putting in his resignation. Wounded buffalo bulls are extremely aggressive and will often attack unprovoked, so acquiring the nickname of 'black death'. At one time

Parks' staff were following the spoor of some poachers close to the boundary near Lobuti and ran across a wounded buffalo. The buffalo attacked and injured a game scout named Sidhlohlo whose leg was broken in several places and the muscles torn. The buffalo stayed on the spot and died during the night. Bruce Austen carried the man to safety next morning and took him to hospital. From then on Sidhlohlo walked with a limp and was Bruce's faithful assistant for years afterwards.

## *Ugly*

Ranger Harry Cantle had a naughty gnu (wildebeest) called Ugly, which used to come into his house at Main Camp. As it grew up it became aggressive and was kept in a paddock by the office. On one occasion Ugly took exception to a government official, Mr. Sexton, who was gored through the thigh. After inflicting this nasty wound, for his troubles, Ugly was banished to the safety of Livingstone Game Park in Northern Rhodesia. Parks also caught a giraffe for Livingstone. They used a land rover, ropes and a harness with old belting to do this job. Tom recalled another wildebeest which got aggressive with people and finally met its match when someone who was attacked by it, beat it over the head with a metal pole.

## *Rastas*

Tom often spoke about Rastas the crow, a nuisance of a bird at Main Camp. Rastas used to do some mimicking and loved impersonating Connie. This bird had a bad habit of stealing shiny things, especially jewellery. National Parks had a list of items taken by Rastas. The list also documented those things that they presumed the bird had stolen. One day someone found Rastas' eye-dazzling treasure trove. The Parks' staff then sent all the missing items back to their respective owners by registered mail. One day Ted Davison had his spectacles stolen by Rastas and the bird flew up into the wide blue yonder. Ted was desperate to get his glasses back and sent some game scouts out with a blanket. While Rastas did wonderful aerial manoeuvres in the sky, the game scouts were running around below with the blanket trying to catch the glasses - if they fell. On one occasion, Rastas also took to the sky with a typewriter ribbon and enjoyed himself doing displays above the office. Jim Gordan a ranger from Kenya was warned about Rastas, but ignored the warning and left his office door open. He had been typing out pay sheets and did not listen to Bruce's

*Giraffe capture by Parks in Wankie for Livingstone Game Reserve 1956 PHOTO Ted Davison for (Game Dept. Annual Report)*

warning. When he got back from lunch at 2.00pm, he found Rastas had reorganized the place. The typewriter ribbon was strewn all over the office and the pay sheets torn up. He had to do it all over again! As Tom visited Main Camp over the years, he also saw Tim's ground hornbill. This bird used to ride on vehicles and peck grasshoppers and insects off the rangers' radiators after they returned from their patrols in the bush. Unfortunately, one day one of the rangers never saw him in the front of the land rover and drove over him. He was doctored and came right.

## *Matetsi*

The Matetsi/Kazuma district was plagued with lions and at least 25 cattle killers had to be eliminated in 1960. This area had good grazing and when there was a drought further south, cattle were driven up from the Plumtree/Marula ranches. Tim Braybrooke and Tom were sent out in a Parks' Land rover to watch both the farmers and the cattle. The cattle needed protection from the lions and the game needed protection from the farmers! The farmers were dead keen for

Tom and Tim to sort out the lions, but did not want to be watched while they shot illegally for the pot. Tom spent some time here on predator control and anti poaching. Bobby Young, whose family farmed at Nyamandhlovu, recalls one occasion when he and his young friends went up to Matetsi. They normally stayed with Squire Cummings on his ranch, but were at this time moving through Stoffels' Vlei. This was a huge grassy area, that stretched to the horizon and they were not allowed to hunt there. These youngsters were up to mischief, having deliberately gone up there to shoot game! They had just shot a zebra when they heard a noisy land rover in the distance, so they hid the zebra and their weapons in the bushes and moved some distance away. A fire was quickly made, pots and pans brought out and water was already boiling for tea when Tom arrived in his short wheelbase land rover. Tom asked, "What are you doing in the area." The reply was, "oh we are just having tea". They told him they were staying at the Cummings place and pretended to be lost. He was very suspicious and interrogated them. Eventually however he relaxed, sat down and joined them with a cup of tea. After he left, they waited for a while to see if he was spying on them and then they quickly returned to Squire Cumming's place. Tom chased Bob and his friends around without success. Later on, they met him at Kazuma pan where he again asked them what they were doing and once more, questioned them thoroughly. Tom was convinced they were responsible for the poaching that was taking place and wanted to handcuff them and take them away. They managed to talk their way out however and it was a narrow escape. He was so stern and fierce that they could not make up their minds whether he hated the human race or just poachers! When they met in later years Tom said to Bobby, "You were one guy I never managed to catch." Another of the youngsters Tom was trying to catch was Mike Bromwich, who later joined National Parks and became a good warden.

## *Gwaai Farmers*

The Gwaai farming community bordering Wankie National Park originally started when the government encouraged the settlement of (biltong) farmers who would want to hunt the game and thereby help check the spread of the tsetse fly. Over the years these farmers hacked out farms and homesteads as they pioneered the new district and cattle ranching became their main livelihood. Many of the farmers also tried (as did other Matabeleland farmers) to grow Turkish tobacco for a

*Wankie Main Camp restaurant PHOTO (1964 National Parks Annual Report)*

while - this was a good money-spinner while the world prices were high. There was often tension between the farmers and Parks' staff in the early days because the lions found the newly introduced cattle easy meat. The farmers' attitude was, "right these are your animals now and we hold you responsible for them." Needless to say, Parks' staff had little time for the farmers. However, when ranchers Tony Coomb and old man Kaneels Van Wyk formed the Gwaai Farmers association, a good working relationship was finally established with Ted Davison and his team. Tom often visited these farmers as he travelled about on vermin control and taught them how to use poisons on baboons and other troublesome predators.

## *Tony*

Tony Comb was a real character that had fought in the Battle of Jutland. He was apparently British upper class with good connections, while Kaneels Van Wyk was a true Afrikaner. For some reason these two very different characters hit it off. While hunting in the Okavango area, Tony was badly mauled by a lion and his leg badly damaged. His servant Chimwara carried him to help and safety some distance to a clinic. As Tony weighed 230 pounds, this must have been an incredible feat. He was then transported to Livingstone hospital, where Godfrey Huggins, a future prime minister of Rhodesia, amputated his leg. During his travels, he came across some beautiful crown land in the Gwaai area, bought it from the Government and decided to name it after his faithful servant Chimwara. His beautiful house, built from the stones of an ancient ruin, was situated near Half Way House. Tony was incredibly strong and legend has it that he could single handed lift a full 44-gallon drum of fuel onto his vehicle and you shook hands with him at your peril! When he hunted lion he would park 30-40 yards from the bait with his headlights switched off, but strategically aimed directly onto it. One of his assistants would sit in the land rover while he sat on the ground in the dark in front of the headlights. As the lions appeared, the lights would be switched on and Tony, with his back to the vehicle, would have ideal conditions in which to shoot them.

## *Van Wyks*
The Van Wyks settled on a ranch in the Kana block, which bordered the Shangani River. This area had an over abundance of lions and Parks' staff were often called in to deal with persistent killers. A ranger named Tony Boyce set a trap gun for a lion there next to a kraal. Sometime later a cow jumped out of the kraal and shot herself when she set the trap off. The Shangani River in the old days was a great fishing spot, with 10-pound tiger, 70-pound vundu and 3.5-pound bream. Sadly, the Tsetse department destroyed trees on the banks of the river, which was the end of the beautiful riverside surrounds. Furthermore, when too many cattle were allowed to overgraze further up stream, the loose soil was washed down the river and this led to it being silted up.

## *Other farmers*
The Venter family consisted of a grandmother, mother and two daughters. This all-woman family lived tough and each one of them could take care of themselves as well as any man. One of the granddaughters has been given credit for shooting the last rhino in the area; she was about 15 when she went out to shoot for the pot one day and that was the end of the rhino. Then another farmer used to legally lure elephants across the railway from the park to crops that he grew there for this purpose. Because the animals were away from the

*Sugar-Sugar 1975 being ridden by Soldier at the Gwaai hotel*
*PHOTO Chronicle*

protection of the Park and causing 'trouble' they could be legally shot. The ivory could be sold and the meat was turned into biltong and sold to the railways – a very profitable exercise. It was common knowledge that some of the farmers on the Gwaai did the odd bit of poaching, so rangers would be sent on patrol to the farms to check for possible evidence. Tim Braybrooke recalls a visit to one particular farm where he arrived at X's farmhouse and stopped his land rover. 'Tiger Tim' as Tim was nicknamed arrived, a door in the house opened just a little bit and about '100' snarling curs came running out. He then saw the curtains moving and X came out with his old .303 and said, "what do you bleep want here?" Tim meekly replied, "I am on patrol sir". X replied, "Everything is fine 'bleep' off". Old Granny X his wife was also a character and could chirp. When they had the Gwaai valley farmers association meeting once a month, she would sit in the front. Every meeting without fail and it did not matter who was talking, she would say in a loud voice, "Cecil Rhodes gave this farm and the government will not take it away from me". She was quite old by this time.

## *Gwaai Hotel*

It used to take forever to get to Victoria Falls from Bulawayo on the narrow winding strip road. These old roads were cheaply built back in the 1930's and made of only two narrow tar strips, but it was a sensible way to build a road in the hard times of the great depression. At every river, you had to wait your turn to cross the narrow bridges and it was convenient to make an overnight stop at the Gwaai hotel. Motorists also had to keep their eyes open for animals crossing the road, particularly elephants in the Mbali area that needed to access the water in the Gwaai River on the other side of the main road. On one occasion, a VW combi from Natal was smashed by an elephant on the road to Victoria Falls and overturned. The occupants slept the night in the upside down vehicle and then walked to the Gwaai hotel in the morning. When the combi was repaired, they refused to have the tusk marks removed from its sides and painted red rings around them. There is no record of what happened to the elephant, but no doubt, he walked off with some satisfaction! When the farm where the present Gwaai Hotel now stands was put up for sale just after World War II, no one wanted to buy it, so the owner put it on a raffle. A Mr. van Niekerk won it and proceeded to build the hotel, which then became the social centre of the district. He kept an African Painted Dog on a long lead behind his store and no one dared come near his unlocked store (the old name wild dog leads to confusion with domestic dogs).

## *Lions*

The local ranchers were continually losing cattle to lions and when the cattle panicked, they could stampede a long way and end up in the park. If this happened, a message would be sent to the owner with the warning that if the animals were not collected they would be shot. Because it was often too far and difficult to collect just a few animals, they were invariably shot and turned into biltong (dried meat) by the Parks' staff. Buck De Vries, a local rancher in the district, built a large strong kraal by bolting mopane poles together. His cattle would be placed in the kraal overnight before being taken to Kennedy Siding the next day to be loaded on the train. One night 300 head of cattle were sleeping there when a pride of lions arrived and although the lions could not get through the thick walls of the kraal, the cattle heard and smelt them and panicked. Desperate to get out, they pushed against each other and the pressure was so great that some of them crashed through the walls of the stockade. Inside many were crushed and others outside the kraal had to be shot because their legs were broken. He lost 80 precious animals that night. Buck never kraaled his cattle again and used to sleep in the Dett vlei with them to try and protect them. He made his bed in his roofless old series one land rover, which did not even have a windscreen. His boss man, called Chiparapata, was a little man who also slept in the vehicle wrapped up in blankets. It was often extremely cold here and temperatures sometimes went below zero degrees centigrade. The little guy would wake Buck up if there was any activity. The lions would chase the cattle into the forest and then Buck had to drive around looking for them. When the lions started choking the animals to death, the cattle would try to fight back. When it was freezing cold in the middle of winter, Buck remembers the lions generating so much heat in their battle with the cattle that they would be covered in sweat, which then vaporized and rose up into the trees like smoke.

## *The Pub*

Permits to hunt elephant could be bought at the nearest post office and old Man van Niekerk made good use of them by shooting elephants to supplement his income. Although most times his hunting was legal, he appears to have been caught once by the Parks' staff for poaching. From then on the rangers were not in his good books so they avoided his hotel and frequented the Dett pub instead. However, there was also a problem there, because many of the tough railway men were habitual poachers who did not like or trust Parks' staff. The rangers did not want to be drawn into a fight and so Bruce Austen and Tim Braybrooke always went together to protect themselves and avoid trouble. When Van Niekerk sold the hotel to Harold Bloomberg and his partners, the new owners welcomed the rangers and it became their regular watering hole. The rangers spent much of their free time there and Tom remembered a few wild parties and one when men danced around like ostriches! Although in later years Bruce Austen became a real gentleman, in his young days he and Tim Braybrooke were wild young rangers. They spent a lot of time in the bush with very little company and no entertainment and when they came out, they needed to cut loose. Ted Davison used to try to keep either one or the other out on patrol to prevent their getting together and misbehaving. Once they borrowed one of Harold Bloomberg's pigs and let it loose in one of the hotel rooms and this caused much merriment. Later when Bruce was warden at Main Camp, he always made sure Braybrooke was there, so they could have a good time with the likes of John Coleman and others. Tim remembers Bruce coming into Braybrooke's single quarters house and saying, "get ranger Thomson and ranger Boyce." After being woken up by Tim they asked, "What rifles must we bring?" "No rifles come". The men then used the old dirt Dett Vlei Road to go to the hotel. However, when the Gwaai Copper Mine came into being, a new road was built to Main Camp and that old road, with all its memories, was no longer used. On one occasion, the men entertained themselves by catching springhares on the road. These were placed in a sack, bundled into the land rover and taken off to the hotel. They walked into the pub and let the miniature kangaroo-like creatures loose and soon they were bouncing everywhere. Harry Cantle also loved to have a good blast and he was happy mixing with the railway crowd, as he had worked on the railways at some stage. After having too many drinks one night, he and his mates were said to have managed to stick a few stamps on the backside of a wild elephant. One of the rangers was so drunk once that his friends gave him a dead terrapin to eat, which they passed off as a meat pie. He happily started to crunch away at his pie! Terrapins are hard and when just out of the water somewhat slimy and smelly. His face was probably a picture when he tried to sink his teeth into it.

### *Harry's Lions*
When visitors at Main Camp complained because they had not heard or seen any lions around, Harry sorted out the problem by playing a tape recording of lions roaring. That evening the tourists were blissfully happy as they listened to lions calling in the distance. In the morning when Harry went outside, he found himself in all sorts of trouble; the whole place was full of lions. They had heard the tapes during the night, moved in and did not seem to want to leave.

*Railway line by Dett*

*Tom on boat with Rex Bean behind offloading bushbuck on mainland 1959 PHOTO Ronald Hadden for Ministry of Information*

## CHAPTER 6
# OPERATION NOAH 1959-1963

*The Filling*
In December of 1958, the Kariba dam wall was finally closed. This was the start of the filling of a lake some 200 kilometres long and up to 20 kilometres wide. In the weeks following, the staff of the Game Dept. with other government departments, started to monitor the situation. The Zambezi banked up the Nyaodza and Sanyati riverbeds and caused the rivers to flow in reverse directions. The fish were ecstatic and fed on trapped and drowning insects that attempted to climb higher up the grasses. Cat fish would shake plants vigorously causing the insects to fall into the water. Tiger fish in fighter plane formation and large Vundus hit their prey in the flooded hinterland. Below the Kariba dam wall, the fish were so thick that black fishermen caught them simply by jigging bare fishing hooks through the water.

*First Captures*
The Game Dept. then started to develop techniques for capturing

*Len Harvey on OP. Noah. Len was later killed by a lion*

game and by the end of 1958; they had caught a variety of small animals and antelopes. The men expected to rescue and translocate animals from the beginning. Using small boats, they caught baboons, monkeys, genets, dassies and small antelopes in the water. Some animals swam well, while others drowned. Guinea fowl were like ducks and tortoises like paddling bowls. The fern Salvinia molesta carpeted the lake, covering up to 75 square miles and in places became so thick one could lie on it. It was so thick in places that man, beast and boat could not move. Trees were submerged and their crowns festooned with spider webs, while millions of insects fled and swarmed everywhere. Dead bodies floated on the water and the crocodiles were well feasted.

## *The Rangers*

Rupert Fothergill was the man chosen to take on the herculean task to save all the animals at Kariba, as the valley began to flood. He and his contemporaries had been doing mostly game control and antipoaching work. He was now to be involved in the biggest animal rescue in history. Other men with Rupert and Tom were Frank Junor, Brian Hughes, Rex Bean, Mike Van Rooyen, Peter Jones, Stewart Claasen, Tinkey Haslam, Barry Ball and Len Harvey who was later eaten by a lion. Tinkey Haslam was a wild, fun loving man who loved to have a

*Rupert and staff tying up bushbuck after capture on OP. Noah. The man on his left looks like Kadiki (later a Sgt in Head Office) who was one of Rupert's game scouts. PHOTO Ronald Hadden for Ministry of Information.*

drink, and a good hunter who was to do much good work for wildlife. These were all tough friendly young Bushmen. The men of Operation Noah had courage, compassion, hard work, love for animals and a typical Zimbabwe/Rhodesia skill for making plans. At its peak there were 19 white men from the Game dept. involved, working with veterinary officials and about 70 black workers. The white men enjoyed nature and for their work received little financial reward. Then there were the tough black men like California, who was a strong valley boy who had also hunted with Tom and Rupert. The black staff were amazed at the strange behaviour of these white men. It didn't make sense to catch animals and then release them into hunting areas. For just down the road at Kariba black folk were being paid a bonus by the government for every baboon tail produced. Another member of the capture team was Crackers the hound, who was often more of a hindrance than help, but always a pleasure to have around. Crackers was a mongrel sausage dog and was the Operation Noah mascot.

## *Boats*

The team used 18-foot and 15-foot diesel powered steel boats, later to be joined by a barge and then in April 1959 the 30 foot Tuna. The Tuna mother ship was used to tow a flotilla of about 6 flat-bottomed craft with 50 horsepower outboard motors and a light ski boat. The flat-bottomed boats were used for the transport of game to the mainland. One of the boats on the lake was named the Hilda Mary. The Ark was the supply boat that kept the men in provisions.

## *Techniques*

The first technique the rangers used to catch animals was to drive 'beat' them off the islands into water where they could be caught from a boat. These could be lassoed, caught by hand from the boat or caught by a swimmer. From here the animals would be dropped off on the mainland or released in shallow water with the complementary ear tag. On one occasion Tom went into the water to retrieve a poor little night ape that was seen in a tree miles from the shoreline. This unhappy creature was on a perch a few inches above the water line. Tom put the creature on his head and swam for the Tuna. As the night ape kept slipping off into the water, he grabbed its tail in his teeth and towed it to the boat where he handed it to the safe hands of Len Harvey. Tom was often mentioned for his ability and bravery in capturing animals on Kariba, from the snakes to the rhinos, but he was one of many. He was particularly expert at rescuing the animals found in the riverside vegetation such as bush pig, bushbuck and vervet monkeys. He made light of his involvement in this operation saying anyone could have done it. "It's easy to save an animal if you like them. In any case, I thought it was rather special."

## *Nets*

With the introduction of nets on large islands such as Irrigation Island, as many as 70 animals a day could be rescued. Net capture led to animals dying of shock and tranquilizers were introduced. A local doctor named Jim Leggert tried adrenalin injections to revive the shocked animals. Game nets were about 10 feet high and up to 200 yards long. The nets were supported by heavy poles and strong ropes attached to trees. The nets were hidden in shallow ditches and camouflaged. The animals were then chased towards the nets by beaters. Whether you were waiting at the nets or chasing the creatures it was dangerous, as you never knew what could suddenly appear out

*Bushbuck being released on Mainland OP. Noah 1959 with California PHOTO Ronald Hadden for Ministry of Information*

of the trees. There was the danger of kicking hooves and of razor sharp warthog tusks. The end of 1959 had seen the rescue of over 2000 animals on Lake Kariba.

### *Phineas*

Once on a drive a number of impala were rounded up in a netted enclosure. Phineas, who was Tom's faithful black tracker, batman and cook, happened to be present. Phineas was avoiding the darting, jumping antelopes trying to escape, and in Tom's words the was, "looking like a mopane tree". A ram broke away from the net and hit Phineas flat in the chest and bowled him over. At first Tom thought the man had been mortally horned right through his body. He was relieved to see Phineas get up and dust himself off. Tom's comment was, "Why didn't you catch him?" The short man who was about 4 foot 4 inches high replied with pride and said, "Do you think you could have caught the impala if it had hit you like that?"

### *Stockings*

The ropes that were used to hobble the antelopes, chafed the animals' legs. An appeal was made for silk and nylon stockings and the response was overwhelming, with tons arriving from all over the world. After the request went out they had something like 1000 pairs of stockings arriving in the first 24hrs. The ladies contributed more than their share, as panties were often sent to the rescue of the wildlife. The Game Department staff soon disposed of these and many no doubt ended up in various townships. After administering drugs to cope with shock, small animals were put in grain sacks, while the larger ones had their legs tied with plaited, ladies nylon stockings. Machillas (animals hung from a pole while carried) were used to carry the animals back to the boats.

## *Honey Badger*
The honey badger was the animal Tom learnt to respect. This tough animal is not scared to take on elephant and I have heard of two lions fighting one ferocious creature. Probably the most comical and impressive capture was when Tom and Rupert took on a honey badger. Mary Ball was sitting in one of the boats on the edge of an island. She saw Tom and Rupert come sprinting out of the bush like Duracell bunnies. The men fleeing for their lives, dived into the boat, as they ran away from the fierce honey badger. Rupert was determined to 'get' this particular badger and said, "I made up my mind there and then that I was going to wipe out the disgrace of having to run for it". It seems the same beast took to water after being driven from the undergrowth. Rupert swam after the animal and grabbed it by the tail, but was soon in retreat from the fierce animal. The badger made for the branches of a submerged tree where it tried to escape observation. Tom now came to Rupert's assistance with the boat. The two men were soon shaking it loose and then chasing it through the tops of mopane trees. It thrashed around until Rupert got a lasso around its neck and it was hauled unceremoniously on to the boat's deck. While Rupert pressed its neck down with his foot, Tom tied its legs. The animal was now wrapped in some canvas and tightly bound with rope. Both men were now exhilarated with their victory, but not for long. Tom shouted, "Watch out the blighter's getting loose." The men scrambled to the escaping prisoner. Its head biting through the canvas, some glaring eyes appeared and it was free. In the chaos the badger plunged overboard and when it hit the surface, Rupert made a grab for it. His finger was crunched for his efforts and he held it tight until they got near the mainland, where Rupert released it in shallow water. There was also a story about a badger escaping from a box on a boat and lots of white eyed, gaping staff, jumping in the water to escape from it. Tom was proud to take the first known picture of a swimming honey badger.

## *Pigs*
The bottom tusks on warthogs are like razor blades and men often had to climb trees. Tom says warthogs on this risky operation nearly castrated him. Warthogs were one of the most dangerous animals they had to deal with. After capture, the snouts of hazardous warthogs and

*Rupert holding bushpig before release OP. Noah PHOTO Ronald Hadden for Ministry of Information*

bushpig were bound securely to a firm object. On one occasion a bushpig turned back after being released and attacked one of the trackers named Sarachekepa. "Look out this character is going back into the water," yelled Tom. The pig went in the water, was tackled again and hauled out of the lake. It then broke loose and hit Sarachekepa full in the chest and sent him into a back somersault. He had a bit of flesh taken from his finger. On another occasion a pig just missed a black catcher, jumped into the water and started to swim. Tom battled to get the boat going, as the engine wouldn't start. When he finally got the engine going and neared the pig it was too late. The sunken pig walked along the bottom and drowned.

## Snakes

The first year on Operation Noah was the worst for snakes. The submerged trees were festooned with them and they often fell into the boats. This normally resulted in the occupants leaping out of the boat into the water. A sable was caught and was put in a boat, but was not held properly by the horns. This animal then flicked a game scout out of the boat into the water. This man now found himself in a sorry situation, as he couldn't swim. When he looked around he saw a nasty looking boomslang on a branch near his head. Suddenly he virtually walked on water back into the boat. Sable antelope were one of the more dangerous animals with their scimitar like horns. Sable horns were held with respect, as they were not averse to using them. One captured sable was released in shallow water. As it wasn't moving to land they tried to throw things at it. They were surprised to see it hit every missile thrown at it with its horns – putting many a cricket

*Bushpig being carried from net in background while Tom and Rupert discuss strategy. OP. Noah 1959. The man at rear left (in the photo) is Gizani who was one of many Shangaans on the operation. PHOTO Ronald Hadden for Ministry of Information*

player to shame. One night the black staff were thrown into turmoil as a dangerous puff adder paid them a visit. Tom rushed off to the rescue, put his foot behind its head and grabbed it by the tail. He stuffed it into a sack. He made a few remarks to them about them being a gang of tsotsis (ruffians) that were afraid of a harmless wriggling snake and then went back to sleep. Tom with his theatrics was caught on film dangling a snake in his mouth, but was no snake catcher like Frank Junor. Frank was a fundi (expert) on snakes and was not afraid to take on the deadly mambas as he shoved them into sacks. On one occasion Frank was bitten by a house snake. He was injected with a serum before an identification of the snake was made and was nearly killed by the serum. There were some well-known snake catchers present on the lake. Mr. Dick Isemonger collected snakes from the game rangers for the Salisbury Snake Park, while Don Broadley was the acknowledged reptile expert.

## *Primates*

Monkeys and baboons were often left stranded in the tops of trees for as long as 4 months, as the islands were engulfed with water. Often they would dive in the water and swim under the surface. The rangers would have to dive overboard and swim after them. Big baboons couldn't swim well under water like the monkeys and had their bums habitually sticking up above the water. Baboons also took to aardvark holes in their attempt to hide on islands. The starving baboons resorted to killing small game to survive on the islets. When the men caught baboons, they were normally released in Zambia, as they were not desirable residents on the Southern Rhodesia side. Tom once saw a baboon in distress as it struggled to swim. He jumped off the flat barge into the water to help the primate. As he closed in on the baboon, it grabbed Tom and prevented him from swimming. He found himself unable to swim and was drowning. The men in the boat seeing his distress jumped in and saved both of them.

## *Aardvark*

Aardvarks would stay knuckled up (safely holed up) in their holes until forced out by the rising waters. Holes had their surprises for the catchers, with a baboon and porcupine found in the same hole, while on another occasion there was a baboon, warthog and aardvark together. Tom and Rupert had to enter an aardvark hole to extract 2 female aardvarks and a young warthog. One day there was an aardvark cornered in its hole, with an observer standing above the hole and waiting for it to come out. Aardvarks and warthogs could suddenly charge from the entrance, so it was wise to stand above the hole. This aardvark decided not to escape through the hole, but erupted straight up through the ground where the man was standing. He found himself in a veritable volcano as it burst out of the earth.

## *Camp Life*

In the open bush camps the men had modest cooking equipment and their camp had rudimentary facilities. There was little good food away from base and lots of tiger fish, bream and vundu on the menu. No animals dying on the operation were to be eaten. This prevented 'accidental' deaths. They slept under stars and mosquito nets, while canvas awnings helped with the rain. Bathing was done in the lake. The mosquitoes came like thick fog and would 'massage' their backs. At night under simple paraffin lamps there was little in the way of

*Tom steering a boat to the mainland with captured game on OP. Noah 1959*

entertainment. Tom could change this by bringing gaiety to any gathering and would produce a series of 'cracks' (comments) with machine gun rapidity that would lift downcast spirits. Tom would often play the rejected suitor. He would assume an air of mock dejection and said that his only option in the matter was to go big game hunting. Tom had a fantastic armoury of rifles, shot guns, automatics and hunting knives. He would appear accoutred like a Corsican bandit and would jokingly threaten a highly unpleasant form of death to anyone who dared to cross his path. Tom was a favourite with blacks who enjoyed his humorous tongue-lashings. When the men were lying in their sodden camp beds in a thunderstorm, it was Tom who rigged up a radio under his mosquito net, under a packing case to tune into the gay music of a Johannesburg nightclub. "Just think of the contrast between our healthy, outdoor life, with the sky as our roof and the trees as our walls, and that of those poor blasé creatures who have nothing better to do than sit in a fetid den, full of cigarette smoke, listening to artificial jungle music," he said mildly. Then to cap his efforts he miraculously produced steaming hot coffee. When bread became stale and bitter, it was Tom who made delicious hot scones to add to their usual fish and tinned food. Tom had some cooking skills and once came to the rescue of the Prime Minister's party with some first class pies. Sir Roy Welensky the Federal Prime Minister had laid the last strip of concrete on the 420-foot high Kariba wall on June 2 1959. This signified the finishing of the largest manmade lake in the world. While here, he met the men of Operation Noah and became great friends with Tom. Sir Roy and

*Tom holding Bushbaby on OP. Noah 1959 PHOTO Ronald Hadden for Ministry of Information*

Tommy got on well together and were always bantering with each other, especially about dogs.

## Base Camp

The base camp at Kariba was well managed by Rex and Gwen Bean. It was named after Peter Moore and given the name Peter's Point. The camp was built up on a peninsula jutting into the lake close to the dam wall. The open rectangular dining room gave a good view of the lake. It had a thatched reed roof and was always a welcome for the men after their hard trips on the lake. It had its own little garden in which it was said Rupert would water his paw paws in the nude. Base camp was a good place to have a few beers and good food. A neighbour Graham Paxton could always be counted on to provide a good meal and warm shower.

## The Press

Before Operation Noah on Lake Kariba took place, the human race tended to look only at hunters as being heroes (with wildlife). Operation Noah probably created the first conservation heroes. This was a turning point for world conservation, man's relations with animals and was a milestone in African conservation. Operation Noah brought a tremendous amount of publicity to the Federation and for its wildlife. The effects of this went beyond its borders to Natal Parks in South Africa, as they were said to have benefited from the attention. At first Archie kept the operation quiet. When he eventually let journalists come down to look, someone came up with an 'Operation Noah on a shoestring' article. The government was so embarrassed that they gave Archie more money for boats and staff. Soon there was media frenzy as the public clamoured to find out what the wildlife heroes were doing. There was lots of pressure put on the staff by newspaper reporters, cameramen, writers, politicians and women. Tom was too busy at times to talk to American and BBC journalists who sometimes got on his nerves. Nevertheless, Tom was also keen, like some of the others, to entertain the press. Tom not only got on a book cover, but found himself portrayed in a full-page photo in LIFE magazine. This magazine is similar to the modern TIME magazine. With many brave, tanned, muscled hunks saving poor animals, it was no wonder that there were many women in camp. Frank Junor was a charmer and he had ladies floating around him like bees at a honey pot. Barry Ball took over briefly from Rupert and found with all the reporters, photographers, research people, VIPs and a whole lot of women hanging around, it was too much. Barry promptly ordered the woman off the island where they were working, including his future wife Mary. As a researcher, Mary was collecting mammal specimens for the national museum and it certainly was not love at first sight.

## *Research*
The Game Dept. had its own researchers now. Frank was the new fisheries officer, while Graham Child was a wildlife ecologist. When Graham first met Tom he was told by Tom all the finer points of game capture and important details. These details included which part of the lake had the worst mosquitoes. Graham tried to get Tom to be more scientific and to write down all he observed, but Tom was not very interested.

## *Wild Pets*
Rupert, like Tom, loved animals and during the years he was with Tom, often kept parrots, genets and other creatures. Rupert would often bring home a hyena, baboon or monkey, which Christine his wife would have to look after. In the bush Rupert enjoyed not having his clothes on. On one rare occasion he was seen nude at his Rhodes Avenue Belvedere home in Salisbury, where he raced out of bed into the yard one night to quiet a young hyena. This pet of the Fothergills had decided to practice its mating call (a somewhat eerie sound in suburbia) and their elderly neighbour came out on her second story balcony with her torch to see what was going on. She saw a nude Rupert and was taken away the next day by ambulance having suffered a heart attack!! True story! On Operation Noah, Christine became a mother to a range of wild animals including 13 orphaned

fish eagle chicks, which had to be fed every day. To feed the fish eagle chicks, Tom would run a boat to get the propellers going. Curious vundu came up to investigate the noise and he would shoot them with a revolver. The men also collected various pets, which included kudus, dassies, genets and a small baboon. Desmond the baboon went to Chester Zoo in Britain to live in style as a VIP and was to receive over a million visitors. Christine also had a young baboon named Zambezi and a small vervet monkey named Sanyati. Sanyati would swing on Christine's telephone wire, as there were no decent sized trees nearby. Tom had a way with some of these animals and pacified poor young creatures by letting them suck his sugar coated fingers.

## *Dangers*

Kariba was wild and free, life hard, tough and dangerous. Men had to spend up to 8 hours a day grappling with dangerous game in water or mud, dealing with mosquitoes, tsetse flies and stinging ants. They would often come back to camp undernourished, with sores, wounds and roughed up. Margaret Haslam back at base camp helped sort out these sick men and the odd animal. In the field Tom acted as the self taught medic, being well read and he handled the first aid kit. He would treat men of all colours and animals, with delicate skill and patience. When the black folk got sick they would go to him for treatment. Often in jest, He would produce a knife and say that amputation was their only cure. When Graham Child met Tom on Operation Noah for the first time, a man named John from the museum had caught his hand between two boats, injuring his hand at the Kariba game camp. Tom, with enthusiasm, suddenly appeared, came to the rescue and took the man to hospital. Frank and Tom caught a small Goliath Heron injured by a monkey, which they medically treated. Later they found it trying to fish pathetically from a small boulder with its impaired vision. The two men caught it and took it back to the campsite. Here they slid fish after fish down the heron's throat. A grysbok that the men caught was in poor condition and was dying. Tom tried to keep the poor creature alive and taking it, wrapped it in his sweater. He took it to his camp bed where he gently placed it between the sheets. After his meal, he went to bed and snuggled up to the grysbok, sleeping with it all night in his arms. He hoped that the warmth of his body would keep it alive. In the morning the animal was barely alive and half an hour after he rose from his bed the animal had died.

## *New Reserves*
Tom was also involved in the early days of Matusadona, before the lake was finished. Here a camp was built for the ranger and staff, roads selected, harbour sites built and bush clearing done at the Sanyati and Bumi complex. Les Gregory started the close by Chizarira Game reserve and Brian Hughes was to pioneer the Urungwe, where the famous Mana Pools National Park now resides. These remote areas were hard to access. The first ranger at Matusadona was the plant loving, Lofty Middleton-Stokes. The tall and bush wise Lofty once had a good-looking wife who originated from Namibia. Ian Nyschens visited Lofty down in the Sabi valley and a shooting challenge was taken up. Ian was a good shot, while Lofty was fairly good. However, when the shooting contest started the men could not match her shooting skills. She was consistently hitting bulls at 200 yards. She had been a farmer's daughter and had been sent out by her father to shoot springhares as Ian joked, 'only when they jump.' Lofty left the country later to settle in New Zealand.

## *With Bob*
Bob Truman was a Land Inspector with the Dept. of Lands and was seconded to the Game Department at Kariba. He was to help with survey work, demarcate the eventual shoreline on the 1590ft contour, peg the various commercial sites and to run levels on the islands to indicate which islands were going to go first, so giving an order of rescue in between other jobs. Tommy and Bob spent a lot of time together particularly during a six-month stretch on what was the Inyamune River, which drained some of the flatter land between the Matusiadonas and the lake. Bob Comments, "We lived bush style under thatch of our own devising with around 20 boys to cut survey lines etc. We had two pole beds under a communal roof. There were leopard and hyena about so the dog slept at the bottom of my bedroll in case. We got on reasonably well and I suppose were quite tolerant of each other.... a rooi neck (though I had been out there 5 yrs) and a colonial! Tommy liked his food. He had a large tin trunk jam-packed with all kinds of tinned delicacies, mostly originating from Macey's, I think. He went off to town to get a refill every two months or so. So, the high spot of the week was Friday night scoff time (not sure how we even knew what day it was sometimes!) And the question was

put... what are we going to have for sweet this time? The undoubted favourite was Honeynut Roll.... such extravagance! There were probably 15 tins of it! Living close together, little things irritate. Tommy had an awful (well, that's what it became after six months) habit of clearing his throat. Only a brief 'huugh', but he did it twice a minute or more. I at one stage probably gave serious thought to strangulation!! I undoubtedly may of course also been guilty of some irritating idiosyncrasy that made Tom feel the same about me.... we lived through it! He habitually toted a colt .45 automatic in a thigh holster and was so persistent that these should be de rigueur that he convinced me I needed one too. Can you believe it? There we were both ambling around like a couple of western gunslingers. Did come up trumps once.... we were walking up what was the old Naodsa dry sand riverbed (can't remember what actually for) and we rounded this sharpish bend to confront five lionesses and a male just on the bank and under an acacia tree. They all stood up as we came into view. We stopped as one; a lioness stretched her legs and began walking towards us looking quite purposeful. I don't remember who was quickest on the draw but we both fired a shot in the air which sounded like a single Blam at which all lions fortuitously departed at speed. So they did come in useful after all! I had a twenty five foot launch called 'Scorpio' which we used to get to and from Kariba Township and also to lay out a gill net to catch ration fish for the boys. Somehow, on one occasion the net found its way to wrap around the prop. Tom immediately took charge. Pushing me (I am a lot bigger) to one side. He drew a villainous looking knife from somewhere about his person, stuck it pirate style between his teeth and disregarding a distinct possibility of encountering a croc (we were only a mile away from the Sanyati gorge) disappeared with a splash over the side to start the unravelling. He came up for air at intervals, finished the job, but as he swarmed back over the side, managed to drop the knife (I swear it weighed all of three pounds) over the side. I was informed that I had to buy him a new one!"

## *Elephant*

Elephants could pose a problem on the islands and Bob Truman records an occasion when 3 elephant were despatched. "It went like something like this: It was actually all seriously unofficial! Rupert had grumpily gone off to Kariba to get permission from Salisbury to drop these three because they just would not leave for the mainland some 3/4 miles away even after multiple risky efforts with boats and were thus obstructing the rescue of everything else. There was a lot of other game there and the situation was urgent. That left Tom, Tinkey and me to await Rupert's return. Tom took out his Rigby .470, but was a bit reluctant to start, yet sort of driven along by Tinkey's enthusiasm. We came up to them just on the edge of the island as we walked some 5 yards apart. I was on the right, Tinkey in the middle with Tom on the left flank. Tinkey called, "everybody ready?" and at that hurled several clods of earth towards the jumbos. Heads came up; circling, they made threatening noises. The middle one's ears came forward, trunk well up to catch our wind and he lumbered several steps quite sharply toward us. I suddenly remembered Tom had mentioned to me a year or so back that an elephant will normally give two false charges and keep coming on the third. It certainly didn't apply on this occasion. All three were now serious; coming at a rate of knots! (Perhaps the previous hassles with the boats had upset them) This was something I had not previously really been involved with and even though in the ensuing minutes the adrenalin was in full flow, I felt my heart beating rather wildly! There was red dust and a crashing sound as they pushed through twig and branch, sounds which seemed crystal sharp to me, then 'Blam' the elephant in front of Tinkey dropped like a stone, coming to rest on its chest. Seconds later and 'Blam' again as Tom took on the left handed one, which was actually coming through shallow water in a small inlet from the lake. It went down on its side with a huge splash, water spurting high. All this in seconds, but it seemed almost in slow motion. The third was a dual effort, the shots sounding almost as one as this last monster beast closed with me, less that 15 yards away now, 'Blam, blam,' almost simultaneously, as both the others decided to make absolutely sure! Rupert was back in camp that evening and rather more cheerful with the OK from town to go ahead with the cull. Tom and I left it to Tinkey to tell the tale!!"

### *Buffalo*

After 1959, Tom was rarely up at the lake, just popping in on special operations. Game such as buffalo, sable, waterbuck and impala had to be brought in from Kariba for Kyle, and Tom would go and help his fellow rangers up at the lake. On one occasion Alan Savory, Tom and others were trying to catch buffalo calves on Operation Noah. Alan went off with Samson and some other staff to try to catch one. They were chasing a group of about 20 to 30 buffalo and were running behind the herd to try to catch the calves. As Alan chased them into a grassy depression, one of the buffalo turned around and came back. Alan mistook it for a calf and as it came out, he stood his ground, waiting to catch the three quarter size buffalo. It charged Alan who tried to grab its horns. His left hand slipped and the buffalo hooked him in the chest and arm and threw him over its back. Alan landed and scrambled desperately as he hit the ground and was on his hands and knees. The buffalo then started to gore Alan who now had his hands around its horns. Alan twisted its neck like he had done with oxen in his earlier days. He managed to twist the animal down and it fell on his legs. The animal was furious and was thrashing its head up and down. While Alan held on, the animal's boss was hitting the ground, but his legs were getting graunched. Samson shouted to him to let go. Alan let go and Samson then grabbed him by the arms and pulled him to safety, as the buffalo rose to its feet. Alan was safe, as Samson had tied the buffalo's back legs in the chaos. Alan was then able to call Tom, Rupert and others. This was the biggest buffalo they caught without drugs. With about 40 men, the team eventually dealt with the animal and heaved it to the shore. While they were near the Bumi mouth, Frank Junor was gored by a buffalo and he was lucky to be still alive afterwards.

## *Later years*
On another occasion, there was a waterbuck bull and a kudu bull in a pen. The team wanted to catch the waterbuck and nobody could get a rope on it. Alan eventually jumped in off the wall onto its neck and pulled it down cowboy style, but was soon in need of help. No one had the courage to jump in there to help him. Tom however being the exception jumped in and helped wrestle it into submission and tie it with ropes. Alan commented that Tom was the guy they laughed at, but was the only one with the courage to jump in. At this later stage the Operation Noah team was working from their temporary bases on the islands and being supplied from their tinned hut headquarters at Kariba. The camps on the islands were very crude and the men often just slept under tarpaulins. There was still the odd researcher. Rupert, who was Tom's idol, now had about 40 black staff and a handful of white rangers. One of the men now on the team was Paul Coetsee who was a talented hunter and was to shoot a phenomenal amount of elephant. Like his brother Clem, he was good with his hands and

wildlife.

## *Operation Ends*
In 1963, the world famous Operation Noah ended with some 6000 animals, birds and reptiles being saved over a period of four and a half years. In this last year, the men had bravely continued their work catching a variety of creatures. Rupert by this stage had had his share of close shaves. On one occasion being targeted by a rhino, he ducked behind a tree trunk that was rotten. The rhino ran right through it and the tree landed on him. Rupert escaped through the back legs of the rhino and ended up with six cracked ribs. He also got cracked ribs after a buffalo caught him. Rupert had now become Africa's most celebrated game ranger. At this later stage, some of the game caught on the operation was used to restock private farms, parks and zoos. Viv Wilson a well-known author and scientist, who started Chipangali wildlife orphanage, happened to be on Operation Noah at this time. He remembers meeting Tom and found him unbelievably dedicated to his job and a useful medic. Viv not knowing Tom asked, "Tom are you new here?" Tom visibly upset replied, "What do you mean am I new here, I started this". In recognition of Rupert Fothergill's efforts at Kariba, Rupert received an MBE (Member of the British Empire) from Queen Elisabeth. However when he heard that the Beatles had also received an MBE for their music, he sent his back with a letter to the Queen, telling her that he was not going to be put in the same category as some long-haired, rock music group, and that she could keep her medal. Just as Operation Noah ended, so did the Federation of Rhodesia and Nyasaland. This was to split into Malawi, Zambia and Rhodesia. With the end of the Federation, it was decided to amalgamate Rhodesia's National Parks and the Dept. of Wild Life Conservation (Game Dept.) to form the Dept. of National Parks and Wildlife Management. It now became one organization, which controlled vast swathes of the country. The Game Department had worked mostly in the valley and to the East of the country, while National Parks had worked either in 'parks and gardens' or in the Wankie/Victoria Falls complex, where there was big game. As National Parks had been tourist orientated, they were a rich department. The Game Dept. bush babies benefited greatly from the two departments becoming one.

*Hartebeest capture in Chipinda area for Kyle, Top left Lammeck, top right warden Tinkey Haslam*

## CHAPTER 7
# KYLE 1960-1966

### *Original Farms*
Kyle Game Reserve came into being when Kyle Dam was built to provide water for the massive sugar and wheat irrigation schemes in the Southern Rhodesian Lowveld. Two farms on the northern side of the new dam were used to form the basis of the new game reserve. Basutos once settled the first, a farm named Ericsthal and the ruins of their stone built houses were still there when the Park was formed. They called it Mutundumushawa 'the place of red earth'. In time, this farm became overgrazed and over cultivated and was acquired by the government who used it as a quarantine area for imported livestock and for controlled public grazing. A German called Leiss who built quality brick stables, outbuildings and a house had pioneered the second farm, Bompst, about the turn of the century. When the dam was built, Bompst belonged to the Swart family whom Tom knew well. As the waters rose, most of the farm was flooded and the government acquired three quarters of it for the new park. Ericsthal

*Putting up the fence in the new Kyle Game Reserve with Lake Kyle in the background.*

Game reserve, was about 10 000 acres in extent and was to become known as Kyle.

### From Scratch

Up to 1960 Tom had spent most of his time under Rupert Fothergill dealing with crop raiding elephants and buffalos, with vermin control and anti-poaching exercises on farms, state land and in protected areas. Now Tom was sent to the Fort Victoria area to pioneer and open up this newly designated Kyle Game reserve. When he started there, he lived in the old Bompst farmhouse, just outside the new game reserve. Starting a game reserve from scratch was a heavy responsibility, but Tom was ready for the challenge and put his heart and soul into this new venture. He undertook all the preliminary work such as surveying, fencing, accommodation, harbours and roads. Quite apart from these tasks, he had to oversee the restocking of the Park with healthy animals captured from other areas. Soon after the lake began to fill, Tom built a game fence consisting of 10 strands of high tensile steel wire and 3 strands of barbed wire. At one point, he found it was too difficult to put the fence over a large hill, so he put it around, so 'liberating' and including a bit of extra land for the reserve. It seems no one apart from a few Game Department staff ever noticed. Fireguards, drains, culverts and roads had to be built all around the park and this took time, as he only had tractor drawn scrapers. Tom was famous for acquiring grader time and fuel from other government departments and using them for the Game department. He managed to persuade government officials grading elsewhere to come and do a 'bit' of work at Kyle where he would provide the diesel. The old Game Department was very short of funds and the staff became experts on improvisation and using their initiative.

## *Buildings*

The first task was the perimeter fence, after which Tom went to work on the buildings. There was nothing there but one little house and most staff lived outside the park. Tom began to pull down old ruined farm buildings and tobacco barns to build new complexes, staff quarters and some of the first chalets, the entrance gate, etc. Frank Junor joined Tom at Kyle as the first fisheries officer in the country. He and his wife Jean lived in a caravan while they built their own house with bricks from derelict barns and at the same time building the thatched laboratory. Tom soon built his own camp within the borders of the Park. This camp, which reflected his outdoor nature, consisted of tents and thatched open style structures built of gum poles, local grass and reeds. It was positioned within a few meters of the holding pens that were used to quarantine white rhino, buffalo and other animals before they were released into the reserve. Tom lived here for a number of years until the game reserve was well established and he then built a small stone cottage/office in the area designated for staff housing. This was not far from the tiniest of cottages that Frank built for himself from the same bricks. It was not until the Game department amalgamated with National Parks, that larger and more spacious houses were built for the staff at Kyle. Throughout the sixties and into the seventies Tom was to work on this park. The roomy, black staff quarters were some of the best built during that era, showing his interest in their welfare.

## *Red Tape*

Tom detested incompetent bureaucracy, red tape and paper work and was outspoken about his dislikes and this cost him dearly in promotion. A good example of his lack of formality was the story about 'the door'. During the early days at Kyle, he needed 3 simple doors for some newly constructed rondavel offices. He phoned head office in Salisbury to ask for financial assistance. Roy Short declined the request on the grounds of 'budgeting constraints', saying there was no money for doors for that particular station. Tom frustrated at the lack of support decided to liberate one from head office and drove up to Salisbury at his own expense. When most of the staff went off to lunch Tom began his work. He was observed using a screwdriver 'attending' to a door as it 'did not close properly' muttering that he was

*Rupert Fothergill and his parrots*

'fixing' it because 'It took field guys to do this as head office staff were useless with tools'. During the lunch break, he removed three doors, including the director's office door and loaded them onto his land rover. He then headed back to Kyle to install them. When Archie and the rest of the head office staff returned from lunch, they had no doors and could not lock their offices! Needless to say, finance was immediately found for their replacement doors! Tom was one of the few who could get away with such a brazen 'theft'. Nothing was said and it seems that the head office staff were too embarrassed to pursue the matter. Tom considered paper work a chore but took it seriously as a necessary appendage to the vital work of conservation. He was occasionally casual at this time with his reports and was once late, when assistant director Phil Evans came down to Kyle from Salisbury head office. Tom charmed him by calling him Uncle Phil and he managed to talk his way out of being late with his reports.

## *Quelea*

Tom was a no-nonsense 5'8" tall package of boundless energy, always wide-awake and on his toes, moving fast here, there and everywhere! From his base at Kyle 'Peter Pan', as Tom was known, went far and wide dealing with problem big cats, elephants, hyenas, quelea, doing game capture and various duties. He had plenty of experience with vermin control and was knowledgeable about gin traps and poison. If there were lion, hyena or leopard problems, Tommy was the one they usually called on to sort it out. However, there were also the lesser creatures like Quelea birds, which were a recurring problem. Tom, Frank, Rupert and a young cadet went to sort out a roost at Beaulie, the Mitchell's farm. The queleas were roosting about ten feet up in a large thorn tree. The rangers placed an explosive mixture of diesel and ammonium nitrate under the tree and moved about 200 to 300 yards away. When they pressed the hammer, there was one humungous explosion. When they went to see the damage, they found only one quelea in its death throes on the ground!

### *Original Game*
Kyle had a healthy population of reedbuck, with some bushpig, steenbok, klipspringer, bushbuck and kudu. When the waters of the new lake started to rise, the animals were forced out of their previous areas onto farms and into the new reserve. Many crocodiles took up their places along the newly formed shoreline. On the sand banks of one of the rivers flowing into Kyle, the Giffords from a nearby farm had shot a 14-foot long croc. This cow eater would have been longer if its tail end had not been cut off. Animals were also brought in from neighbouring farms. When Mrs. Gifford threatened to turn her overgrown pet reedbuck into biltong if someone did not come and deal with it, Tom quickly went to the rescue and brought it back to its new home in the Kyle reserve. An albino eland, which normally lived in the park, had taken itself to a nearby farm and had to be brought back. Tom and his game scouts did succeed in retrieving the animal, but it proved a difficult exercise. Tom used to help Alf Gifford with his massive baboon problems, as they would maraud through his mealie lands. Tom would come out and place poison bait. Alf however dealt with his own problem leopard and he once lost 40 calves in one year alone.

### *Poachers*
Before the reserve was finally fenced off, Tom spent a lot of time trying to catch the poachers who were having a great time killing off the reedbuck and kudu. One night he was sure he had caught them red handed. He heard a vehicle that should not have been there, so he parked in his land rover on a side road and waited. Finally, he was going to catch them. However, when they came past on their way out, he started his vehicle and found, to his horror, that his back tyre had gone flat. So they got away. He warned most of the well-known poachers of Fort Victoria that he was after them and they then gave Kyle a miss, as they knew that eventually they would be caught.

## *The Zoo*
When the game fence was completed, it was time to reintroduce all sorts of species that had disappeared from this area. A lot of preparation went into building an animal hospital and a treatment area; stock rooms for capture equipment, storerooms for animal feed and rations, plus a cluster of miscellaneous huts, all adjacent to the quarantine pens and Tommy's cottage. All the new animals had to be quarantined, weighed, measured, tagged and examined for parasites, before being released into their new territory. Every effort was made to ensure that no alien diseases were introduced into the area. Kyle was known at this time as the 'Zoo' and many of the animals became a great attraction to Fort Victoria residents.

## *New Animals*
From 1960 to 1963, some 210 animals were introduced to Kyle including white rhino, zebra, giraffe, buffalo, eland, sable, waterbuck, wildebeest, impala and ostrich. In the years following oribi, tsessebe, hartebeest, bushbuck, grysbok, aardwolf and nyala were added. In most of these translocations, Tom was a key figure. Blesbok were also brought from the Orange Free State. Tom brought in some Oribi from Chipinga and the tsessebe came from Central Estates. Truckloads of eland, sable, impala, giraffe, zebra, buffalo and wildebeest were brought in from Wankie National Park. Tom also had some young 'chirping' painted dogs (wild dogs) that he had in pens near the rhino stockade. Bruce Austen often helped Tom and they ranged far and wide over the years catching animals in the Lowveld, Eastern Districts and Wankie. Tom repeatedly headed off to Wankie where Ted Davison organized the lassoing of game from land rovers. Some of these operations were given names such as 'Operation Road Lift'. Most of the animal capture was still being done the hard way with no helicopters or dart guns. It was tough physical teamwork. However it was extremely satisfying and when the job was well done, there was great camaraderie over a beer and a braai. Tom was an amazing storyteller and a wonderful guy to have in camp, with his innumerable and humorous stories.

## *Bruce Austen*
During this time, Bruce was the Regional Warden based at Great Zimbabwe. Tom was often there for dinner where the two of them would talk late into the night about game matters and occasionally

there was a staff party. Together they did a bit of quail and francolin shooting and shot bushpig in the Zimbabwe Ruins area. One day Bruce thought Lawrence of Arabia had paid him a visit, but then recognized Tommy under all the paraphernalia and said, "What are you doing with all that stuff?" Laden with bandoliers of ammo, rifles, knives and the rest, Tommy was so keen to get going on their planned game capture trip to the Lowveld that he had turned up a couple of days early!

## *Drugs*

Drugs used for darting animals were still in the experimental stage and often in short supply. There was always a problem with the odd animal dying from an overdose. The Department staff would habitually eat the meat obtained from the capture team. There was a jail in the reserve for criminals and on one occasion, a prison guard got his hands on some of the meat. He and his girlfriend had lots of beer and meat that night. Early in the morning, she suddenly keeled over, as she was getting ready for work. The surprised boyfriend reported the incident and she was carted off to hospital. Later, while he was on duty guarding prisoners, he also suddenly collapsed and the prisoners carried him down to the offices to get help. He and the lady both recovered in hospital. An investigation discovered that the drugs in the meat had caused all the drama. The staff thought it was hilarious, but there was a casualty in that someone's child died from eating the meat. Forty years later, this prison camp was being used as a Parks' staff beer hall.

## *Nyala*

In 1965, Tom and the team spent some time on the south banks of the Lundi River in the Benji Springs area of the Gona-re-Zhou trying to catch Nyala. Black staff from the tsetse operations helped them to drive the nyala into the nets. To everyone's disgust, they were only able to capture three of these beautiful animals. They proved to be clever and wily and one of the three subsequently escaped. Tom spent many hours with the captured animals feeding them, talking to them and giving them extra care and attention and some of the Nyala became quite tame.

## *Hartebeest*

Lone Star Ranch in the Lowveld was now the only place in the

*Catching hartebeest in Chipinda area, Lammeck top & Warden Tinkey Haslam on left, centre Alan Savory?*

country where Lichtenstein's Hartebeest could be found. The owner of the ranch, Ray Sparrow, had done an awesome job looking after this rare animal and eventually built the herd up to about 100 strong. Some of them moved into the Chiwonja Hills where they joined others that had been brought in from Gorongoza in Mozambique. In later years, the advent of war damaged the population as poachers killed most of the Hartebeest, although a few were taken to Triangle and McIlwaine in the 1970's. Rupert Fothergill actually shot one of these animals at Lone Star for meat for Sir William Peverill Powlett who was camping at Chipinda for a few weeks. Ray, who ate some of the meat, regarded it as being some of the best game meat he ever had. The Department decided to restock the Kyle reserve with Lichtenstein's hartebeest and in September 1965 Tom, Mike Bunce, Charlie Williams, Don Stott, Tim Braybrooke and Bruce Austen camped near the small Chilovega River on Lone Star ranch to undertake the capture exercise. After they had set up their nets, they caught an eland bull by mistake and when Bruce asked, "What should we call it?" Mike said, "Chilovega". Tom piped up, "ja that's a good name." So after that the eland was called Chilovega and sent off to

Kyle. A bit trivial, but it shows how haphazard and primitive game capture was in those days. This was also about the time when they first tried a new drug called M99, which Dr. John Condy was experimenting with. One day, when Tom visited the Lone Star homestead, he started to casually play around with the dart gun. He darted the Sparrow family's pet monkey and nearly killed it with a drug overdose. He got a real telling off from the girls in the Sparrow family. The crossbows that were fired near waterholes from hides with M99 were mostly useless. With a great deal of effort, the team managed to catch only two of the cunning hartebeest, then the rains began and the exercise ended. Both animals were taken to Kyle where they soon became tame and ended up feeding out of their captors' hands.

## *Zebra*

When catching zebra for Kyle on Merrievale Ranch, the team encountered problems getting the animals into the nets. The beaters had to drive the zebras a long way and they were not moving fast enough when they got to the net line. When the zebras saw the nets, they would break back through the beaters and dash off to freedom. Round the campfire with Bruce Austen and Tim Braybrooke, Tom came up with this brilliant plan. He would sit on a termite hill 60 meters from the nets and when the zebra passed him, he would stand up with his two revolvers and fire shots into the air to keep the beasts moving. Tom duly put his plan into action the next day and as the zebra passed him on the way to the net line, he leapt up shouting and firing into the air. This certainly got the zebra moving. So well in fact that the stallion was watching him instead of where it was going and it ran straight into a mopane tree, breaking its neck in four places. Bruce Austin walked up to a rather embarrassed Tom and said in his sonorous voice, "Tommy, we are trying to get these animals to Kyle alive!" He took quite a bit of good-humoured flak around the campfire that evening. On the mound with Tom was a young wide-eyed 10-year-old Charlie Davey. Charlie later became a good businessman and probably the biggest safari operator in Africa. He would become famous when his daughter dated Prince Harry of England. His father Tony owned the Zimbabwe Ruins Hotel.

## *Buffalo*

Catching dangerous buffalo using primitive methods led to Tom and

*Lulu the giraffe at Kyle 1966*

others spending an embarrassing amount of time in the trees. They did manage to catch three buffalo in the Umtali area and they transported them to Kyle. However, once there, the buffalo took to the water and swam across the lake. One was shot and the other two were caught on the nearby farms. The two survivors had to be imprisoned in the rhino enclosures for a while. After a while, Tommy soon had a nice population of about 30 buffalo in residence at Kyle. They were so tame that he was able to get out of his vehicle and walk in among them, talking to them all the time as though they were cattle. Whilst the captured animals were still in the holding pens at Kyle, they were treated for pests and minor injuries in the 'hospital' pen. Sometimes, when the mangy buffalo were being doused with Multi-Benex, things got out of hand and a Wild West Rodeo ensued. The animals had to be held until the treatment was completed and this was not an easy task. One game scout, Mahash, was determined to win the 'hold on for the longest' trophy. He hung on grimly to a young bull's tail, when all the others had let go. The agitated buffalo dived so hard at the retaining pen's walls that he broke some of the thick poles and soared over the remainder. To every one's amazement, the game scout sailed on with him through the splintered gum poles. The buffalo was dazed and came to a stop with his 'handler' still firmly attached. Due to Mahash's heroics the animal was soon safely back in its pen. Luckily, neither man nor beast was injured.

## *Porky*
Tommy had a great affinity to animals and often preferred them to humans. One of his best-loved pets at Kyle was Porky the

porcupine. Tom used Porky to peel his potatoes! He would give the potato to the animal and once Porky had gnawed all the skin off, Tom would take it away and give him the next one to peel. When Tom left Kyle, he gave Porky to the Great Zimbabwe hotel where he shared a pen with some guinea fowl, ducks and fish (in a pond). With a change of management, all the animals were released. The guinea fowl hung around, but Porky disappeared and soon afterwards a porcupine began to raid the nearby fields. He proved to be very cunning but was eventually conned into entering a trap. He was released in the bush a long way from human habitation, where hopefully he found a mate.

### *Leopard*
Two young pet leopards were brought up to Kyle from Lone Star Ranch. They were probably in the house for a short time as there is a story of them ambushing Tom, pouncing on him from the top of a cupboard. There was also a very wild leopard, which was kept in a large wired enclosure, whilst a suitable release site was being sought. It used to lie on a large tree trunk in the middle of the pen and Jean Junor remembers an occasion when her little daughter ran past the cage and the leopard immediately sprang and smashed itself against the wire trying to attack her. Tom used to shoot leopards or trap them and relocate them.

### *Lulu*
A giraffe at Kyle, called Lulu, had become partly tame through tourists feeding her apples. The staff felt she was probably a hermaphrodite and this could have been the reason why she was rather unpredictable. It was definitely risky to leave her alone with children. It may have been this giraffe or one called Pongolani, which liked biting peoples' hats and grabbing women's headbands. Black ladies with headscarves were very special and it used to try to mount them and make love to them. It was responsible for destroying a Game Scout's bicycle, then kicked in a vehicle windscreen and so had to be put down.

### *Ostrich*
During one winter, Tom kept orphaned ostrich chicks in the kitchen to keep them warm; otherwise, they would have died from the cold. There was a large male, which behaved like a black and white Zulu warrior doing classic steps and whirling to show off his amazing

feathery costume, all to impress his drab female companions. It may have been this same male that was particularly dangerous and nearly killed a game scout. A convict from the prison who was serving time for a wildlife offence got a taste of his own medicine when he was attacked by one of the ostriches. In later years, an ostrich went into Mathias the game scout's kitchen and laid an egg!

## *The Staff*

Tom spoke reasonably fluent Shona and was well respected by his black staff. They were dependant on him to patch up their minor wounds, see to any illness, arrange time for shopping or take their orders when he went to town. They came to him for advice about family troubles and other woes. He made a good father figure, but was at times rather strict. He would allow them only one wife at a time and they were only allowed to brew traditional beer over weekends. The bachelors used to bring in ladies of ill repute for company. At one beer drink, there was an ever-widening brawl. This started over change owed to the beer brewer by a jail guard who was otherwise preoccupied with his hired lady. Tom discovering what the problem was, jumped into the five-ton truck and drove off to the staff quarters, where he loaded all the 'ladies of the night' onto the truck. He dropped these professional hookers on the outskirts of Fort Victoria and drove back to the reserve. After this incident, he instigated a form of pass that held the scouts or guards accountable for their visitors. This included family members, they were allowed only a couple at a time and there was a time limit to their visits. Some family members became spongers, hangers on, quite a nuisance to the game scouts and so, to a certain extent, the scouts were pleased about the new restrictions.

## *Babies*

Tommy was at Kyle in 1963 when Boyd and Kate Reese were stationed at Chipinda Pools. Kate was pregnant with Elizabeth and because it was her first child, she was told she would have to have her baby in Fort Victoria. Kate found temporary accommodation in a cottage on Ray Stockill's farm. Tom told her that he was just a phone call away and if she ever needed help, he would be there. Elizabeth arrived early! Boyd was only able to visit Kate occasionally and when she went into labour, he was back at Chipinda Pools. Tom phoned Kate just to check that things were OK and got into a panic when she did not answer. He then found out that she was at the maternity home, so he set off to visit her. However, she never saw him, because when he got to the door all the staff congratulated him as they thought he was the father. Poor Tom, it was too much and he took off like a long dog! Boyd Reese was brought up in Zambia by his American missionary parents. He loved the African bush and thrived in National Parks (his African name was 'Kapipe', as he always had a pipe in his mouth!). Tom was enlisted, once again, to be on stand-by to take Jean to the maternity home when Frank Junor was away on a field trip, as the birth of their first child was imminent. This made him extremely nervous and he spent most of the day near their caravan with the vehicle fuelled and ready to take off at a moment's notice. He became the Godfather of their eldest daughter Jane-Elizabeth who, to his great relief, was born the day after Frank returned.

## *Bristows*

One of the people whom Tom and Bruce worked hand in hand with was Ozzie Bristow, who ranched near Beit Bridge. The Bristows were always taking in stray wild animal orphans and ended up with a whole menagerie around the house. The media heard about this and photographers and film crews started to come from overseas to use their animals in wildlife documentaries. The family decided it might be lucrative to start their own game farm with animals in captivity in big paddocks, so that it was more convenient for the foreign tourists to come and take pictures. As Great Zimbabwe was a tourist attraction, they bought and moved to Le Rhone farm nearby. Ozzie Bristow kept ostriches and baboons. The young baboons would for their own entertainment ride as jockeys on the ostrich. Tom had his government wildlife sanctuary while Ozzie had his private sanctuary.

## *Garden Sharks*

While the waters were rising and before the roads in the park were constructed, most of Tom's visitors had to cross the lake in a boat. He would then take them for rides in his open short wheel base land rover. From an early age, Tommy loved short wheelbase vehicles. His treasured land rover was called the 'drinker of the wind'. He always drove with his goggles on and the windscreen was often down. Wherever he parked his land rover, a trusty, faithful fox terrier would be on guard. The garden shark (dog) would be obedient and sit there until he came back. Tom at this time had a couple of fox terriers and

*The 'Drinker of the Wind' land rover at Kyle in early 1960's*

these were the longer legged, pointed nose types and were without brains. There was brown dog, red-dog and black dog. Rookie was to excel himself at humping everyone's legs and Muffin was a sweet little – well, not much of anything. He used these for hunting lions and acquired a reputation on the Sabi where the dogs would bay the lions and he would sneak in with his rifle for the kill.

## *Bachelor*

In 1965, the Regional Warden's headquarters were still across the lake at Zimbabwe Ruins. One day Tom's boss went across the lake, with a visitor called Trevor Edwards, to visit Tom at Kyle. Although this was a routine inspection, he also wanted to see how Tommy was getting on in his new home – the newly built warden's house. On reaching the other side, they found Tom at home and received a warm welcome. However, when they entered the house, they were amazed. Every room was bare except for one which had a Parks' issue Houndsfield stretcher bed and sleeping bag in one corner and a few clothes in a pile in another – nothing else! Mess tins and cutlery were beside the braai stand outside. Tom then received a lecture on how a ranger was expected to aspire to a much higher standard of living than was apparent in this house. Furthermore, Tommy was told the public looked on a ranger much as they did their doctor and they expected him to be married and a family man. Alan Savory thought Tom would

*Kyle 1961 at Bompst homestead. Tony Web crouching on left and Tom with his foxies Rookie and Muffin.*

remain a bachelor all his life, however there were a few lady 'friends' during these years and being near Fort Victoria made it easy to socialize. The image of a die-hard bachelor leading his solitary life, which was true when he first went to Kyle, was to later change. During the early days, when he was stuck out in that abandoned farmhouse, he did get quite lonely and would suffer fits of depression from time to time. There were no tourists and very few visitors when they were building up the park. However, he was very friendly with the Mitchell family who farmed nearby and often popped in to see them after work. After some friendly chatter and a few jokes, he would soon revert to his cheerful self. He seldom stayed for supper, as he had "reports" to write and send off. Tom would not let his apprentice rangers bring woman to Kyle and would admonish, "Get them out of here you hooligans". Tom did have a girl friend of his own at this time, which the guys ragged him about. Tom's advice to his apprentices was, "if you start thinking of a woman, just go out and shoot an elephant to take your mind off her".

## *Crocodiles*
It was always hard to tell Tom something when he was on his own

mission. An order once came through to go and "shoot all the crocs causing problems on the Mtilikwe River". He took the command "shoot all the crocs on the Mtilikwe" literally and proceeded to equip himself to undertake this momentous task. The command was rather vague, the number of crocs and the length of the river rather daunting and so Tommy asked for clarification as to which crocs and where. He was told "Oh the ones that are troubling". Thinking of all the crocs on the river Tom replied, "That's impossible". He was then ordered, "You will go and shoot those crocs over in the Mtilikwe". So relishing the thought of a long camping trip, Tommy planned to start at Kyle dam wall, work downriver and annihilate every croc on the river. He prepared carefully, packed his kit and vanished. Later his superiors were looking for him and visited the farmers along the Mtilikwe River trying to locate him. He was eventually found way down the river living like a real bushman and eliminating any and every croc in sight. He was said to have been nearly 100 kilometres down river near the Chiredzi River, where he was happily camping and chasing the crocodiles.

## *Cupid*

Kyle was becoming busier after being opened to tourists officially in 1965. On one occasion, Tom had a phone call from an anxious wife in the middle of the night. Her husband had gone fishing on the lake and had not returned home. Doing his duty as the rescuer of both man and beast, Tom headed out onto the lake in a boat to find the lost husband. Eventually after searching every nook and cranny, he found the husband's boat tied up to a tree. He quietly approached and found the man was very busy enjoying himself with another lady. Tom quietly sabotaged the man's engine and made off. The next morning cupid could not start his boat and suffered an extended period stranded on the water. Tom arrived later, sorted the engine out and gave him a good rev.

## *Rangers*

The initial hard work of fencing, building and roadwork was complete and it was a time to get down to normal ranger duties. Tom was to be joined by two rangers whom he sent out on foot patrols, on horseback and in boats. Tom's apprentices at Kyle were Barry Duckworth and John Stevens, both of whom had been specially chosen through an SAS selection course. A warm hearted and generous Tom looked after his two apprentice rangers like a father. They were charged 10 pounds a month for their board and lodge whilst they stayed with him. For hours, they sat and listened to all his fascinating bush stories. They often saw him with a huge bunch of keys, his dogs and then there was Manyuki his cook. In later years John became one of the best safari guides in Africa and Barry was one of Zimbabwe's better known hunters. Other young ranger scientists and game rangers came and went under Tom. These young rangers and the youth in the Fort Victoria area often got up to mischief. Tony Davey had to boot them out of the Zimbabwe Ruins hotel when they got out of hand. A ranger, remembered as Mike, caused some mayhem when he placed his pet crocodile in the hotel swimming pool and this certainly stopped the tourists from swimming that day! Another prank here was when a leopard cub was placed in the hotel pub and this sobered people up very quickly.

*Tom on Nyala capture ca1965 in Gona-re-Zhou PHOTO Mike Bunce*

*Natal Parks 1962 with drugged rhino, Ian Player on left, looks like Magqubu Ntombela on right*

## CHAPTER 8
# RHINO 1959 – 1968

### *OP Noah*

The Game Department were pioneers in the capture of black rhinos during Operation Noah. At first, the men would try to just chase the rhino off the islands, but with new drugging techniques, they were to later dart the rhino. In 1959, Tom was assisting Rupert in trying to drive a black rhino to safety, which they named Greta Garbo. After Rupert had escaped a close personal encounter with this animal and nearly got a horn in his back, Tommy quipped, "Rupert, you certainly hold the hundred yards world record over stones and thorn bush!" Rupert asked, "How far was she behind me? I daren't look round, but I could hear her thudding at my back." Tom replied, "She was about three yards away". Tom had raised his rifle to his shoulder when it seemed that his colleague was about to be flattened. "If she had come six inches closer, either she or you would have died", Tom commented. Later rhino were caught and many were translocated to Wankie's Mandavu dam, while others were landed on the Kariba

*Black Rhino capture 1965 Sizemba. Tom helps place rhino on sledge*

shoreline. Tom was privileged to play a small part in this pioneering work with the black rhino. On one island, they had to catch a cow and calf. After darting the mother, the men now had the headache of dealing with a moody little black rhino. This youngster was too small to dart and as they battled to subdue it, they found themselves short of ropes. In desperation, they came up with the idea of tying it up with some overalls. Tom then suggested, "Put it into the overalls." So, after a fair amount of struggling, they did manage to put it in the overalls and then tied the overalls' legs and arms and slung the rhino up onto a mopane pole. The baby was walked across the island to safety snugly wrapped up in the overalls.

## *Sizemba*

In 1964 and 1965, 30 black rhino were taken from the Binga Sizemba area near Kariba to Wankie, where 9 rhino had previously been reintroduced from Kariba. In 1965, the operation lasted about six weeks and Tom was sent there to help Rupert Fothergill. Using a compressed air Cap-chur gun and crossbow and experimenting with the new drug M99, the exercise was a success. Morphine sulphate had been the drug used before. During these operations, Ron Thomson had tried trap guns without success, while Rupert tried moonlight darting. At this time, M99 was in an experimental stage and was tried out on eland, roan, zebra and hartebeest.

## *Capture*

Stalking rhino was hazardous due to the crackling of dry leaves, as one walked through the jesse bush. Some of the rhino also ran with elephant herds to avoid being caught. Then there were the intrepid oxpeckers that would give the game away with their chatter. One time Rupert was nearly gored and said, "The good old tree saved my backside from being punctured again. Made it with practically no seconds this time!" Rupert would approach to within about 10 paces and once the rhino was darted, a rope was slipped around its leg. Once trussed up it could be loaded onto a truck. Tom spent some time here caring for the rhinos after they were caught and he would then translocate them to Wankie. One young bull and a heifer did die after capture, due to previous lion and hyena injuries, so it was an important undertaking. He used classical music to settle them down, much like he was to do with white rhino. Normally they were fed lucerne, but Tom would place paw paw (papaya) on a long stick. The rhinos would try the paw paw out and the juices would dribble out the sides of their mouths. He found Black Rhino loved this fruit and Tom used this to coax them between holding pens.

## *Mandavu*

Tom would drive the rhinos in a 5-ton truck from Sizemba, on the Sengwa mouth, to Mandavu dam in Wankie where they were released. This trip was over some rough roads and steep inclines. On particularly steep and rocky slopes, someone would walk alongside the truck armed with rocks to put them behind the wheels when necessary. This was a necessary safety measure as one truck nearly had a bad accident. One male rhino was named Chavuta. Tom claimed this was the longest black rhino he ever saw and claimed it was built like a dachshund. This fearless bull would rear up on his hind legs with his front legs on the pen walls at Sizemba. From this position, he would rock back and forwards and try to break the poles. When he arrived at Wankie, he was taken to the pens below Mandavu dam, which had not been used for a few years and were in need of strengthening. Tom parked his truck near the pens to offload the big cheeky bull. Jeremy Anderson had come to see Tom release the rhino and parked his land rover on the road about 200-300 yards away. Jeremy walked up to the pens, leaving his cook and dog sitting in front of the land rover, with instructions for them to keep quiet. Tom with the help of his black staff, tried to get the hesitant Chavuta out of the crate into the pen. Eventually it got out of the crate into the pen, where it ran around trying to stab everything with its horn. Tom wanted to turn the unsettled animal away from the gate, so the men could sort out the poles there. He stood waving his arms and shouting to get the rhino's attention. It charged the side of the boma near where he was standing and the whole side of the mopane boma, riddled and eaten by termites, shattered and collapsed. The rhino vaulted out like a show horse and escaped down the road, thundering straight towards the land rover parked in the distance. It ran up to the land rover and thumped it a few times in the radiator, bumper and bonnet. The bull terrier jumped out of the land rover and took off after the rhino and both disappeared into the distance. The cook just crouched down behind the dashboard, with wide terrified eyes.

### *Gored*
The hazards of rhino capture were borne out when Rupert had his stomach gored and his right arm broken. He had approached two feeding rhino behind some trees and a termite mound, with the intention of darting one. They were only ten yards away when a third rhino appeared from behind and Langton his accomplice shouted a warning. Rupert tried to climb a tree, but slipped down and the rhino dashed in and hooked him to one side. Rupert then managed to retreat behind a tree where he was safe. He had been gored in the stomach, his intestines were sticking out and he then pushed them back in himself! Later, in the hospital they found that there was also damage to his appendix. His staff took him to a truck about a mile away and he made it back to camp. Tom was in camp organizing pens, etc. having just come back from taking some rhino to Wankie. He immediately went in to see Rupert and found him lying down totally unconcerned for himself. Rupert's only worry was that Tom was looking after the rhinos. Tom contacted Wankie via the radio network, where messages were relayed to Salisbury and a helicopter and aircraft were mobilized to help. Tom organized three fires and sent his cook to hang up a sheet. The cook placed it on a large baobab and when the RRAF plane came over the escarpment to drop morphine, they could not miss the site. A helicopter flew in and Rupert was

flown up to Salisbury for medical attention. Rupert's later comment was, "this is the worst accident I have had, there was a hole in me this time!" With Rupert injured, Ron Thomson was to take over the operation and Tom was sent on other missions.

## *Natal*

White rhinos had become extinct in Rhodesia and at one time were whittled down to a paltry few hundred on the rest of the continent. 1962 was a momentous year in Rhodesian conservation, with the arrival in the country of the first white rhinos from South Africa. Tom was privileged to be a key man in this historic translocation. Before collecting the rhino though, weather permitting, Tom was kept busy during the early part of the year preparing strong bomas and fences at Kyle in preparation for their arrival. In July, the white rhino advance party of Tom, Rupert Fothergill and John Condy left for Umfolosi Game reserve in the Natal Province of South Africa. These men were a rough looking bunch of Bushmen compared to their Natal counterparts. On arrival it was said, a suspicious secretary mistook the men for poachers. However, once they were identified as VIP rangers they were treated with great respect. As there was about a month's delay in the exercise, the party was fortunate to be taken around and to see some of the great game reserves of Zululand, going as far north to Ndumu and across to the Drakensberg. The Rhodesian party included a National Parks' ranger from the Matopos named John Hatton. John was an ex policeman and nicknamed 'Ndebele' by the Matabele people, as he was a talented Ndebele linguist. Ted Davison was a key man in the team and 18 black staff, of both the Game Dept. and National Parks backed up the squad.

## *White Rhino*

The Natal Parks' staff did a brilliant job catching the rhino and did a great service for the future of African wildlife. Ian Player, John Clark and 6 foot 7 John Tinley, were some of the rhino men at this time. A capture team consisted of two rangers in a land rover, with 2 mounted black riders and about 15 other general hands. The horsemen had crash helmets, rain proof kit and they and their horses were padded to protect them from thorns. They would first locate the desired rhinos in the right terrain. The action would then begin, with the land rover charging at maximum speed, regardless of small trees, termite mounds, rocks and holes, until within a few yards of the rhino. The

*Horsemen and land rover ready to chase down white rhino in Natal 1962. Looks like Ken Rochat sitting on the vehicle on the right, with Ian Player on the left holding the dart gun.*

land rover would come alongside the rhino and the beast was darted in the rump. Often one of the horsemen would go to a prominent point to see in which direction the rhino went after darting. The horsemen would then follow the drugged rhino until it was down. The rhino were endangered at this crucial stage, as they could in their drugged state fall over cliffs, or hurt themselves in the rough terrain. The horsemen were at risk from dangerous animals and once a rhino cow tossed a horse in the air. After being given a small antidote, the beasts were brought groggily to their feet and then pushed and shoved into crates, with ropes and many strong hands. From here, they were taken to holding pens at the main camp, where they would be fed teff hay or lucerne. These rhinos frequently had very fussy feeding habits and some were reluctant to feed at all, in contrast to the readiness of the black rhinos caught at Kariba. At least 24 hours before leaving Umfolosi, the Rhodesian rhino were confined to their stout crates, with their heads facing the rear of the truck. Each rhino was in a 5-ton truck, while land rovers with radios carried the vet, game rangers and mechanic. Canvas covers were used to help cover the animals when needed. One animal Mashayezonke took an intense dislike to her plastic drinking bath and would only drink off the floor. This cow and one called Mabaleni both went to Matopos and lived for over 40 years. Mashayezonke (hits everything) and Chianna were nervous and fought their pens, with the former breaking her horn off against the crate.

## *Storyteller*
During the course of this operation, it was noticed that Tom was a pretty good talker and that John Clark of Natal Parks was another great storyteller. The other rangers decided to put the two together and laid bets on who would out-talk the other. Tom was soon yarning about his exploits and problems shooting elephants in thick jesse bush and his respect for the game scouts he worked with. John joined in with stories and more than held his own. At about three in the morning they gave up, the others declared that the contest was a tie and knocked off for bed.

## *Departure*
Although torrential rains initially delayed the departure of the rhino, the 11 vehicles were soon on their way north, leaving Umfolosi at 0800 on the 30th August 1962. As they travelled through Durban, a police motorcycle escort accompanied the convoy through the city. The first night was spent in the Fort Mistake show grounds at Pietermaritzburg, where there was a heavy frost. It was cold as a miser and there was only one large rondavel for the 6 senior Rhodesian men involved in the rhino translocation. Rupert Fothergill and John Hatton were the first to get in and hastily grabbed beds. John Condy and A. Smith of CMED (Rhodesian Government Central Mechanical Engineering Department) were the next to get comfortable. This left Tom and Ted Davison. Ted soon got into the double bed and Tommy came late, as he had been looking after the rhino. He came in and quickly saw that all the beds were occupied and when his eyes swept across to the double bed, he saw Ted with a sheet up to his nose and two eyes peering over the top. Tom probably thought getting into bed with Ted was too much and with a remark, he was off and he went to sleep under the truck in the bitter cold.

## *Kyle*
On the 2nd of September, the convoy assembled at Beit Bridge at

midday. Here the convoy split, with Tom taking Babs, Nyoni, Ngazana and Nqoloti to Kyle/Ericsthal Game Park and the other four were taken to the Matopos. Babs was named after Dr Toni Harthoorn's wife and the other three were named after the places where they were caught. The next day Tom arrived back home at Kyle, after a 1 200-mile journey of 5 days and 4 nights with the two female and two males. As the trucks passed through Fort Victoria, they stopped at a filling station and here the rhinos caused a sensation, as both black and white folk crowded around the trucks to look in. The four rhino arrived with abrasions on the hocks, which were apparently due to a shortage of bedding. The unusually dense and dry mat of the grass in the park was 4 feet high in places and constituted a fire hazard, which would have endangered the rhino. For their safety, they were retained in their pens until the first heavy rains fell in November. They soon settled down in their new home on the fenced peninsula.

*Tom's Rhino*
The Kyle rhino became known as 'Tommy's rhino' and were like babies to him. Tom was so concerned about the success of these rhino that he built a little African style, mud hut, next to the rhino pens. He slept there to make sure his new protégés were under 24-hour control. The hut was built out of the local msasa trees and woodborers loved the soft wood. Boring at a great rate, these borers caused so much dust, that Tom slept with goggles on to keep the dust out of his eyes. While lying next to the great fortress like rhino pens, he would play the radio to try and get them used to people and he said they preferred classical music. The rhino often leant against the side of a pen to be closer to the radio. Tom was said to have liked country and western music and especially Burl Ives. The Kyle rhino got so tame that you could eventually call them. He also managed to habituate the big male Ngazana so he could walk up to it and it would roll over for its belly to be scratched, like a pet poodle. This was always a risk, as one female nearby often wanted to get him and he had to move to the other side of the male for protection. The local people regarded Tom as crazy, as he liked going into the pen with the rhino. Noel Swart visited Tom at Kyle where the two men went into the rhino pen together. Tom first used a radio to quieten the rhino and then the two went in and both sat on different rhinos. Noel had the privilege of sitting on the rump of big Ngazana. The Junor family loved and got to

*Rhino from Natal 1966 arrive in Rhodesia at Kyle. Driver getting into lorry Ken Rochat of Natal Parks Board*

know Ngazana and his tribe well. They found watching the visitors who came to see these huge dinosaur looking beasts, much more amusing than the animals themselves. There would be a squealing and frantic leaping away, when a horned giant got tired of being gawked at and made a mock charge, right up to the slotted gate where the visitors stood.

## *More Rhino*

In 1965, another 6 white rhino were brought up to Kyle from Umfolosi. This was followed by a larger operation in 1966 and 1967 when 'Operation Rhodesian Rhino' took place. This operation lasted for about 7 months and about 74 rhino were brought to Kyle, Matopos, Wankie, Victoria Falls and McIlwaine. Kyle received 21 rhino and Wankie 36. Transit trucks covered a total of 115 000 miles. Almost every day of every week, the men were capturing, driving, repairing or servicing vehicles. Tom was very involved in a pivotal role, with this work. The trip down to Natal was about 1 200 miles and was done in a minimum of about 36 hours. These committed drivers, game rangers and veterinary surgeons were continually up and down on exhausting trips to Natal. It would often be only about 3 hrs from the darting of the rhino until they were on their way north. The rhino sent to Wankie went to the hastily erected pens at Manga vlei. It was here that Rob Gee had to chase elephants away from the pens with a shotgun. The elephant were trying to access water and threatened to destroy the enclosures built for the rhino.

## *Capture Again*

In Natal the Black scouts on horseback were out at 3am in the morning looking for suitable rhino. Once the rhino had been found, the white rangers (like Ken Rochat) would stalk them on foot and dart them with a gas gun, or rush up to them with a land rover. They used the drug M99 with a Palmer carbon dioxide gas gun, or a powder charge gun to project the dart. The mounted game scouts then followed the rhino for approximately 12 minutes until the rhino was down. When it had been confirmed as unconscious, a loading truck was called in. This was not always straightforward. Often trees had to be cut down and a rough track constructed. A rhino is a large animal and an adult can weigh more than two tons. On the truck would be a secure container of some sort, strong ramps to give a gentle slope down from the rear of the truck to the ground, a winch and quantities of rope. The winch had to be attached to ropes that were cradled round the rhino, in such a fashion that the rhino was not hurt in any way. The rhino would then be taken to a boma (enclosure), lowered onto the ground and left until it came round. Once it had settled down in the boma, arrangements would be made for it to be re-darted, crated and dispatched to a new destination.

## *Empangeni*

Tommy was normally the man in charge of the Rhodesian crew during the white rhino run. He took his responsibilities very seriously and gave lectures all the time on how the rangers should behave in uniform. During the trip down to Natal, the Parks' staff had been given instructions as to what to take, where to go, where to stop, how to treat the blacks in reserves, how to treat the rhinos, etc. On one trip he went ahead in his land rover to Natal and was later joined by Paul Reid, Kim Hodierne and Peter Wright. They were bringing rhinos up to Matopos, Wankie and Kyle. In South Africa on the first morning of their arrival, the three men were planning on loafing around the capture camp and doing some servicing on the trucks. Tom then arrived in his land rover and invited them to go with him to Empangeni. The three men cleaned themselves up and set off with him. On arrival in town, Tom dropped them off, went to have his land rover serviced and to attend to some other business. The three walked up the main street and back down again. While mooching around, they saw a man sweeping out a pub and decided to pop in. It was only mid morning and they found a few regulars were already escaping the heat. Naturally, all they could do was join them, while waiting for Tom to find them. Tom searched in every nook and cranny and at last found the men in the pub. He was furious to find his team rather wobbly and full of high spirits. After having toasted Ian Smith (the prime minister of Rhodesia) and the boys, for a large part of the day, they now were chewed out by Tom for having let the uniform down, which was met with cheers from all.

## *The Road*
One of the tricks used by the Zulus to get the rhino moving into the crates, was to bite their tails. The rhinos had to be sprayed with water in hot weather and they were treated with drugs. If a rhino came round from the anaesthetic in transit, Tommy had to give it a further shot. Often Tom just travelled on top of the crate and talked to the rhino to keep them tranquil. To get the needle into the rhino necessitated the dispenser hanging precariously head down into the crate, with one hand holding on for dear life and the other holding the syringe. Inserting the needle into an agitated rhino took nerve and accuracy. It was impossible to give a rhino just the right amount of anaesthetic to coincide with the length of time of the journey. The rhinos often revived and began to beat the woodwork and frequently lost horns for their efforts. Some of the animals were very aggressive, destroyed the sides of the crates and tore holes in the canvas buck sails. At other times, they were still "out" on arrival. The crate would be slid onto the ground and then one person positioned on the top of the crate, would prise open one end. The animal would then either charge out or stagger slowly out, depending on its anaesthetized state.

## *Telegram*
When the rhinos left Umfolosi and arrived in Rhodesia, a telegram was sent back heralding a safe arrival. A typical one read "Big sister minus horn otherwise both fine". Another telegram that was probably from Tom, as he once had a breakdown at Loskop read, "Mechanical breakdown. Smallest sister handed to relations at Loskop. Three others fine despite 40 hours." Loskop was an overnight stopping point

*Alan Henderson and Alfie Wilson run from a released rhino on Doddieburn 1970 PHOTO Chronicle*

and was used as a drop off zone in case of emergencies. One bull and two cows were left at Loskop after a breakdown and an accident in which a diesel truck overturned at Potgietersrus.

*Arrival*

When Tom arrived once in Livingstone he was so tired, he just fell asleep in the driver's seat. When he woke up, he was a bit confused and did not know where he was. Some rhino were also taken to Kafue and released in a sandy fenced area. The rangers took advantage of the empty space on the returning trucks and once loaded three sable and a roan at Wankie and dropped them off at the Matopos. On one of the 'Rhino Runs', Tom arrived at Wankie quite late one evening, with a truck carrying White Rhino and he parked close to Arthur Wood's house. After he had made sure the rhino had water and feed, he came to the house and had supper with the Woods. They offered him a bed for the night, which he declined, saying that he would sleep out with the rhino. An hour or so later there was a knock on the door which, when opened, revealed a very wet and smelly Tommy. On being asked what had happened he said ".... I've been s**t on from a great height many times, but this the first time I've been peed on by a b****y rhino." It transpired that he had bedded down under the truck and received the full contents of a rhino's bladder.

## *Smuggler*
Once when Tom was bringing some rhino through the border, the customs official started to get a bit difficult as the papers were not entirely in order. Tom put the keys on the desk and said, "Well I am leaving the rhino with you and if they die, you will have to explain to the government how they died – I am not going to be responsible". He then turned and walked out. Not long after that the customs man appeared, frantically begging, "Hang on, hang on" and so he was allowed to bring them through. Rhodesian cigarettes were the best you could get in those days and Tom received an urgent request from the Natal Parks' staff to bring some down. He obliged and arrived at the Border post on one of his trips to go down to collect rhino. He was by now well known by the Custom's staff and the official asked, "Anything to declare Tom?" Tom replied, "Yaa, a crate of beer and 10 000 cigarettes". Laughing at the joke, the man stamped the pass and waved him through. The 10 000 cigarettes were a fact and the Rhino crate was stacked to the brim with Lion and Castle beers, which he had all dutifully declared.

## *Care again*
Once the rhinos reached their new homes, it took time to settle them in and staff spent a lot of time caring for them. Tom spend a great deal of time at Kyle caring for his new rhino (like the earlier ones), sleeping next to the Rhino pens, so he could talk soothingly to them during the night, as they adjusted to their new homes. He also made the young rangers, John Stevens and Barry Duckworth, stay with the rhinos and play music to them the whole night. One night Barry fell asleep and Tom came down and kicked him awake saying, "What are you doing asleep?" Sadly, when they were released into the Kyle Reserve one of the rhino cows died in a wallow while having a mud bath.

## *Poached*
The Wankie rhino were fed on lucerne and molasses at Manga, but preferred grass. Some of them were soon to break out of their pens

and scatter all over Wankie and even into Botswana. One was even hit by a train down near Sawmills. During the next few years Tom and other members of staff, were regularly tasked with retrieving these animals back into the park. Two of the rhino brought to Wankie were killed. Communist fighters killed one and a young local white farmer shot the other. This man who I will name Y was a skellum (rascal) and boasted in a pub that he would be the first to shoot a white rhino, since the last had been shot out in Mashonaland in the 19th century. Not long after that, two white rhino were seen feeding daily in the recently burnt Dett vlei. Both animals then walked through an open gate at a grid and into the Forest and onto private land. One of these rhino visited Kana and came rushing past a car that was driving along the road. Its shoulder barged the car off the road and into the bushes. Mr. Y of Kudu ranch heard the rhino had moved through the Dett vlei gate and went to look for them. He passed a black police sergeant who was cycling nearby who saw him get out of the car, go through a paddock fence and then get in his car and drive through a gate into the paddock. The sergeant cycled on, but saw Y stalking something in the open veld, after which Y fired a few shots. Later Y had various stories about how he mistook it for an elephant and that he had shot it in self-defence. Tom who had been looking for the rhinos stated in his diary, "contacted rhino 3 times, no joy, heavy rain, rhino actually seen by Mrs. Jordaan, ranger Wright sees murderer why did he kill the rhino." The case was remanded and Tom tried to influence opinion against him, by organizing some of the local Wankie school children to demonstrate against him at the courthouse, much to the displeasure of the magistrate. Y was fined 250 pounds and his rifle was confiscated. After this Y nearly died when a black servant, who he had underpaid, put some poison in his orange squash. Y lived, but was to leave the country soon afterwards.

*Next page, some of the 1962 Rhino team (Left to right) Rupert Fothergill, Nick Steele, John Tinley, Ted Davison, Ian Player, John Condy, A. Smith Rhodesian mechanic, Man from Rhodesian Broadcasting Corporation, Newspaperman possibly Rhodesian Chronicle, John Hatton, Ken Rochat*

*Tom in the Game Dept. with a mob of poachers caught while in the Lowveld*

## CHAPTER 9
# GONA-RE-ZHOU 1957-1964

### *To Gona-re-Zhou*
Tom spent much of his time in the late fifties and early sixties in the wild Gona-re-Zhou elephant country in the South East. The protection of fences, law enforcement, crop protection, assistance to game ranchers and dealing with game issues kept him busy here. Before Mabalauta was built, Tom often went down to the Nuanetsi River on his various missions. Tom stayed at the District Commissioners sub office named Malapati built by Allan Wright. Parks, Police and other government officials used this camp, situated in a beautiful spot shaded by big trees. It was a tranquil place visited occasionally by elephants. Allan was very instrumental in the formation of the Gonare-Zhou, particularly the Mabalauta side. At first he was at odds with Parks but found an ally in Bruce Austen, the National Parks Regional Warden who was also pushing to have the area protected and formally designated as a National Park. District Commissioner (D.C.) Wright was named Chibgwe (rock). If he did not want to show sympathy to the Shangaans, he would state his heart was like the stone on his desk in front of him. He used to say, "If you can get blood out of this rock you can get what you want." One day a Shangaan who heard this in

his office replied, "Only God can do that". That rather took the wind out of Allan's sails.

## *Chipinda*
Boyd Reese was the first Game Department ranger to be permanently based at Chipinda Pools in 1961, which was at the North Eastern side of the Gona-re-Zhou on the Lundi River. Other Game Department staff had worked there before and after, but they do not seem to have stayed permanently. Later it became a National Parks' base with Mike Bunce helping put up the first prefabricated Parks' buildings in 1965. Originally Chipinda was the Tsetse main camp in the area, where the white Tsetse staff based themselves and they may have been involved in building the old house. They were certainly instrumental in building the road network there. The Tsetse staff were a tough bunch and enjoyed a good party. The black Tsetse hunters were named Magochas and they did most of the hunting. They lived two in a hut in rough scattered hunting camps, positioned so they could monitor the fence lines. They were given 10 rounds of ammo for their .303's and would patrol up and down the fence lines, trying to eliminate all the small game they came across. Later they would hand in the tails and would be given more ammo and return to the slaughter. They racked the meat, dried it and tied it in bundles, which they then sold as their part payment. Most of the meat was sold in the nearby Tribal Trust Lands. Tom's other neighbours included the odd lonely policeman on the border and a few traders. Tom recalled seeing tree houses in the Gona-re-Zhou area made by earlier migrant labourers and travellers, which had been built for protection against man-eating lions.

## *Poachers*
By this time Tom's forte was catching poachers and he was very successful. In earlier days, white poachers from the Shabani and Fort Victoria areas were a problem. A few were after ivory but most were after biltong. South African poachers would hit the Sengwe and Mateke hills to the South West and even some Catholic priests were once recorded adding to their meat supplies! The master poachers in the area, however, were the local Shangaans who were known for their bow hunting skills. They knew Tom well and he became famous for arriving at court and telling the magistrate that he would have poachers there to stand trial the next day. "Well, where are they?" the magistrate would ask. Tommy would only repeat, "They'll be here

*Shangaan poachers stalking an antelope. Tom made them do a hunt so he could photograph it*

tomorrow sir," before leaving. Sure enough they would be there the next day, along with Tommy as witness for the prosecution. This never failed to astonish the magistrates. The Shangaans hunted in groups with their scrawny dogs and could kill up to fifty or more warthog and/or impala on a hunting excursion. After apprehending them, Tom would command them to send someone on a bicycle to tell their women to come and collect the meat. The men were ordered to come to court the next day. Tommy would take off in his land rover and the next day, after having walked all night, all the accused would duly appear in court. These poachers used old muzzleloaders, bows and arrows and the odd .303. They often brought the weapons in from Portuguese East Africa. Their courage was praiseworthy but not always sensible. A hunter near Dumela tried to kill a leopard that he had caught in a trap by the foot. When an assault with bow and arrow failed to subdue the beast, he approached it with a club. Instead of beating it to death, he received a serious mauling and the leopard eventually freed itself by chewing off its foot.

### *Pambwulani*

When the Shangaans were caught, they often outwitted their captors by escaping. Pambwulani a well-known elephant and buffalo hunter was caught for poaching and escaped from the Nuanetsi police camp at the end of 1963. Quite a few of the men in Pambwulani's community were put in prison for elephant and buffalo poaching. Unfortunately, this left many of the wives and children without any providers. One day the Super Express chicken bus arrived at Tom's camp with a load of stinking buffalo meat on board. They reported to him that they had found a poached buffalo near Chikombedzi village. It turned out that Pambwulani had used an old muzzleloader to shoot it. Tom and his men tracked him across the Nuanetsi River where they found some huts containing strips of buffalo meat. Soon after this, the police caught him again and Tom helped to press charges against him.

### *Teaspoon*
Tom related once how he was passing the pole and daga (mud) hut prison where a Shangaan poacher was awaiting trial. This man so the story goes, was guilty of killing a buffalo. Anyway, on the first night in the prison, this poacher used a teaspoon to tunnel his way out. Tom happened to be walking past and behind the makeshift prison and saw the man desperately digging out. Considering that his family was starving and that he was a better hunter than those who had caught him, Tom felt sorry for the man. He drove the man down the road and released him, leaving him to fend for himself. This is an interesting story as it shows that Tom had some sympathy for those poaching to simply feed their families.

### *Hanyani*
Hanyani Musengi was another skilled poacher-hunter who used a .303 to keep his village supplied with game meat. He had an accomplice named Engeleshi. Hanyani was picked up at Boli for killing and wounding at least 5 buffalo in the Gezani area. He escaped when Tom was away from Twiza siding by opening his handcuffs and was soon back to his old tricks (these poachers often used snare wire to escape from handcuffs). Later on, Tom captured him and took him to Nuanetsi to stand trial. The magistrate sentenced him to pay a large fine or go to jail and asked. "Do you have this money?" Tom wanting to make sure Hanyani did not end up in jail shouted, "Whoa there" from the back of the courtroom. To which the annoyed magistrate replied, "Five pounds for contempt of court. Now what do you have to say Mr. Orford and remember you are not driving a team of oxen". "I'll pay the fine for Hanyani your worship", said Tommy. So Tom paid the two fines and the case was closed. The reason Tom did this was that the rangers often employed ex poachers as game scouts in order to utilize their skills. On their way to camp Hanyani sat between Tommy and Mac the game scout. When they got to the camp Tommy then issued Hanyani with a uniform, a .458 rifle and a belt full of

ammo. "Ah white man, you must be mad", exclaimed Hanyani. "Tomorrow morning, I will be in Portuguese East Africa hunting for a big bull, sell the tusks and pay you your 'hundred' pounds." "You won't leave me," said Tommy matter of factly. Hanyani never left Tommy and did a sterling job as a game scout. Hanyani was also a nanga (medicine man) and used muti (medicine) for his hunting. To help Tom he would put muti on Tom's clothes and weapons. Tom was not allowed in the baobab tree where Hanyani kept his medicines. Hanyani said this was because Tom's spirit was different to his.

## *Ray Sparrow*
There were other characters who lived adjacent to the Gona-re-Zhou that Tom had dealings with and one of the most interesting was Ray Sparrow. Most ranchers could only lease land in the South Eastern Lowveld during the early years and Ray Sparrow was one of the first people to own his own ranch. In 2004, Ray was an elderly man with a thickset beard. He still wore khakis, a pith helmet, his WW2 army belt and walked around with a walking stick. After many years of pioneering in the Lowveld, he had built a house on the top of a sandstone hill. On the one side was a magnificent view of game filled plains leading to the Mahenya hills and the Gona-re-Zhou. On the other side, one looked down onto the large scenic Lone Star dam, which was 7 kilometres long. The garden was frequented by tame but noisy Natal Francolins, who came onto the lawn to be fed and if they did not eat all the food, the Vervet monkeys would try to clean up, only to be chased off by Ray's dogs. The house was spaciously built, with well-designed colonial verandas, louvered windows and fly screens. The lush well-watered garden boasted an enormous baobab, tropical palms, plus selected exotic and indigenous trees. His ranch was now one of the best game viewing areas in the country. Ray's philosophy was that there are three tools for wildlife and these are fire, water and the bullet. In Tom's 1964 diary he noted that Ray Sparrow was building a dam and said, "This should make an ideal small game reserve." Forty years later, we now have Malilangwe, one of the best private game parks in Africa.

## *Ranch Life*
In those days, there was little western civilization in this area and the Shangaan people were masters of the district. The Sparrow and the Stockill families were some of the few that had mastered the

Shangaan language. Ray Sparrow spoke Afrikaans, English, Shangaan, all the Shona dialects and some Portuguese, Ndebele and Zulu. The locals gave him the nickname Reki (possibly Shangaan word). The Sparrows had to get their supplies from Fort Victoria and the roads were all dirt, with countless farm gates to drive through. In the rainy season, the flooded and swollen rivers would repeatedly prevent them from leaving the ranch to shop for essentials. On one occasion, Ray had to shoot an arrow with a message attached, across a river to some people, asking them to pass on a request for supplies. Bitter salt from some springs was purchased from the Shangaans and honey was used for sugar. Life was wild and beautiful, with spectacular trees, bordering the huge Lowveld rivers. This was before the Tsetse Department raped the big rivers of many trees and vegetation using bulldozers. Fort Victoria, the nearest centre, was about 240 kilometres away, so they had to make their own entertainment - there was no Chiredzi town in those days.

### *Ray and Vermin*
Before Ray decided to push for wildlife on privately owned land, he and many other ranchers battled to make a success out of cattle ranching. He brought 500 head of cattle down from Melsetter, after buying them from farmers who had sold their farms to the Wattle Company. On horseback, he and his uncle drove the cattle for three weeks down to Lone Star ranch. It was a wonderful experience, but as they hit the Lowveld, they hit the lions. Every night they had to fend them off and for many years, Ray was forced to shoot lions to protect his cattle. Ray had a 16mm film camera, which he swapped with Tom for a 7mm Mauser rifle. From then on Ray always used this weapon, as it was deadly accurate. He killed at least 200 lions that were after his cattle, shooting nine in one morning. He spent days in blinds on the ranch waiting for lions, but never used anything bigger than a 7mm rifle - he relied on accuracy rather than the heavy calibres. Game had no commercial value in those days and all predators, including the Painted Dogs, were regarded as vermin. Their tails were collected and farmers paid by the authorities for every tail they handed in. It was a worthwhile exercise for Ray to take the tails all the way to the Zaka District Commissioner, where he was given money for them. There was no value in the animal skins in the early 1950's, but this changed later on when the Game Department officials began to assert themselves and the protection and utilization of wildlife

*The Tshlotsho cliffs on the Lundi River*

gained favour. Ray was one of those who became a strong advocate for wildlife utilization.

## *Lone Star base*

Rupert and Tom spent much of their time together in the East of the country and in the Lowveld. Rupert was a level headed guy, not a great talker, but a good companion for Tom. For years the two would make Lone Star their headquarters because the Lone Star phone worked and everyone could phone the Game Department there to come and deal with problem animals. Tom and Rupert had a tented camp under some Brachystegia trees and from here they would spend up to a month roaming as far as the Chipangayi and Chipinga. They used a Bedford 1.5 ton truck and then graduated to the first land rovers, but still used the truck. The Veterinary Department seems to have been the first to use land rovers in the South East of the country. At this time, the Sparrows had a small brick cottage, under thatch and were busy building a larger house, which they finished in 1958. On the foundations of their new house, they grew pumpkins and bred rabbits. The Sparrow family enjoyed Rupert and Tom and had particularly pleasant times with Tom, who they called Deng Deng. This came about when the Sparrows had some refugee Dutch girls staying with them from Java. They began talking about different types of fish dishes whilst having dinner one night. Tom mentioned a fish dish that no one recognized until one of the girls in broken English said, "deng deng". Tom said, "Yes that's it". So Tom was nicknamed Deng Deng. It was noted at this time that Tom's heart and soul belonged to wildlife and he was very sentimental about it. When Tom visited Lone Star, he often helped with lion and cattle issues. The Sparrow kids idolized Tom in his uniform and he regularly played with them and told them entertaining stories. When Tom was there, he was part of the family and even went to the farm church services.

## *Wild pets*

Ray had a menagerie of game animals around his homestead, which included eland, kudu, buffalo (that were milked), impala, duiker, bushbuck, reedbuck and a honey badger in a semi captive state. Lofty Stokes from the Game Dept. brought in a baby elephant, but it did not last long, as young elephant were hard to feed. There was a hilarious occasion when Ray's honey badger came rushing into the room where Tom and Rupert were sleeping and jumped on one of the beds. Tom and Rupert woke up in a panic thinking they were being attacked and there was a big hullabaloo. In later years, Ray and Tom were to both comment that the best place for wild animals was in the bush.

## *Twiza*

In 1964, Tom was transferred to the Gona-re-Zhou on a permanent basis to work on the tsetse corridor fences and to do problem animal control. He soon had an organized and immaculate bush camp at Twiza (Tswiza) siding (meaning giraffe), which was along the Rutenga-Malvernia railway line. These fences in the Chipinda and Galuene/Chefu areas were built to prevent the movement of game, especially elephant and buffalo into non tsetse fly areas. This had a dual purpose of stopping the spread of tsetse fly and of foot and mouth, which were carried by the wild animals. The fence line Tom worked on was first bulldozed, after which Tom put up the fence. National Parks and the Game Department also had the sad task of eliminating the big game animals like buffalo and elephants in the tsetse corridors. Tom had a large area to cover from the Sabi Lundi junction and Chilojo cliffs, through Nematongwe, Twiza, and Chikombedzi, along the Bubye River, down to Crooks Corner, in Buffalo Bend and along the Nuanetsi River.

*Authority*

Tom believed in good manners and fair play. He was outspoken when necessary, sticking up for what was right. He had a heart of gold and was a gentle soul until something upset him and then he was like a bull terrier. He would latch on and leave no stone unturned until the matter in hand had been resolved to his satisfaction. One day one of his superiors arrived with some paperwork, marched into his tent at Twiza and threw the papers onto the table. Tom went ballistic and threw them out of the tent onto the ground. Tom's later response was, "a man's home is his castle." A senior member of National Parks at this time used to get irritated with Tom, due to his radio 'chat'. When the man did the radio schedule, he put Tom last as he knew Tom would talk a long time and hold up the whole proceeding. Tom would say, "good morning Uncle X, this is your little ray of sunshine on the net". The answer was a rather unenthusiastic, "morning Tommy".

*Play Time*

At Twiza Tom would occasionally put the land rover in gear, pull the hand throttle and sit back relaxing, letting the land rover drive by itself on the service road next to the railway line. The sandy banks of the road were so high that the land rover would stay faithfully in the ruts. The railway was always a good way to get in supplies, whether from Portuguese East Africa or Rhodesia. There were the prawns and demijohns of Portuguese wine, which he and his friends could access. There wasn't much to do at Twiza in the way of entertainment and the Police Camp at Malvernia (the border post down the road) was the nearest and best stop. When the Gona-re-Zhou later became a National Park and the headquarters were built at Mabalauta, Tim Braybrooke's staff would go there at the end of every month with their monthly reports and get their orders for the next month. They would be given two days to go off to the border Police Pub at Vila Salazar, which was a well-known watering hole for anyone within 150 kilometres. Ben Kaschula, a young assistant D.C at the time, used to see Tom down at Malapati while on his way to the Sengwe T.T.L. He remembers enjoying Tom and Tim Braybrooke's company while drinking the Portuguese Cerveja beer and eating smelly goats milk cheese. Tom had obtained the cheese from P.E.A and it was high and smelly, but great on brown bread. Other visitors here at Malapati were policemen such as the young Rob Hopkins. He remembers sitting with Tom and others around campfires. Rob was doing a 6-month patrol around the Lowveld while Tom was on antipoaching. In the evenings, the gentleman would get together and regularly have a good yarn. Tom was often quiet as he did not drink much and he always took the opportunity to warn Rob about the dangers of smoking and drinking. Tom taught Rob about weapons and the importance of learning from the black people about the bush.

### *Tim Braybrooke*
Tim Braybrooke had spent many years in Parks, some time in South Africa with Ian Player and a spell in the French Foreign Legion in the Sahara. In later years, he took to hunting and his love of fishing. Tim was famous for his involvement in the shooting of the famous elephant Dhulamiti in the Gona-re-Zhou. This 132 lbs and 107 lbs tusker was one of many large elephant shot in the area and the second largest recorded from Zimbabwe. As Dhulamiti's tusks were so large, there was some debate afterwards whether sport hunters should have hunted it. The largest tusker recorded in Zimbabwe was an elephant shot by Potgieter in the late 1860's. Potgieter wounded it between the Vungu and Gwelo rivers. Later it was found dead and the tusks were sold to a trader in Bulawayo. The tusks were 9 feet in length and had a combined weight of 300 pounds. Big bulls came regularly through from South Africa to the Gona-re-Zhou.

### *Mabalauta*
When Tim came down as warden of the South East Lowveld, he stayed in one of the district commissioner's houses at Mpakati, while Mabalauta was being built in the south of the Gona-re-Zhou. Mabalauta was to become the headquarters of the Gona-re-Zhou and much of the Lowveld in the earlier years. It became one of the two main camps in Gona-re-Zhou (the other being Chipinda in the North). Tim had chosen the Mabalauta site, as it was a non-tsetse area, a great place to be and had less poaching problems than the Chipinda area. Two staff houses were completed here in 1965 on the banks of the Nuanetsi River – which had tiger fish in it! On one occasion Allan Wright, the District Commissioner said to Tim, "I've got the DC from Beitbridge coming up... John Tapson. We are going to fly over this whole area and show him what I have done, so would you like to come?" "Sure" replied Tim. So they got into the airplane with John and flew around and near Mabalauta. Tim said, "Mabalauta was looking really lovely. I had done it up and the fruit trees were growing

and everything was nice, fencing and everything. I said to him, 'sir would you mind if we do a circle around Mabalauta'. And so we tipped over and had a look, and John Tapson the DC said, 'that's a nice place Allan Wrights built'. And I said, 'no I built it, that's my b****** station'. 'Sorry he said - I never realized that'". Tim built up the station with a great workshop and he had all the kit a garage needed, including pits, joists etc. The station bordered the Buffalo Bend on the Nuanetsi River and was surrounded by towering canopies of Wild Mango, Natal Mahogany and Nyala trees. These enormous trees produced a cool, shady, cover for humans and animals, on those hot Lowveld days.

### *Elephant*

Tim Braybrooke had just arrived at Mpakati (District Commissioners camp) and there was no radio at the time. In these remote areas, radios were the chief means of communication between staff, as there were no phones in the remote bush areas. Gona-re-Zhou elephants are famous for their huge tusks, smaller bodies and aggressive attitudes. Tom often dealt with crop raiding elephant in the adjoining Tribal Trust Lands. One of Tom's first meetings with Tim here was when he roared into Mpakati in his short wheel base land rover and came up to Tim saying, "Jeff Gillette has just been hammered by an elephant". The two of them jumped into the vehicle and went off to investigate. Jeff Gillette was the senior tsetse officer and worked quite a lot with Tim, as National Parks did plenty of elephant control in the tsetse areas. Jeff and Ruth Gillette had been going down the road along the fence near Gorhwe pan with two assistants, when they came across a herd of cows. As the vehicle appeared, a calf was suddenly separated from her mother. The cow elephant then came boiling out of the bushes and smacked the front of Jeff's vehicle, pushing it back down the road and putting two nice holes in the front. Jeff grabbed his .425 rifle off the rack, managed to lean out of the vehicle and shot it. On another occasion, Bill Nash was sleeping next to his land rover in a camp near Naivasha when a passing elephant attacked his stationery land rover and severely damaged it. Then there was the Portuguese mechanic who came down from Fort Victoria to do work for National Parks. He said, "Never again" after being threatened by several angry elephants. From then on Tim Braybrooke had to go to Fort Victoria and collect the spares himself. Early one morning Tom drove around a sharp corner and bumped into a strange tree trunk on the side of the road and this had not been there before. The vehicle thudded to a halt with a big bang. It was an elephant bull feeding with his head in the bush and his hind side in the road. It screamed, gave the land rover a kick and took off. The bumper was kicked against the wheel and Tom had to get out and use a mopane tree stump as a lever to free his wheel. Another time Tom drove down to Malapati and he was chased both on his way down and running the gauntlet, was chased on his way back on the same day. His diary records that two days later, elephant chased him again!

## *Guns*

Tim Braybrooke the warden based at Mpakati suggested to Bob Cole (later Tom's lawyer) and a friend that he visit Tom at Twiza. Here they would be able to see all of Tom's beautiful guns, "Guns like you've never seen before". So Bob and his friend went to Malvernia, drank some wine and on the way back they visited Tom and he showed them all his firearms. Tom was described then as a dedicated conservationist, a highly intelligent bushman and knowledgeable on anything in the bush. Tim was right, Tom had an arsenal of very beautiful guns and would gladly lend them or give them to anyone who needed them. His knowledge of guns was exceptional. He could quote the grain size of bullets and data about a great variety of weapons. By this stage he appears to have favoured heavy weapons and did not trust .375 rifles on elephant. He formed a lifelong love of the .505 Gibbs, which was a great elephant gun. Some of the National Parks' staff like Tim Braybrooke coped well with the .375.

## *Control Work*

During this period in the Gona-re-Zhou Tom did very little hunting compared to those that came after him, such as Richard Harland, Chris Kay, Mike and Johnny Bunce, Ollie Coltman, Charlie Williams and others. Under Tim Braybrooke these men were to find themselves busy shooting elephant in large numbers. Mike Bunce once shot 27 elephants by himself on one morning from three separate herds. One of the Parks' rangers was said to have had a tracker who regularly smelled that elephants were getting closer while he was tracking. Allan Wright, the local District Commissioner would send messages to the Parks/Game dept. staff, requesting something along the lines of, "please destroy elephant damaging pipeline", or it could be "2 lions killing cattle". Then the Parks/Game Dept. men would decide on the nature of the problem and deal with it. Tom tried thunder flashes on the nearby farmlands to chase elephant away, but without much luck. He also tried blasting hippos under water without success. They had to revert to their tried and tested shooting of crop raiders.

## *Tom hunts*

On one hunt, Tom walked for 6 hours after elephant with a colleague called Bob and both came back defeated and in much pain. Tom walked back with a stick, after hurting his back and he suffered for some time afterwards. On another occasion, he was chasing three crop raiding bull elephants through some Musimbiti thickets. While tracking, he came across a large tusker, so he left it in peace and went after the two smaller askaris (term for young bulls following a huge tusker). As Tom was pressing the trigger to shoot one of the younger bulls, it moved its head. The resulting bad shot with his .505 smashed its teeth out. The elephant fled and Tom chased after it trying to get in a side shot. It then ambushed Tom who nearly ran into it. Enos the game scout shouted a warning and took a wild shot with a .470. Tom found himself 10 feet from the elephant, which tried to reach him with its trunk. Four of Tom's six shots were fired within a range of 10 yards and due to the dense timber not one got within 6 feet of the animal. He was lucky to get out of the situation alive.

*Tom Elephant hunting in Game Department*

*KAMCHACHA*

## CHAPTER 10
# BIRCHENOUGH 1964-1965

### *To Birchenough*
Tom was transferred to Birchenough Bridge in the east of the country, which in those days was a wildlife Eden. His area of jurisdiction was from the bridge all the way to the Mozambique border below the Sabi/Lundi junction and then east across to the Chirinda forest, including the whole Chipinga area and the wild unspoilt Mahenyas. The Birchenough Bridge area was hot and beautiful and huge trees edged the river. Tommy loved the grand old bridge, which could be seen from miles away, arching across the romantic Sabi River. His predecessors included Danie Bredenkamp; a quiet and private man and Kevin Blizzard. Tom operated on nearby ranches and within the Tribal Trust lands. His work on the ranches included game counts and ascertaining quotas for culling specific species so that the owners could crop and manage the wild animals efficiently. Commercial game utilization was increasing at a remarkable rate, with meat and skins sales rising to more than 350 000 pounds per annum and about

49 ranches were involved. There was now a detailed administrative process to go through before any game could be cropped. So many requests for help came in from farmers that Parks were short of staff to do quotas. There was also the usual elephant and vermin control, supplemented with anti poaching work.

## *Tom the Character*
Tom was totally self sufficient with his immaculately packed short wheel base land rover stacked with jerry cans and fox terriers, a .505 Gibbs rifle, three tin trunks (full of pots & pans/clothes/bedding and washing kit) winch and cable, medical kit (sufficient for a hospital!) a game scout, one .357 S/S handgun, tow rope, camp bed and mosquito net. Tom's land rover had everything that opened and closed. It was like a motor show. He had a great first aid kit and probably the best medical kit in the world. He somehow managed to get drugs like morphine, which he should not have had. He would joke that if his medical capabilities did not work, if all else failed, he always had a pistol to finish off the patient. He loved tea and avoided alcohol. He was an amazing storyteller and a wonderful guy to have in camp, with his countless and humorous stories. He never repeated himself. Tom was always good to and liked by the black game scouts and other members of staff. Tommy, to all intents and purposes, was a confirmed bachelor and all that he had in the huge ranger's house, just downstream from the bridge, was his standard issue equipment, i.e. 1 x camp table, 1 x camp bed, 1 x kettle, 1 x bucket, 1 x folding camp chair, etc. There were no curtains on any of the windows and the lounge floor was ankle deep in magazines such as Farmers Weekly and Popular Mechanics. They were not stacked - just lying loose and scattered everywhere! He spent very little time though at his Birchenough Bridge base and travelled everywhere in his light green land rover with a canvas top.

## *Patrols*
Kevin Thomas would accompany Tom on his patrols to the Chipinga 'A' Hunting Block, the Mahenyas on the lower Save (Sabi) River and beyond into the Mt. Selinda area and Chirinda Forest on the Mozambique border. They spent many of their patrol nights camping at Rupisi Hot Springs and for a young "bush mad" schoolboy such as Kevin, those were exciting times. Tom built the initial camp within the Chipinga 'A' Hunting Area and undertook many intensive patrols, as

there were still a few black rhino there in the sixties. Tom was brilliant with teenage schoolboys and always tried to encourage them to join National Parks (it worked with Kevin and John White). Kevin would have liked to hear more about Tommy's early experiences when he was a young ranger on Operation Noah, but Tom seldom spoke of it. Tom's needs were very simple and he ate the same food as his game scouts. Whenever Kevin was with him, Tommy focused far more on anti-poaching than vermin control.

## *Sabi Beauty*
There were many pans along the meandering Sabi with not thousands, but millions of aquatic birds. Ducks unlimited blanketed and darkened the skies as they flew up from the pans. Ray Sparrow used to shoot them with a .303 while they were flying. There were so many that you invariably brought some down, however poor your aim. They used to breed on the best water bodies on the eastern side of the river. These shallow extensive pans within a few miles of the sandy river were up to half a kilometre wide. The chains of glistening pans there reminded one of Mana Pools. There were few human visitors to the thick forests along the river, but an abundance of game. Tom also remembered with nostalgia sitting on a rock in the beautiful Chipangayi valley where he looked down and was able to observe two tiny, blue duiker "bulls" fighting each other over a female.

## *The Hotel*
The Birchenough hotel is just a stone's throw from the river. The Parks' base was nearby and in those days it consisted of the ranger's house, a braai area, a camping ground and its own well signposted road. The thick riverine vegetation and the waters of the river gave a cooling effect to the settlement. In the distance the local black people would walk down to wash themselves in the river, while crocs lazed in the sun. The hotel was the social centre of the district's white community. Here one could sit in the small bar or on the wide verandas - either looking at the bridge or the looming mountains of the Eastern Highlands in the background. Then there was the frequent motorist coming by who would stay the night, or stop for a drink, on his way to goodness knows where. Visitors included dedicated government officials, tourists, miners, tough farmers and the odd alcoholic. The gardens of the hotel showed their colourful bougainvilleas and striking Sabi Stars. An airstrip even served the

hotel at that time. The hotel and Parks' house started to fall apart later during the 1970's civil war. Dick Stock, who was one of the owners of the hotel, used to spend most of his time hunting to supplement his income. He struggled on, but became so broke that when he saw a car coming down the hill he would disappear, as he was scared it might be a creditor. His wife Ruth would then look after the pub and fend off any creditors. Later on, Graham Paxton and his partners took over. Graham built himself a house with one wall constructed entirely out of beer dumpies. One of the local residents was Robert 'Bob' Carshalton who bred bulldogs and frequently had a few too many toots (drinks). His favourite party trick was to nip quietly out of the pub during the evening and then some time later you would hear, "helloo, hellooow" and everyone would go out to see Bob right on top of the 70 metre high arch of the Birchenough Bridge. This was one of the first major bridges in the world to use high tensile steel and contains some 1500 tons of metal.

*Valley Residents*
The Lowveld and Sabi valley had its share of characters, which included Ian de la Rue. Ian had a naughty sense of humour and used to invite people around for dinner. Later he would inform them the delicacy they had relished was hyena, baboon or some other strange creature. He enjoyed their reactions!! Tommy was notoriously shy in mixed company and although a number of well meaning local people tried to get him married off - it was to no avail. They became convinced he would remain a bachelor forever. However, Tom's memory of the Afrikaans girls at Chipinga was that they "were so strong they could load the RMS trucks themselves with bags of mealies." Whenever Tom went up to Chipinga village, he used to pop in to visit his friends and they thoroughly enjoyed his company. He once settled down for a drink in the local pub only to hear two Afrikaans men talking to each other about the young 'rooinek' in their midst. Later they were surprised and embarrassed when Tom spoke to them in perfect Afrikaans. For company Tommy often visited the Whittal family on Humani Ranch nearby. During the school holidays the Whittals used to host orphans from the Fairbridge Institute in Bulawayo. Many had been abandoned by parents or orphaned in the UK and had a difficult start in life. Even though some of the older ones were caught poaching by Tom, they still regarded him as a good chap. He used to joke that he had gone to Tokai Academy, which he

inferred was either a reform school or an orphanage. This gave the impression to some of the locals here that he had also been an orphan.

## *Townleys*
One of the most interesting couples in this area and friends of Tom, were the Townleys on the Devure (Devuli) River. Denis and Bill (Mrs.) were real bush people who hunted crocs in the Sabi River for a living and Denis was very creative. She would wade in the river with a night lamp on her head and when a croc's eyes shone in the light, she would shoot it. With a knife and rope tied to his belt, Denis would then swim to the croc, put a noose around its jaws and drag it back to the bank. On one occasion, he did this to a croc he thought was dead. Struggling, he managed to hold the jaws closed and his wife came, put the gun to its head and finished it off. They also had numerous crocs conditioned to come to feed; one in particular, a 14-foot specimen called 'Wandoko', responded to his name. Both Ruth Stock and Denis Townley wore monocles and Bill smoked a pipe to keep the mopane flies away. In later years when all her teeth had fallen out, she could not hold her pipe any more. Although upset, she was undeterred and took to smoking disgusting Portuguese cigars!

## *Elephant*
Much of Tom's work was vermin control. Tony Osborne, who worked with Tom, sent a letter to his boss with Osborne V.C. (Vermin Control) written at the end. This looked suspiciously like Victoria Cross and J.C. Tebbit, the Director, was not amused. This work was eventually known as P.A.C or Problem Animal Control. Much of the work was in the Maranke and Sabi Tanganda areas, where elephants were the main problem. Mike Bunce, another tough ranger based in Chipinda, would frequently come across to help Tommy. Tommy used to patrol the Crown Lands across the Sabi River in order to keep track of the elephants that travelled up and down the valley. He had to shoot several that persisted in raiding the peasant farmers' crops. One of his predecessors at Birchenough was Ian Nyschens who would follow elephant tracks here for 50 kilometres or more until he caught up with them. The Ngungunyana thickets were extremely dense and Tom had to retreat in haste on one occasion when he ventured in after some aggressive elephants. These fearless elephants had got to the point where they would not run away, but would 'Buta' when the firing started. Buta means they would bunch up and then the whole

herd would charge the sound of the rifle fire. You had to be on your toes and it was a nervous and tricky job. Tom had his .505 and Tony Osborne used his .470. Tom remembers one occasion when, "I was sitting with my back against an ancient mopane tree down in the Sabi, once watching a female elephant. It was just after a rain and I was just enjoying the smells and sounds, when I feel a trunk feeling me all over my neck and back. I turn slightly so as not to move too much and there is this baby elephant touching me all over. Then it goes over to its mother and blows air into her mouth. Without a second thought, she curled her trunk in tight, laid back her ears, and charged straight for me." Tommy got out of there fast!

## *Hyena*

Apart from springhares and hippo, hyenas were a big problem on both sides of the river. As the farms in the Chipinga area developed, there were more and more clashes with hyenas. Cyanide pellets were used to kill them. While setting out baits in Chipinga, Tommy accidentally poisoned himself - luckily it was a mild dose and he was only ill for a short while. Tom was dealing with problem hyenas near Mt. Rudd in the Tribal Trust Lands and the hyenas had totally finished off the cow they had eaten. Tom normally used the leftovers to attract the hyena back and commented in his diary, "All meat that could have been used as bait has already been eaten. This was a blessing in a way as Mtema is 250% overstocked. This area could do with at least 2000 hyena." This showed that his sympathies were with the wildlife and he did not like the encroaching civilization here.

## *Hippo*

While doing hippo control Tom had an interesting experience. He shot a hippo and his staff went into the water to retrieve the carcass. One man enthusiastically rushed ahead of the others to get to the meat. As he arrived at the carcass, there was a commotion - he screamed and lifted his arm and his hand had been completely sliced off. Years later Tom was still convinced that this had not been a crocodile, but rather a shark that had come up the river from the sea.

## *Tribal Poachers*

Some enterprising poachers ambushed animals from platforms in trees by the pools along the Sabi River and others used poison to kill fish there. Many bows, arrows and ancient muzzleloaders were captured when these men were apprehended. However, the poachers in the Birchenough area repeatedly intimidated Parks' staff by their numbers and one poaching gang at Rupisi was about 50 strong. On a patrol near Marumbini, close to the Sabi/Lundi junction, Tommy and his staff came across seven poachers with bows and arrows. A game scout was stabbed in the leg as the team tried to overpower and arrest the poachers. Tom had to fire a warning shot to bring things under control and then take the wounded tracker to Chiredzi for treatment. It was about this time that Tom caught a notorious poacher who was boasting about his powers of witchcraft and relationship to hyenas. Tommy felt he needed a lesson, so he tied him to a tree near an animal carcass in a lion prone area. To add a bit of spice to things, he had already placed a fake human corpse nearby. He pretended to leave the man alone by getting someone to drive off in the land rover while he actually stayed nearby. When evening came, Tom then made a few nocturnal noises (some hyena 'whoops') so the prisoner would think the predators were coming. The terrified man believed he was going to be eaten like the corpse nearby and things were not looking so good. However, in the early hours of the morning the land rover came back and Tom 'sort of arrived' to find a very scared poacher who certainly did not want to get caught again. He seemed to have had a life changing experience!! On another occasion, a tyre was the only thing available when Tom needed to handcuff a recently apprehended poacher to something in an empty storeroom. The poacher and tyre were stored away and the room securely locked. When it was opened later in the day they found the man had escaped and run away still attached to the tyre. They caught up with him miles away and as with many other poachers, he was later employed as a game scout.

## *Poachers*

There were also a few notorious white poachers in the Umtali/ Chipinga area and Tom was always threatening to bring them to book. He was quite convinced that anyone with a name of Van Staden, Van Rooyen, or Swanopoel had to be a poacher. And it didn't matter if the guy was innocent - he regarded them as all poachers - anywhere in the world! However, Tom sometimes made mistakes. The Chief Justice Sir Robert Tredgold and Dr James Kennedy of Ndanga were friends and enjoyed camping together in the Lowveld winter. They were once walking down the bed of the Mkwasine River and had shot a guinea fowl for the pot. They soon heard a rapidly approaching land rover and from it emerged National Park's Game Ranger Tommy Orford, who enquired as to who had shot the bird in this area of government-owned State Land. Sir Robert confessed at once that it was him and Tom said, "You are under arrest". "Do you know who this is?" asked Kennedy. "No" was the reply and Tom was then told, "This is Sir Robert Tredgold". "And I'm Tommy Orford and he's under arrest!" said the young Parks' man. There is no record of a subsequent prosecution, as Dr Kennedy had been provided with a permit to shoot for rations. On receiving a tip from an informer, Tom made plans to catch a white croc poacher who was going to be busy on the Chiredzi River on a certain day. Tommy went there with a policeman to wait for the man. They waited for a long time but no one came to shoot the crocs. On returning to their vehicle, they found the poacher had paid a visit as there was no air in their tyres and the two of them were stranded. It was a long, long walk home.

*Graham*
Graham Hall (ex Parks) had this to say about Tom. "To some extent I used him to gain entry into National Parks (my life's ambition). I was a number one notorious poacher (mainly crocodiles), and my chances of getting into Parks were less than zero, however I made it my business to befriend Rupert Fothergill and Thomas Patrick who was after all, my wife's cousin. When I had to quit professional crocodile hunting to marry (and become a townie) I took a job as a baby food and chocolate salesman with Nestle, hating every minute of it, and ended up using my issued company car (an Austin Westminster) to go poaching crocs with over the weekends, with a small boat strapped onto the roof carrier. If Nestles ever found out about that, I needless to say, would have been fired. One of my sales areas was Umtali (now Mutare) and I knew that Tommy was based at Birchenough Bridge at the time. I decided to sell my chocolates and baby food, and "extend" my trip from Umtali to Birchenough to introduce myself to Tommy with a view to gaining an ally to put a word in for me in my quest to join Parks. I drove into his camp at Birchenough Bridge towards the end of the day and introduced myself to him. He seemed a little wary of this "dude" in a silk shirt, tie and suit, but eventually we clicked and he suggested I spend the night and set up a stretcher for me under a tree. We ate sadza and meat at the campfire and he talked about my fancy clothing saying that I looked nothing like an ex pro hunter. On the question of clothing, I recall his

*Tom and game scout view an elephant Tom had shot up at Sizemba in 1965. He left Birchenough briefly to do Rhino work. This cow elephant had been snared by poachers and was shot to prevent it suffering. PHOTO (Donald King for Ministry of Information)*

saying that his favourite attire was 'jockstrap, top hat and spurs'. I heard him use that line on several occasions in later years, a genuine 'Orfordism'. Anyway he put in a good word for me at head office and so did his close friend Rupert Fothergill and I got into Parks sometime later."

### *Generosity*

Whilst at Birchenough Bridge Tommy made a special trip up to Salisbury to see Tim Braybrooke who was sick in hospital. He barged his way past a big nurse and gave Tim a book on poetry. Tim well remembers Tommy's legendary generosity. On two occasions, Tim had to argue with him after finding gifts in his land rover. Sometime after having shown an interest in Tom's 7mm rifle, Tim found it in the front of his vehicle. Another time when he was about to drive off, he noticed a fly rod tucked in the front of the vehicle. Tim managed to get Tom to take back the gifts, but it was dangerous to show too much interest in Tom's things, as he was liable to give them to you. If he felt it was needed he would give you the shirt off his back. Many of his expensive technical items - night sights, rifles and much of his camera equipment went that route!

## *Weapons*

Graham Hall had this to say on Tom's weapons. "Now re Tom's weapons... When I could not take selling baby food any longer I was offered a job as a gunsmith with Jason Cambitzis at 'Springbok Arms' in Salisbury. Just before U.D.I. in +1964. I saw more and more of Tom because most of the Parks guys used to frequent Springbok Arms for their ammunition and rifles etc. Tommy came in one day and we got into a discussion about weapons and which were best for a given purpose etc. He told me about his magnum Mauser .505 Gibbs, and when I mentioned that I was about to go on a hunt at "D" camp on the Zambezi he absolutely insisted that I use his beloved .505, which, believe me was a great honour because he was very protective of his weapons and I felt really privileged at the gesture. I used it, shot five or six buffalo and a couple of elephant with it, and returned it to him in a better condition than when he gave it to me in that I re-blued it and had the stock polished by our Italian stock maker. The .505 was a magnificent weapon; I often wonder how Tom handled its recoil being a small man in stature (but not in heart). One day he walked into the shop with the second love of his life being an original Oberndorf Mauser, a 7mm, with the full length stock (right up to the end of the barrel). It was a priceless gem among rifles. He plonked it on the counter and said that he wanted an aperture sight fitted to it and I was the only one he trusted to do the job. I told him he was mad, especially when he added that he wanted the stock cut off and reduced to a normal length, about 2/3rds down the barrel. He insisted I do it and I carried out the distasteful task of unsweating the beautiful German rear sights and replacing it with a plain utility Parker Hale military type 'peep' sight. I well remember the day I took that 7mm to the rifle range to test fire it with six or seven other rifles, all with newly fitted telescopic sights. I made a habit of attaching the targets to the rifles as I tested them for the customer to see. When I walked back into Springbok Arms that day, I put the rifles into the gun safe, and showed Jason Cambitzis the targets. He singled out one of them marked '7mm - Orford' and remarked on the five bullet holes touching each other in the bull's-eye, asking me what magnification scope sight was on the 7mm. When I told him that this was the only weapon tested that day with 'iron sights', he didn't believe me. All the other targets were unimpressive by comparison in spite of being equipped with high power scope sights. I didn't feel so bad about having 'desecrated' it when I handed Tom the weapon with the remarkable target attached. I had never fired a more consistently accurate weapon before that, or what's more, in later years in spite of many thousands of expended rounds of various calibres. I don't know what became of the 7mm or for that matter the .505."

## *Buffalo Beans*

Tom was a deep thinker, always planning some new tactic or development. This trait, combined with his sense of humour and close affinity with nature, could have some interesting results. Just before UDI circa 1964, at the breakup of the federation, some politicians who were visiting from the UK became very unpopular with the local white community because of their tactless comments. Tom decided to try and get rid of them. He approached the Special Branch bodyguards protecting these V.I.P.s and asked them if he could put some buffalo beans in their clothes. They gave permission saying, "Go for it". Now the Buffalo bean is a creeper that grows in various parts of the country and produces wicked irritating hairs on the outsides of the pods. The best way to prepare them was to place the fresh hairs in a small pipe and then let them dry inside the pipe. After they have dried they are then at their itchiest. Once he had permission, Tom got access to their clothes in the hotel room and blew some of these irritating hairs onto their underwear. When they donned their underwear the next morning they were in agony. They thought they had some strange venereal disease or something. The excruciating pain was enough to convince them to leave immediately, which they did.

## *Uniform*

While at Birchenough Tom, always a stickler for correct dress code, recorded in his diary that, "the so called game scouts are still looking like a lot of tramps due to lack of uniforms." National Parks' staff though, were now beginning to receive uniforms from headquarters, which was pleasing to some but others felt this destroyed individuality. Barry Ball, while operating in the Beitbridge area, once had a problem with head office concerning the lack of game scout uniforms. Having absolutely no uniforms for his staff except boots, he put his men on parade with boots, guns and nothing else. He took a photo and sent it to Salisbury as a form of protest requesting they treat the matter with some urgency. Certain officials thought he ought to be tried for pornographic photography!! However, nothing came of that and he managed to get his message across.

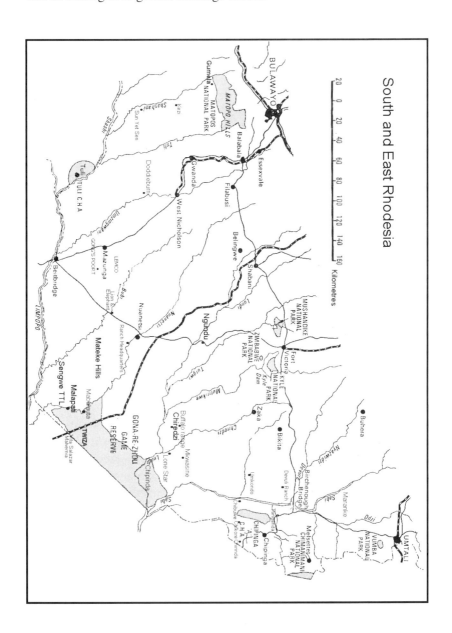

*Culling in Wankie 1980, Looks like Clem Coetsee PHOTO Chronicle*

## CHAPTER 11
# WANKIE HUNTING & CAPTURE 1966 –1968

### *Bumboosie*
While Tom was still bringing up the rhino to Rhodesia, he was posted to the Lukozi and Bumboosie hunting area at Wankie. Although the headquarters were officially at Bumboosie, Mbala was a much better base. The Bumboosie camp was rough and Tom complained about his rent and accommodation here. He wrote to head office in Salisbury about the 'bird cages'. The humorous reply from head office came back with, "It is noted that you have now moved into 'palatial tents' and 'broken down bird cages' at Bumboosie. Your rent charges will be reduced to 1 pound per month for sub-standard accommodation with effect from May 1967 (No charge will be made for bird seed)." Tom was further charged 13/- per month for unpurified pump water and purified water was 25/- per month (Tom had to purify his own water). It continued, "It is regretted that no exception can be made in your case, although it is noted that the Bumboosie water has been highly vitaminised by creatures in the past. Perhaps the vitamins in the water will prove beneficial to your health." A number of the Park's

*Capturing baby elephants in Wankie for the USA. Thomas (?) on top right, bottom Jim Fowler central with Marlin Perkins behind him, left was an employee of Perkins, the bottom right is Ronnie Van Heerden PHOTO Africa Calls 1967*

camps were rough and basic. Jackie Pringle (Myburg) remembers living at Marongora, where they had to collect their domestic water from a dam. They and their kids were forever sick and they could not understand why. The problem was solved when they saw the dam filled with maggots and detected a terrible smell wafting off a dead buffalo. Their accommodation here was a tent with no lights and some rustic buildings. There were no locks on the doors and the windows were broken. Jackie's daughter of a few months old always seemed to have German measles and cried all night. One night Jackie awoke to see a black sheet of bed bugs streaming down the whitewashed wall and that explained everything.

## *Camp work*

Tommy was given the task of building the hunting camp at Bumboosie. He did a fine job using one of the old Bedford trucks to carry sandstone slabs to the lodge. He carried a couple of large stone slabs, one of which was used to build a large table. However, the incredible job was marred, when the weight of this large rock, broke the back of the truck. He had a little explaining to do. There were

*Tom helping test cross bow (with Van Rooyen?) at Main Camp 1960's*

many amusing moments in the hunting camp; for instance, when some of his friends sneaked up on a nervous client's hut at night, pretending to be lions. In addition, there were also tense moments, when clients shot the wrong animal and wrongly presumed that Tom was, "a good guy", but found him to be inflexible and instead they were penalized. During one of the hunts Tommy was busy sorting things out at the camp when the clients returned all by themselves. They told him that their game scout and the trackers had run away with their rifles at nine in the morning. The men were still missing in the late afternoon, but eventually turned up tired and triumphant with a poacher whom they had spotted and chased. Most of these hunters were South African biltong hunters. They could either get a Parks' ranger to accompany them or were allowed to hunt on their own. With Kenya closing its doors to hunting, many of the East African hunters had relocated to Southern Africa and this had stimulated the growth of modern sport hunting in Rhodesia. The Matetsi/Wankie area began to attract more and more trophy hunters. During the February auctions, Dan Landrey (one of the East Africa professionals) would buy hunting camps for two weeks at a time. Dan had vast experience with both big game and plains animals. Some of the clients (particularly farmers) often made the mistake of thinking they knew what they were doing and therefore walked into problems when hunting big game. This is why Tom had to accompany several big game hunts in the neighbourhood. Tommy recorded an elephant hunt in his diary: "2/6/67 0400 Nobody up yet. 0800 Leave camp for springs area to hunt elephant. 0930 to 1030 sort out spoor. 1130 Contact and shoot lone bull with 50+ a side. Ferreira shot first in Hellish cover. I put two .470 into elephant at 10 paces. Elephant finished by Dr Keevy. Great joy. Nobody saw any buffalo all day in whole area."

## *Len & Lion*

Just before Tom arrived in the Bumboosie area, Len Harvey had been hunting a lion with two clients. One of the clients shot the lion, which then dropped into the grass. They thought it was stone dead and the second hunter asked to be allowed to shoot a second animal not far away. Warden Harvey left the first hunter with two game scouts, with instructions to be careful, whilst he went off with the second hunter after the second lion. Shortly after his departure, he heard a roaring and ran back to find out what was going on. When he got there, he found the first hunter sitting in a pool of water, with the dead lion only a few feet from him. The lion had charged the man, biting him in the leg, before being shot dead by this same hunter. Meanwhile the game scouts were hiding under the water trying to make themselves invisible.

## *Big & Small Cats*

Tom also had his lion experiences here. The lions took to eating 11 semi wild domestic cats at Mbala lodge, with one badly wounded lioness taking one in broad daylight. The lioness was reported to be extremely weak and left pools of pus and blood in her wake. The game scouts also complained about a pair of male lions chasing cats near the dam. When one of the male lions passed the camp at 2100 hrs going to the dam, it was quite amusing when 5 men, all tried to get through one door in their escape. Tom would wait up all night for these lions, using mange-infected impala as bait. Diseased animals were often shot by National Parks to prevent the spread of disease. One very old and fearless male lion made a habit of terrifying the workers in the Bumboosie compound. So Tommy tracked and unfortunately, wounded it and that night the hyenas kicked up a

*Sable hunt in the Wankie Hunting area late 60's*

racket. Tom spent the whole of the next day with his dogs trying to finish off the lion, finding pools of blood and places where the lion had lain down. Tom commented in his diary on his dog Rookie, saying, "worked well in cover and was a great help", but he does not record if he found the lion. This was interesting in that he was using dogs to hunt the big cats on National Parks' land. The big wild cats were normally never a threat to humans if approached with caution and respect. However, they are opportunists and the following tragic incident happened whilst Tommy was stationed in Wankie. A three-year-old black child wandered away from Dett towards Mambanje and entered the Park. On the third day his body was finally found half devoured up a tree, with leopard spoor evident. It was impossible to ascertain whether he had died from exhaustion/natural causes or had actually been attacked by a leopard.

### *Lion Hunt*

In his diary, Tom describes one hunt he conducted with a French client saying, "1745 Contact lion. Lowerdes shot one, which disappeared into some hellish cover at the base of a kopje. I sprinted in after it, only to be confronted by a lion, which I shot thinking it was the wounded animal. Lowerdes also shot at the lion. Somebody near the vehicle or on it shouted that there was a lion behind me. I spun around and shot at what subsequently turned out to be the first lion,

*Elephant shot in Wankie Controlled hunting area by client 1967*

lying three yards from me. Both lions were young males and were eating a bush pig." Thirty-five years later, he told this same story with a twinkle in his eye. "I took out this Frenchman once, who wounded a lion. It ran into some tall grass and I had the Frenchman wait out in the clearing. I went in with my double shotgun with my doctored rounds. This time it was #6 with wax." He continues referring to the lion that he shot close by, "The lion only stuck his head up when I was about three paces away and I let him have it with both barrels right on the nose. It was so effective that it blew away the head of the lion and the two ears fell, one on either side. The Frenchman was furious and I guess if you are trophy hunting, using this technique is not the best. But it sure is effective." He had taken a #6 or SSG shotgun shell, taken off the cardboard end and poured wax in. With wax alone, a shotgun can shoot through a piece of wood two inches thick. Put wax into something that has lead and it becomes a serious cannon to soft skinned animals.

### *Hunting Rifles*
Tommy experienced problems at Wankie with his .470 double rifle while working on elephant. He then reverted to his trusty large calibre

.505 rifle, which he said would be able to "knock those things over" (referring to big game). Tom was proud of his .505 and was all smiles, knowing it would get him out of any trouble. Ted Ottey was an extremely knowledgeable master gunsmith and National Parks' rangers relied on him heavily for advice and assistance when they went to Bulawayo. He fixed Tom's rifles and later went to go and work for Musgrave in Bloemfontein. As the Parks' staff earned thirty-two pounds a month in the early days they had to scrounge around to fix up their rifles. They would pick up a Mauser square bridge action here, a cast off barrel there and then get a woodcarver to fit this lot to a tree they had cut down and they would have a rifle. On one occasion, John Osborne accompanied Tom out onto the airfield at Mabalauta (Gona-re-Zhou) to fire Tom's beloved .505. However, after much discussion, Tom decided that John was too big and that he would not be able to ride the weapon (ride refers to shouldering the kick of the weapon). So John was not allowed to fire the .505. Throughout Tommy's life, he was convinced that big weapons hammered big guys, because they tried to resist the kick of the weapon.

## *Culling Team*

In an attempt by scientists to prevent, what they felt was a degrading of Wankie's vegetation; National Parks took to the culling of elephants, buffalo and wildebeest, to reduce the numbers. Many now feel that this was unnecessary, as there were no endangered species and little permanent damage to vegetation within the park. At the time though, this appeared to be the best solution to what appeared to be a major problem. The culling was to have real benefits though, as much valuable scientific data was obtained and experience on how to cull large numbers of animals. One of Tom's friends, Tinkey Haslam was in charge of the culling operation for a while. He was once seen standing before an approaching bull elephant with no rifle. He stood there and threw his hat at it at close quarters and the jumbo took off. Others on the culling team over the years were the hard working Jeremy Anderson, Ronnie van Heerden, Rod Hill (big man called Gomo), Len Harvey (nickname Gatooma), Bruce Couper (nicknamed Super Dooper Couper), Paul Coetsee, Norman Payne, Willie Koen and Clem Coetsee. Outside of culling, Paul probably shot more elephant than most and during culling operations, his younger brother, Clem, probably shot over a 1000 elephants in his career.

## *Willie de Beer*

Another ranger who joined the culling team was Willie de Beer. Before he joined Parks, he had been an Honorary Parks' officer who came from a military background. He used a .470 double and was chosen for his skill as a hunter. He once felt sorry for an emaciated lioness, which had cubs. He spotted it just after having shot an impala nearby. He lifted up the antelope, walked towards the lioness and threw it down for her, which was quite an act of courage. Another time Willie was sitting in the front of his land rover at Chirisa (hunting area in north of country), with his scouts in the back, whilst he watched some rhino. He did not see a cow elephant approaching the land rover. The scouts shouted and banged the truck, wanting Willie to get moving. Sadly, a brand new scout, as of 8.00 am that morning, jumped off and ran for it. The cow stomped him into the ground and he was dead by 12.00 noon. Willie shot an elephant cow nearby the next day hoping it was the same one, and he had to shoot it to prove to the black staff that the incident had been revenged

## *Shapi*

Tom stayed briefly at the Shapi culling camp, some 30 miles west of Main Camp and then, like a yoyo, would pop in to assist with culling and game capture when needed. The first Shapi camp was flooded out and it had to be rebuilt on higher ground, and while the building was going on, they camped under canvas and thatch. When it was finished, it consisted mainly of huts made from crude mopane poles and mud, with the odd caravan here and there. The wives decorated the insides of the huts and a lighting plant operated at night. An airstrip was built nearby so that aircraft could help locate animals.

## *Dart guns*

Game capture and the culling of animals were still in the experimental stage in the 1960's, with different techniques tried and tested. Ray Field was an electrician and used a lathe to make darts, which he gave to the Parks' staff to test on various animals. He used a .410 rifle modified to shoot a dart and this produced a reasonable dart gun. The crossbows used, often killed more animals than they should have, with the dart going right through the animals. The use of a cross bow in dense bush was difficult and one had to have an absolutely clear view of the target, because the smallest twig could deflect the flight of the dart. The dart gun was better than the cross bow and was quieter than firearms. Ronnie Van Heerden had a narrow escape when putting down his dart gun. It went off and the dart penetrated his flesh near the collarbone. Being a soft skinned being, the needle went right through the flesh and the drug was ejected into the air. This is a muscle relaxant and he could have died from not being able to breathe. He was rushed off by John Hatton in a land rover to the airstrip, airlifted to Wankie hospital for treatment and subsequently recovered. In the end heavy firearms were the most reliable weapon for culling as the hunters could do brain shots easier, their rate of fire was quicker and they stopped the animals better.

## *Elephant Cull*

Planes were used to count elephants and they estimated that there were approximately 5000 within the park. In 1966, the first year of culling, approximately 1000 buffalo and 500 elephant were killed and the culling was to continue for years afterwards. Elephants were shot in groups, while buffalo were killed at night with dart guns and the drug succinyl scholine. A private contractor used his plane to locate the elephant and then dropped messages to the culling team below. The members of the team, consisting of wardens, rangers, biologists, scouts and the meat handlers, would get themselves into place. They tried to shoot no more than 15 elephant a day, because that was the number of carcasses that the contractor could handle in one day. They shot the elephant in the morning, as early as possible, after which they would look for buffalo. The marksmen would approach the elephant herd with the warden in charge in the middle, flanked by other gunmen. The men on the flank would shoot any elephant trying to make a break for it. The matriarch would be shot first, followed by the other large animals, until only the babies were left alive.

## *Baby Elephant*

The culling team used to catch baby elephants by either 'stealing' them from the herd or catching the little ones left over after the adults had been killed during a cull. Baby elephants had to be about 4 foot high in order to be old enough to survive successfully and adapt to captivity. When 'stealing', the cull team would watch the herd for some time and pick out their victims by assessing the babies as they walked past the mothers. The team would then dart the chosen baby and pull back for about 10 minutes or so. The baby would fall down and sleep for about 20 minutes. The upset mother would often try to raise it with her foot and this was the time when the land rover would rush in. As they approached the herd they would shout, scream and perform, to try to intimidate the mother - or in some cases the matriarch. They would then grab the baby. If the irate mother attacked them, she would be killed, with six cows killed in this manner when they tried to protect their calves. Although this was a sad necessity, it was, in those days, accepted as part of the culling process. There was an incident when an enraged cow elephant, charged the darting vehicle and her tusks penetrated the bonnet area. She also attempted to open the wooden crate on the back by breaking it, as it contained an elephant calf. The captured babies were taken back to camp, given antidotes if necessary, and then placed in pens where they were given every care. Most elephant calves were taken out of the country for zoos. On one occasion three elephant calves were taken to Shapi where they settled down and became tame and manageable. At night they were confined in their pens and were allowed free range of the Shapi area during the day. Lions visited the pens at night and were chased off, but hyena mauled one of the babies, which had to be destroyed.

## *Buffalo Cull*

The culling team would try to take off about 15 buffalo at night. The buffalo herds normally drank after dark or in the afternoon and this was when they were likely to come to the open areas around the pans. While observing one of these herds, it was noticed a bull at Ngamo was totally blind. He used to stay with the herd by listening to where they were going. Using this drinking habit, the culling team would - after locating a herd - collect their drugs and chase the buffalo down with land rovers. The buffalo were killed with dart guns and a carefully measured dose of the muscle relaxant scoline. The first buffalo was marked with a black flag and the last with a red. The colours showed the team when they had their quota for the night. Paul Grobler would follow the shooters with his 10-ton truck and pick up the carcasses. The lions soon learnt that whenever the culling team arrived there was free meat coming. The big cats would follow the land rovers and try to 'rekill' the buffalo. On at least one occasion, the lions jumped on a land rover and eventually some animals were left for the lions, as they were so hard to drive off. Willie tried to use thunder flashes to scare them off, without success. Many of the hundreds of buffalo killed were used as rations for the Parks' staff.

*Wildebeest*
When Bruce Austen was the regional warden, impala were sometimes shot for rations and members of staff or the culling team would carry out the task. Rangers' jobs were varied and a culling mission could end up as an anti-poaching exercise. The culling team worked with Tom when they were shooting Wildebeest at Makololo and on the Ngamo flats. Tom was warden of game capture and was working on poaching and construction work at the time at these places. Leaving Shapi at three in the morning, the culling team would drive along the railway to Ngamo in two land rovers towing trailers behind them. They would arrive at first light, shoot about 10 wildebeest, cut them up and take them back to base. The method was to drive as close as they could to the animals and then let them settle down until they could shoot them quickly and efficiently. Willie de Beer used a .300 and Tom a 7mm rifle in this operation. Tommy became known as the Peter Pan of the Parks Department. He was forever childlike (in his enthusiasm and inventiveness) and youthful and this was shown in his experimental hunting at Ngamo. He was once battling to shoot the now suspicious wildebeest. He got four scouts together with him under a mosquito net and they sang and walked towards the wildebeest. These alert animals watched with great curiosity, but ran away when this strange creature got too close. Tom then jumped out and hid behind a tree and the mosquito net retreated with lots of singing. The wildebeest were still curious and followed the mosquito net back to where it had started. This gave Tom his chance to shoot the gnus when they came close to his hiding place. Tom also used a grass shield attached to a shooting stick to stalk the animals.

*Processing*
Ian Henderson and Paul Grobler had the contract for the animal carcasses. After the animals were killed, researchers like Basil Williamson would take measurements and collect specimens. Elephants were weighed using 300lb scales. After skinning and cutting up the meat, Paul would then take the meat to Shapi. Here they had set up the infrastructure to make biltong in a hot-air drying room and the rest of the meat was sun dried on wire racks. Paul also had a large refrigerated room, which the gang of about twenty workers kept filled. Some of the bone and blood was used for making pet food and there was a commercial use for just about every part of the carcass. There was always lots of good nyama (meat) for the black

staff and this kept them very happy. The culling operation received a lot of publicity and the Prime Minister Ian Smith paid a visit and shot some elephant. This was in his support for the management of wildlife in Wankie.

*Len Harvey*

Len Harvey was a well-liked, quiet person and slightly older than the others in the team. He was a good mechanic who had learned his trade in the Air Force. He undertook most of the administration work, while the younger staff did the heavy culling jobs. Now Shapi had a bone pile, where offal and old bones were deposited. In the day there were flocks of vultures and marabou storks. Every night there would be about 4 or 5 hyenas and the odd jackal and there were always plenty of lions around. The pole and dagga huts the rangers stayed in had open slots for windows and low thatched roofs. In 1972, after Tom had left Wankie, one particular lioness began to prowl around the camp on a regular basis. She was thin and in poor condition. Willie, in particular, recognized the danger and wanted to shoot her. However, Len had got into trouble on a previous occasion for shooting a lion under similar circumstances and was reluctant to do so. Then she became bolder and entered a storeroom containing mealie bags covered in blood (obviously meat had been carried inside). She was looking for food and soon helped herself to some of the camp chickens. Then disaster struck. Len and his wife had just arrived back from honeymoon and set up a temporary home in one of the pole and dagga huts. One night, when they were fast asleep under a mosquito net, the lioness jumped through the open window onto his wife. She was badly hurt, but managed to wake Len who grappled with the lioness and took its attention away from his wife. The lioness bit Len on the head and killed him. During the melee his wife fell out of the bed, managed to get out of the room and went to start the lighting plant. The rifle bolts, rifles and ammo were locked up in different strongholds (Len was very security conscious), which meant it took longer to access the firearms. Willie and one of his relatives went to the rescue and Willie was scalped when he put his head through the window in an attempt to aim his rifle at the lioness. In the following confusion, one of the people trying to assist was accidentally shot. Willie did eventually manage to kill the animal. Lions were to maul Willie twice in his career. Partly because of the lion incident and also because it was closer to the railway, the culling camp was moved to

*Henry Pringle, Bertie, Barry Duckworth and Tinkey Haslam resting on game capture at Wankie PHOTO Richard Aylward*

Umtchibi.

## *Game Capture*

Tom was made Warden in charge of Game Capture at Wankie and spent a fair amount of time on the Ngamo, Makololo and Kennedy flats. This was during the period when the rangers wildly chased animals across the plains with land rovers and lassoes. They would ambush the game when they went to water and as they fled, pursued them over the rough ground, hoping to beat them to the tree line. They would riotously drive alongside a giraffe with the stripped down land rover and using a Rhodesian lassoe, rope a leg. This was quite dangerous as you could get graunched by the rope. A giraffe would be slowed down and a harness put on to guide it where you wanted. Due to the roughness of the terrain, the Robins camp area was a little more dangerous and Tom nearly went over a cliff at the Deka. He and Rob Gee had some narrow shaves, chasing the game in the hills and grassy vleis. Tommy was involved in the capture of giraffe, buffalo, sable, waterbuck, roan and eland. Some of these animals went to the Okahandja zoo park in South West Africa, while others went to National Parks and farms around Rhodesia. The captured animals were normally placed in their own individual mopane pens. Roan antelope frequently died from the shock of capture, so Tom believed that darting and sedation would be more suitable for this animal. Some special foot and mouth free buffalo, collected by the veterinary department from tsetse operations were transported in RMS trucks from Lusulu (east of Wankie) to Buffalo Range in the south of the country. Tom accompanied them, stayed in the trucks with the calves all the way down to Buffalo Range and would blow into the calves' noses to settle them down. Talking of capture, a number of zebra were caught on the old landing strip at Wankie Main Camp where a Dakota used to land every day. Two of them ended up at the Gwaai hotel. These tame zebras, called Sugar-sugar and Dube, were still around in the 1980's and had produced crosses with donkeys, making zonkeys or debras. The Gwaai zebra were rideable and one day people may ride zebras as a tourist activity.

## *Fellow Rangers*

Two of the people that Tom worked with during these game capture operations were Rob Gee and Kim Hodierne. Kim was the lucky survivor of an encounter with a crocodile. He and a friend were skin diving in Kariba when he felt himself being pulled slowly by the foot. He thought it was his friend, but it went on too long and he looked around to see a croc with his flipper in its mouth. He pulled hard but it held on and managed to get some teeth through into his foot. So he wrenched his foot out the flipper and swam like mad until he reached safety. His foot took a long time to heal. Rob Gee was later instrumental in starting up the Victoria Falls crocodile farm.

## *Glamour Kings*

For some Parks' staff it was, 'how much money do I get, how many camera shots a month do I get, or am I in the newspaper'. These few individuals were glamour kings and the only thing missing was lipstick! Most of the rangers in Parks though were like Tom and were very dedicated to their jobs. During game capture exercises Tom often had to deal with film crews and their 'stars'. One day an American company called Don Meier productions, with the famous Marlin Perkins and Jim Fowler arrived. This intrusion meant capture operations had to be switched to chasing giraffe for photo purposes and this took up ten days of valuable time. The action man in the film series was Jim Fowler, who was a good-looking hunk of six foot three. One of the film crew was overbearing and rude in his dealings with Parks' staff and Tom took a dislike to him. Tom was no respecter of fame and hatched a plan to teach him a lesson. His opportunity came when he found himself driving the capture land rover with this particular cameraman in the back. They spotted the animals they wanted to capture and Tom started the chase. When the time was right, Tom angled the vehicle into an antbear hole and then into a convenient Camel Thorn tree. During 'the accident', the bad guy went flying and his expensive film equipment was flung out, with reels of film strewn all over the ground. Tom was satisfied and his boss John Hatton put in a report that the, "terrain was getting a bit rough!"

*National Parks get together in later years L to R, Mike Bromwich, Howard Shackleton, Alistair Hull, Sherri, Rob Francis, unknown, Richard Peek, Rob Gee*

*National Parks staff at Wankie discuss strategy. They are - from left to right - Bruce Austin (Regional Warden Wankie, Henry Pringle (Ranger Main Camp, Dave Rushworth (one of pilots in WNP and Warden Robins Camp),? (Pilot from Bulawayo), Charles Williams (Ranger Main Camp), Colin Bickle (farmer from Byo with his own plane), Ozzie Bristow (in dark glasses - with his own plane) and Dave Higgins (Research officer Main Camp). PHOTO Jackie Pringle*

## CHAPTER 12
# WANKIE & GWAAI 1966 –1968

### *Gwaai farmers*

The Gwaai farmers near Wankie National Park had to make a living and the carrying capacity of the Gwaai sand veld was only about 1 cow to 40 acres. So if they had 10 000 to 12 000 acres they could only ranch efficiently if they stocked about 250-300 animals. Any more than that caused over grazing. This was not enough to live on or to cover their expenses. The veld had little grass, was very sandy and through overstocking the vleis had been damaged. Huge gullies had formed over a short period, some bigger than a house. To make money the farmers resorted to shooting the game, which was competing for grazing with their cattle. In the old days, the farmers were paid by the District Administrator to kill predators, painted dogs, jackals and there was a 5-shilling reward for a baboon. To prove they had killed the vermin they had to produce the tail of the animal. If they had a major problem that they could not deal with, they could phone Parks to help and they would normally be there that day. Parks' staff taught farmers how to use chemicals to poison some of the predators. Unfortunately, the terrible poison used at that time would often get into the food chain and even the vultures and jackals feeding off the poisoned baboons would die. Although Parks' staff were friendly with the farmers, they never hesitated to take action if their friends broke the law. When one of the Gwaai farmers shot an elephant illegally on his property, Parks' rangers caught him through some smart detective work. Tom recalled how the man cleverly tried to avoid capture by taking an elephants foot and making prints all round a water point and then through his own crops nearby. He then deliberately damaged the water tank and pipes. The idea was to convince Parks that the elephant had been shot legally because it was damaging his property. He certainly did not convince the game rangers and his scheme was exposed.

## *Buck*

Buck de Vries trained as an aircraft engineer in the South African air force, after which he was recruited by the British government to build a wind tunnel in Salisbury Rhodesia, for the testing of the new Viscount aircraft engines. When this job was finished, he worked for a Mr. Boshoff as an assistant tobacco farmer near Salisbury. Mr. Boshoff treated him like his own son and because he was such a good mechanic, always asked Buck to accompany him on his business trips to Angola and Zambia. On one of these trips, on their way back from Zambia, they stopped in the Gwaai area and each of them bought a farm from Harold Bloomberg. Later Boshoff sold his farm to Buck for about £6 000. Buck finally ended up with four farms in the area, two of them being Lion and Dahlia. When he initially moved there, he made his living by fixing tractors and machinery. Buck was one of the first ranchers in the Gwaai to do professional hunting in the 1970's. They hunted with the clients and it was a profitable way to get rid of the many elephants, lions and leopards that interfered with cattle farming. Buck was well known in later years for his domesticated elephants and his game-pioneering role in the district. Using quality shotguns, Bruce Austen and Tim Braybrooke used to hunt ducks on Buck's place and francolins and doves on the Gwaai River. This was their sport and how they spent their leisure time and it was good for the pot. Tim, being a fisherman, also spent many happy hours catching fish in the Gwaai River. Occasionally, when everyone in the area got together for a party, Parks' staff would shoot a young buffalo as a contribution and Buck would buy a pig from the Chatham's. Using some of the venison, the pork and maybe some beef, he would make beautiful long boerewors sausages. Over the braai, with lots of beer and the boerewors fat trickling out of their mouths, the farmers and Parks' staff would have themselves a good time. The farmers in the Gwaai used to play a rough but friendly game against Parks. This involved jumping on each other and the result was often broken arms and legs, with someone once ending up in the Wankie hospital. There was a big sign at Buck's ranch saying, 'Wankie Game Reserve corridor'. As there was not much water in the park, thousands of elephants would go through this corridor to drink at the confluence of the Gwaai and Shangani rivers. Every day they crossed the main Vic Falls road and many continued to sleep alongside this road even after it had been tarred. Often there were so many elephant it was difficult to drive through to Wankie town and the Victoria Falls, so occasionally people would just give up, turn around and stay at the Gwaai hotel for the night. The corridor went from Buck's fence to Dett and then to Mao Pools on the Gwaai River.

*Entrance*

The main entrance to Wankie National Park was at the Dett Vlei where you were welcomed by a giraffe skull and cross bones sign. Before you were allowed into the Park, your vehicle had to be sprayed for tsetse flies. There was a big metal building at the bottom of Dett Vlei on Buck de Vries' ranch, which was used for this purpose. The vehicles were driven into this building and the doors were closed. In almost complete darkness, the bodies of the vehicles were sprayed and the underneath and the engine were thoroughly doused. The Park closed at 5.00 p.m. and any latecomers (generally South Africans) were forced to camp outside until the next morning. Sometimes there were as many as 50 cars parked for the night near Buck de Vries' house and he found himself providing essentials such as tea and water.

## *Main Camp*

As a tourist you passed along the Dett vlei and would arrive at the humming Parks' base at Main Camp. By the mid sixties, the sleepy headquarters of Ted Davison here was just a fond memory. Main Camp was now a thriving and growing centre with ever expanding tourist facilities. New construction, more money and more staff were changing the character of the place. Rangers lived in prefabricated, galvanized iron, round houses called 'lion tents' which had been rapidly installed for the new members of staff. However, living conditions at Main Camp were like being in a 5 star hotel compared to some of the other Park's stations. The original office at Main Camp, where Ted had worked, still stood under a huge acacia tree, but only just. Staff waged a constant battle against a colony of very determined white ants in trying to prevent the complete collapse of the unit. One stormy night a Camel Thorn tree was blown down onto the office and a new office block had to be built. In 1966 while John Hatton was Regional Warden, he had a funny little tin hut as an office, as the new offices had not yet been built. Wild animals still moved freely amongst the staff houses at night, particularly zebra and wildebeest, while lions killed a wildebeest right in front of Peter Wright's house. Gardening was a futile exercise as the elephants visited frequently and demolished everything. Lions also took to chewing hosepipes.

## *Development*

Along with the burst of structural development, Main Camp saw the arrival of new land rovers, an ambulance and a Piper Super Cub airplane. More happened in a short space of time than had happened in the last 10 years. Government allocated $47 000 for the development of roads within the Park. It was recommended that this be spent on an all-weather route from Main Camp to the popular new camp at Sinamatella and this enabled both camps to be kept open throughout the year. Main Camp was completely replanned to provide for orderly development and future expansion and work began on 13 new tourist cottages. Water supplies for both animals and humans were improved, with the addition of seven new boreholes - two close to Main Camp to help with camp supplies. Picnic facilities were set up at sites on the Deteema and Mandavu dams to cater for the over twenty-two thousand tourists who were now visiting each year. Individual visitors were mainly from Rhodesia and South Africa and the increasing number of tour groups came mostly from overseas. The

United Touring Company transported their groups in VW Combies on Flame Lily tours. Tourists were flown in courtesy of Central African Airways and more often than not, the planes had to circle overhead while a land rover chased all the wild animals off the landing strip.

## *Romance*
The landing strip was right in front of the staff houses and the rangers used to line up when the plane arrived, to see what 'birds' came off the plane. If you were a single girl living at Main Camp and you weren't completely cross eyed, wore orthopaedic shoes and braces, or had a figure like Miss Michelin (type of tyre), then you were in demand. There were few girls around and some of the girls had colourful backgrounds. The army, air force, SAS etc. would all pass through and put extra demand on the girls. A few rangers and their lady companions, used to make love under the sprinklers on the lawns on hot nights, as it was a 'cool' thing to do. They had to watch out for the lights of passing land rovers returning from the Waterbucks Head bar. One enterprising ranger was caught using the pump house to entertain his lady friend in private. To many females, a game ranger was a romantic figure and many of the young men took full advantage of this free and very effective advertising. Tom was described at this time (by a girl from Main Camp) as having Elvis Presley features and quite a nice stocky figure, a humorous round face, a cute retrousse nose and sparkling brown eyes. Being a good talker, he was quite successful in chatting with the girls. Main Camp had its own bar called the Waterbucks Head, which was used by visitors and Parks' staff. One day the tall and thin Peter Thomson pinched a girlfriend from Tom here and was later engaged to her in rather short order. The engagement did not last all that long and after a period of heartbreak, he concluded that Tommy and he were both probably better off without her.

## *Bruce*
When Tom was in Wankie he used sleeveless jackets and was full of bounce, having great energy, enthusiasm for everything, was fast-talking and had a huge commitment to wild things and wild places. But he could be a quiet man of few words when he came into Main Camp. He made it his policy to mind his own business and to get on with his own work, which he did well. Regional warden Bruce Austen replaced John Hatton at Wankie. Bruce was a friend of Ian Smith the

prime minister and had gone to school with him. When the Prime Minister and his wife Janet arrived at Main Camp on a formal visit, a cocktail party and dinner was organized in their honour. Bruce and Pat Austen hosted it at Bruce's picturesque thatched house with its exquisite garden and manicured lawn. Despite having helpers in the kitchen to serve the 30 odd guests, Pat was unable to cope. Pat and her friends commenced dishing up spare ribs, veggies and gravy and a new helper soon came in to alleviate the responsibilities. Here Tommy helped serve the spare ribs and gravy. Not only this, but he helped with the dinner plate shuttle service and so in no time at all, the dinner service was under control. Thanks to Tom, the ladies could also sit and eat.

### *Fences and Patrols*
Game fences erected to control foot and mouth and tsetse, ran from Mlibizi down through to the bottom of Wankie National Park. The fencing was made of Mopane poles and any animal close to the wire was shot. A tsetse control unit based on the other side of the Shangani River used DDT poison to control the spread of the dreaded fly. It was only some years later that scientists discovered that this chemical was extremely harmful to the environment. Both the Wankie fence and the Botswana border were constantly patrolled and although some patrols were carried out in vehicles, they were more traditionally done with donkeys. National Parks (sometimes with police) and Veterinary patrols alternatively checked the fence every day. Patrols heading for Sibanini were sent out every few days. This meant that, at any one time, there were always at least 4 white and about 10 black people patrolling the fence. Tommy came to love the donkey anti-poaching patrols and had a high regard for donkeys. The Wankie donkeys learned to know their routes and night stops well. After having a drink at the waterhole, they would automatically walk up to their tying up spots at the end of the day's patrol. They were conditioned to ignore lions by listening to tapes of lion sounds and having lion fat rubbed all over them. They became so familiar with lions that when confronted by the cats, the stubborn creatures would just stand and stare at the confused lions. Tom recalls a time when a patrol arrived with their donkeys at a waterhole and without checking around, allowed the donkeys to rush down to the water for a drink. The donkeys still had their kit on when the lions rushed out and killed at least one of them. Once, when Tom was on the Botswana border doing elephant control,

he came across some policemen, one of whom was a British aristocrat sent out to get some experience in the colonies. J was related to the queen; however he never seemed to wash and wore a shirt until it seemed to decompose off his back. On patrol when he sat down at the fire, you would nearly faint as he stank so much. This man asked if he could test Tom's .505. To start with, he had difficulty lifting the weapon and when he started shooting, he fell down on the ground in a heap. Tom's only concern was whether his beloved weapon had been damaged! When Tom was patrolling with his game scouts near Makwa pan one day, he noticed vultures overhead. He decided to go off by himself and investigate. He found a freshly killed zebra near the pan and while he was looking at it, three lions arrived and surrounded him, cutting off his escape. Tom had forgotten to bring his rifle and found himself in a precarious position. The last thing you do is run from lions, so Tom just sat down. After about an hour his concerned game scouts went to look for him and found him sitting on the ground, with the lions also sitting and waiting patiently around him.

## *Water Supplies*

Tom spent an extended time based at Wankie bush camps. Here he did antipoaching, game capture and he built many of the game water supply troughs. The water troughs were built by digging a circular trench and then they were filled with concrete. The walls were then built up on the concrete ring, the centre scooped out and the base left to eventually form a natural hard pan. On their regular patrols through the Park, the rangers were expected to check these troughs and the windmill pumps for damage. Tom recalled that quite a few men were fired for failing to check these installations. Bruce Austen was very fond of the local Bushmen and he used them to spy at water holes. They would hide messages under stones with information on whether rangers had checked water pumps properly etc. In later years, water pumps were to be permanently attended by pump boys. When Tom was camped at Ngamo he took to growing pumpkins. He not only ate the pumpkins but the leaves as well, which were cooked with peanut butter and eaten with mealie meal. The local Tsholotsho people living along the fence would bring beer for him and his companions and in return, he provided them with meat. A police patrol came across Tom and some other Parks' staff at Ngamo and were invited to join in the midday meal. They sat down to lunch amidst a huge grove of Ilala palms. One of the policemen asked, "Tommy why are there are so many palms here?" Tom replied with tongue in cheek, "Maybe it was the Arabs camping." Another perky and cheerful chap piped, "It must have been one helluva party, as they are all over the place."

## *Foxies*

His fox terriers Rookie, Reddy/Red Dog and Muffin always accompanied Tom. Phil Evans, who was one of the chief officers in head office, decided that no family stationed in a camp was allowed to have more than two dogs. On hearing the order, Tommy took his three dogs, placed them on John Hatton's desk and said, "Right you want to apply this rule, you choose which dog I must get rid of". No choice was taken and Tommy kept his three dogs. While camped out in the south of the park, Johnny Johnson found Tom with a bunch of long-nosed fox terriers tied to different trees. Tom presented one of his foxies to Johnny and it became a great dog. When Johnny was stationed at Vic Falls it used to go down to the Victoria Falls hotel and get a lift with the girls on the bus out to the airport and then, after an inspection and many hello's it would then catch a lift back. It also hitched rides into Zambia. It might have been at this time in Wankie that one of Tom's dogs was sleeping under his bed. A leopard jumped through the open window as they were snoozing, grabbed the dog under his bed and jumped back through the window. He woke up when the dog made a noise and it was too late to rescue the animal.

## *Nyamandhlovu*

During the sixties Henry Pringle built a new game-viewing platform for tourists at Nyamandhlovu Pan, which still stands today. Henry, a good welder and expert ballroom dancer, was six foot four, so the local people gave him the nickname Baas Donsa Iwguba (Boss Pull up the Blankets). The pans at Wankie were stocked with a dozen 3-foot crocodiles from Binga, which increased the population in the Park to over 50. When they first arrived, they were kept in a swimming pool before being released into the larger pans. One of the older and more famous crocs here was an 'ex' pet who was named after a judge called Beadle. Beadle used to travel between Nyamandhlovu and Dom pans and when the elephant pressure was too great, he would take up residence in an ant bear hole. The crocs at Nyamandhlovu could often be seen taking advantage of elephant disturbance to catch the local catfish. Bruce Austen regularly

*Giraffe at one of the Wankie pans Tom was working on*

instructed his staff to catch spring-hares for Beadle and Tom joined others in pampering this hungry reptile. Soon Beadle associated land rovers with food and would rush out the water whenever one arrived. There was an occasion when some VIP's drove up to Nyamandhlovu Pan and were astonished to see Beadle rushing towards their land rover and they feared that they were on his menu. When Tinkey Haslam fed Beadle at Nyamandhlovu he would walk right up to the water's edge, place a wildebeest leg near the water and then just take one step to the side. Within seconds, the croc would shoot out of the water and grab the meat. That he was never taken was a miracle. Having heard for years about the wonderful properties of catnip oil, Tom and his friends thought it was about time its attraction to cats was put to the test. So they smeared some on the tyres of a land rover being used by some VIP's. The experiment worked!! When the vehicle arrived at the Nyamandhlovu waterhole, a pride of lions approached the vehicle and much to the annoyance of the VIP's, kept patrolling round the visitors and made it quite clear that they didn't want to leave!

## *Dandelion*

At Mandavu Dam one day, a lioness charged some people for no apparent reason. She therefore had to be shot and it was subsequently found that she had three cubs nearby. One cub was already dead and one had been badly burnt in a bushfire but subsequently recovered, while the third was fine and Ranger Stott took them back to camp. The two cubs were kept in a chicken coup, from which they once escaped with lots of growling and roaring noises. The game scouts had to play a game of catch to recapture the two cubs that were now the size of ridgebacks. One of the cubs may have been the lion called Dandelion who, as a youngster, took a liking to the warmth of children's beds. When he lived at Main Camp, he loved the hot water boilers close to the tourist toilets and these were a great place to warm himself in winter. A real upper class gentleman decided it was time to do his ablutions. Off he went properly garbed in a lovely long white bathrobe to the ablution block. The young lion found the robe irresistible and gave chase. The terrified gentleman took flight and in his terror dived into one of the chalets. He went through the mosquito gauze and landed (almost naked by this stage) on some ladies. Dandelion later found a new home with Ozzie Bristow down at Le Rhone farm near Fort Victoria. Tim Braybrooke was the warden in charge of Kyle National Park when Ozzie brought Dandelion, now a big handsome lion, along for some filming. A film crew was shooting some scenes with rhino in the background and Tim said, "Osswic if that lion looks twice at one of my rhinos, I will shoot it." And Tim was there with his weapon watching beadily all the time. When he was about four years old, Dandelion was moved to Brits in South Africa near Pretoria. He was still a very docile cat; he had often slept on rangers' camp beds and remained gentle and friendly with humans. A film engineer named Jimmy Chapman placed his camp bed near where Dandelion was enclosed in a tennis court. Dandelion managed to get out the court and tried to sleep on the occupied camp bed - much to the surprise of the occupant, who sat up in alarm and got a reactionary 'clout' (with sheathed claws) from Dandelion across the head, which broke his neck. He died without any other wounds. Dandelion was quite upset at what he had done, but had to be destroyed because of the reaction of the people around.

## *Poachers*

Tom hated poachers and unfortunately, there was a great deal of poaching going on in Wankie. This was done mostly at night in the northern hunting area and plenty of vehicle tracks indicated that this had gone on for a very long time. Most of the poachers were from Wankie town and they operated along the border of the park. Tommy made the problem of white poachers his top priority. He spent many nights in cold riverbeds waiting in ambush for these poachers to sneak into the hunting area, with little success. He did manage to apprehend three white poachers at Gobo Springs, complete with rifles and hunting lamps and they were fined £50 each, or 50 days hard labour

*Hans van der Heiden with donkeys at Main Camp PHOTO Richard Aylward*

and their rifles were confiscated. Many of the white poachers from the railways would drive their cars in at the Dett vlei, sneaking in at night and you would hear a shot or two. Buck de Vries, a local farmer, would go and investigate and would drive around and find nothing. In the morning, he would see the vehicle tracks and where an eland had been loaded. The poachers strategy was to shoot their quarry and then leave immediately afterwards. They would then come back early in the morning when the antipoaching team had given up the search and they would load their prey. To mark the site for the later pickup they would use a stick or marker by the road to show where they had shot the animal. Many train drivers were also guilty of poaching. They could pick out the eyes of animals in the lights of the train from a long way off. They had specific time schedules to adhere to and if they lost some time by stopping or slowing down between points, they could disguise it by speeding up later on. The time sheet could also state 'game on track'. If they saw the likes of a sable, eland or kudu, they would put on the brakes, pull out the rifle and then shoot. Small game hit and killed by the train could also be picked up and eaten and train drivers on this route never had to buy meat. On one occasion, a driver spotted a dead buffalo that had obviously been hit by the train that had gone before him. When he got back to Dett he got into his Opel station wagon with a friend and drove out to the site. They cut off the four legs and left the remainder of the carcass next to the railway line.

It wasn't long before the driver had the police drive up to his house at Dett, where they found blood in his vehicle and all the rest of the evidence on the property. He and his mate were charged with taking a government trophy. Their defence was that they had left the head behind which was the trophy, while the meat was not. The magistrate was unimpressed and sentenced them anyway.

## *Bush meat*
Most of the black poachers came from Tsholotsho. The man best suited to deal with them was Don Stott, the champion poacher catcher, who was then based at Main Camp. Don once caught 50 odd poachers who had been laying snares. He and his scouts handcuffed them to a windmill in a remote area overnight, which must have been terrifying as there were lions around. The next day this troop of bad guys was marched off to Main Camp. Don's Alsatian dog then had the job of guarding them and if they moved it would rush towards them to ensure they did not escape. This dog was invaluable in anti poaching operations and was afraid of neither man nor beast and he proved it by losing an eye when a zebra kicked him.

## *Progressive*
Tom was progressive in his choice of vehicles. He appeared at Main Camp in about 1967 with his first Toyota Land Cruiser. Most people still used land rovers in those days and Ronnie van Heerden had a Willies jeep. All the men walked out to look at it. They kicked the tyres and laughed and someone commented saying, "aghh this will never catch on". They laughed about the Land Cruiser, saying that as it was Japanese, it would never work. Well, we all know now that Tom was right. When Tom bought one of the first .357 handguns, everyone at Main Camp made fun of him and his 'cannon'. They said, "He wouldn't be able to shoot a barn at 500 yards, blah blah and what could he do with it." One day Tommy accompanied a number of rangers and they stopped at a pan in Gwabazabuyu Vlei for lunch. The subject of Tom's 'cannon' came up and some started to make fun of him. So he quietly went and sat down on his haunches on the west side of the pan and took aim at a tree stump on the other side, about 25m away. When he rapidly emptied all the rounds into the stump, they all shut up immediately. They could see the impressive results and Tommy's ability to handle it. He once tested his .357 out by shooting a buffalo.

*Guvalala platform UTC advert 1967 Rhodesia Calls*

## *Johnny Uys*

Johnny Uys, one of the last white game wardens out of Zambia, was extremely knowledgeable about the habits of wild animals. He would confidently go very close to elephants while working with tourists on the edge of the park near Wankie Safari Lodge. He occasionally did brave things like smacking them on their backsides. One night when Johnny said, "I know elephants", Tommy commented, "One elephant one day will not recognize you!" Years later Johnny was taking clients on a walk close to a cow herd, when an elephant cow charged. He hit the elephant on the trunk with a small stick, but she did not turn. She picked him up, killed him by pushing him through the sand and mutilated his body terribly, as she pierced him with her tusks.

## *Research*

Traditionally the Field and Research Departments were often at each other's throats. Some of the researchers were very good, but the field staff felt others needed plenty of help. However just as many of the field staff had learnt their trade through trial and error, so now the research staff were doing the same. Tommy, being Tommy, was outspoken and dismissive of fancy scientific stuff. He was irritated by some of the long-and pompous language, but sharp enough to know good sense from non-sense. Two experiments that did not work at this time in Wankie were the marking of elephants with coloured tail bands and ear tagging them with aluminium discs, but Tom was more

*Tom with foxies at Wankie late 60's*

concerned about the serious mistakes he saw in twenty-one years of Parks. Some of the research mistakes were quite amusing though. Elephants were darted for various purposes and valuable data recorded whilst they were still sedated. One researcher got a fright when placing a thermometer up a darted elephant's behind - the animal reared up and ran off taking the thermometer with it. Tom spoke about the good scientists later on in life, "...These being the men who went or came into the department of National Parks and Wildlife Management or the old Game Department as field rangers, ran stations and got a taste of life other than the rarefied attitude in the universities - where they are basically and still are parasites of society, maintained and paid for by doting parents and other organizations and then came out as so called ecologists, who were attached in their heyday of the professionalism in Parks, from the 1960's to various parks. It would be an interesting study to document the ecological disasters, aided and abetted and sponsored by these so-called ologists. The best biologists and I say this with utter feeling, were those young men who, after working within the department, or other departments, then went to university as mature adults, clear thinking, human beings with a heart." Some of the well-known and better scientists of this period in Wankie were, John Rushworth, Bruce Couper, John Herbert and later Basil Williamson. Temporary researchers like Ray Smithers and Don Broadley later became very well known and respected in their chosen fields. A great deal of experimentation and research work was being done on the botany of the park, specific animal habits, animal movements, culling, fire damage and fire control and on the carrying capacity of the Park. Tom was quite often involved in controlling fires raging through the Park. He ruffled a few feathers because he was outspoken about the fact that not enough was being done to stop them. He was proved right because that same year he complained in 1968, a huge fire swept through the veld near Robins. It came in from Botswana on an 80-mile front, having been started by hunters in Botswana to assist their hunting. The Parks' staff had to grade a road in order to back burn from a distance of 10 miles in front of the fire because it was travelling so fast. Even that was not enough - the grader (Gallion) and the driver - poor old Mafikizolo - were burned in that fire, as they could not get away quickly enough.

*Nyamandhlovu Platform in 2007*

*Staff at Wankie. Standing from L to R - Top Row -
Kim Hodierne, Dave Rushworth, Don Stott, Arthur Wood, Rod
Hill, Peter Thompson, Billy Thomas, Norman Payne, Boyd Reese,
Louis Myberg, Fred Grant, Tinkey Haslam, Don Hutchins, --
Sitting L to R - 'Jordy' (Hendrik) Jordaan, Rob Gee, Gerry
Buckland, Tommy Orford, Fred Balestra, Jeremy Anderson,
Ronnie van Heerden, John Hatton*

*Tom with his rhino at Kyle*

## CHAPTER 13
# ROVING WARDEN 1965-1972

### Witch

In the mid sixties Tom was driving to Sun Yet Sen in the South West of the country in his land rover on an anti poaching trip. He found an ostrich chick and brought it to the local police station at Kezi. This being a live chick, it seemed the best place to take it. Any evidence found by Parks, if possible, had to go to police in those days and that included poached animals. This was great for the police who used to eat the evidence, as once all the details had been recorded they had to be disposed of. There were no refrigeration or mortuary facilities available at any of the bush stations. Later this ostrich grew up and loved chasing the cyclists as they passed the police station. It sadly ended with a cyclist being kicked to death by the bird. Tom picked up some poachers in the nearby hills on this trip. One of these was a woman who was charged for murdering some people by burning their grass-roofed huts supposedly by witchcraft. The police cells at Kezi were new and had asbestos roofs so they should have been fire proof. However, soon after she was locked up the roofing timbers caught alight, even though she had been thoroughly searched. When the case was heard in the High Court, a Kezi Policeman named Kevin, gave evidence against her. She was sentenced to death, but before she was escorted back to the cells, she shouted to Kevin, "You will die by fire". Later on in the year on the 10th November 1965, he was stationed at Dett and was called to go to Wankie Police Station to prepare for the Independence Day declaration the following day. On their way back to Dett, between the Kamativi crossroads and Dett village, about 5 kilometres down the road; the vehicle went up in flames. He died with about 6 other policemen and the cause of the fire was a total mystery.

## *Head office*
At Salisbury head office, Tom would appear as the game ranger personified and had the clothing to show, being proud of the Department uniform. A short, stocky, cocky, first-class talker, often in traditional Parks' uniform, broad hat, complete with pugaree and badge, ironed shirt, a little too long shorts, evenly matched stockings and brown shoes with his brown leather briefcase. After official business was completed, he would happily sit down with the office staff, share a cup of tea and regale them with his stories. He once commented that, "he didn't know why he was in this dump called Salisbury," and that coming into town was his worst nightmare. Once Tom started talking, they could not get rid of him! Normally when the rangers and wardens came to town, the wives would wait patiently outside in the cars knitting or keeping African time. The men would move around the town, getting rations, bits and pieces. Tom seldom came to the Parks' pub called the .470, but he would come and have a coke and chat. If there was a party here the odd character would get 'screaming, blindly, drunk and try to run up the walls', while Tom always maintained his composure. He was a tea totaller and drank tea by the gallon. When in civilian attire and visiting friends in Salisbury and having to dress up for the occasion, he would wear his cowboy, "string tie and toggle," instead of an ordinary tie and was in the habit of giving presents to everyone. Tom was like a pocket dynamo, always humming with energy and full of boundless enthusiasm.

## *Dragons*
Once when Boyd Reese arrived at Head Office in Salisbury, he saw Barry Ball climbing out of the window in hysterics. Archie Fraser's wife Tess was the receptionist at the time and she and Tommy were

talking to a Mrs. H, who was in a terrible state. She had just seen a Unicorn and wanted someone to go with her to investigate. They tried to interest Boyd, but he made his escape by saying that he had to go and collect his camping gear. This same Mrs. H later went to Bulawayo, where sadly, Tommy had waved to her on his way to the old Head Office, in Main Street. Mr. Tebbit was in charge and Georgey Du Plessis may have been in the reception. Mrs. H followed Tommy into the office and complained this time about dragons. Tommy introduced her to one of the young innocent rangers present and told her he was the great "dragonologist", made a polite but hasty departure and left the poor man to find his way out of the predicament.

## *PAC*

On one occasion when Tommy was involved in Problem Animal Control, he unwittingly walked into an interview where two Green Peace Movement members were grilling Arthur Wood, the Chief Warden. This organization was giving the Department a hard time in the press, on their 'excessive' use of firearms. Tommy was wearing his normal khakis, vellies and bush hat, together with two crossed bandoliers (one filled with .375 bullets and the other with .458 ammo). Around his waist, was a belted side arm, with bullet loops, filled up and complemented with a hunting knife. Imagine the impact this had on these sensitive people. They were horrified and asked Tommy if he was going to war. Tommy's reply was (with a straight face), "...Oh no I'm just collecting more ammunition to continue my conservation programme." And when asked what that programme was, he said again with a straight face, "...Quelea control", saluted and walked out.

## *Croc*

It might have been at this time when Tom and a game scout were drinking from a pool at Chipinda Pools area with a fox terrier. With only centimetres between them, they were stooping from the bank and slaking their thirst on a hot day. Suddenly there was a splash and clap and Tom looked up to see a ripple and the white of the foxy disappearing into the depths of the river. A flat dog (croc) put an end to that fox terrier.

## *Buffalo Charge*

Tom spent some of this period at Binga/Gokwe doing anti poaching work and dealing with problem, crop-raiding elephant and buffalo and then the odd lion in this period. On one occasion, he found a snared buffalo, which then charged him. Tom held onto the horns and was saved when Johnny Bunce shot it. Tom had other interesting experiences shooting a buffalo in his earlier days. He once shot a cow for rations. Bushes hid her horns and when he walked up to the dead animal, he found she had world record size horns. He also took a chance with a .22 rifle on another buffalo and managed to shoot it dead, even though it was a small calibre rifle.

## *Man Eaters*
In 1968, he had an encounter with man-eating lions in the Mujere area of Binga, where two black tribesmen were eaten. An old lioness with poor broken teeth, was teaching her three sub-adult cubs the art of human hunting. Tom drove his green land rover to the area and while his men were setting up camp, he went for a walk with his 7mm rifle, fishing rod, worms and went fishing. While ambling along, he found a partly eaten man. As the lions appeared to be hiding nearby, Tom pulled out his poison, made some cuts in the body with his knife and inserted some strychnine capsules in the man's body. He then went off to do his fishing. When he came back later, he found the lions all dead around the carcass. So as not to offend the villagers, he then moved the lions into various positions and shot them. When the local villagers came running to see what was going on, they found the lions shot by the great white hunter. After much ululation, they placed the man and the lions in a pile and burnt them together. This might have been to appease the spirits.

## *Bulawayo*
It was about 1968 that Tom was transferred to Bulawayo and appointed Warden Roving Control (later to be known as Problem Animal Control). Tom was chafing at the bit about being sent to Bulawayo and was never sure whether the transfer was some kind of punishment. He took his assistant Fat Boy (Rambuwene Nhongo) and game scout Alois Shaiwako with him. Fat Boy was a quiet and faithful gentleman who would undertake anything from servicing vehicles to making tea. Tom went off for weeks to parts of Matabeleland and Midlands in his land cruiser, with a fox terrier, tracker, sergeant and a helper. The black staff were treated well by Tom and they loved to hear his stories. When doing PAC in 1970, Tom's vehicle was always

organized to perfection, with the jerry cans, miscellaneous items, scoff (food) box, baked beans etc. When Tom arrived at a problem area, he would camp away from people and do his own thing. His staff would dig out an ant heap and bake bread, so Tom had fresh bread every day. Tom was once sent out to deal with what was presumed to be a leopard on Roger Greef's ranch at Plumtree. This animal killed about 70 cattle and later turned out to be a clever hyena. Tom asked Roger to shoot one of the many wild donkeys on the ranch so they could use it for bait. Tom then cut off the head and buried it in the ground, so only the ears of the donkey stuck out and he then placed traps around. Tom was sure this would attract the hyena, but it was far too intelligent to fall for that one. Roger did eventually manage to kill it by laying out poisoned bait.

## *Dawn*

In April 1969, Tom was tasked with manning the National Parks and Wildlife Management stand at the annual Trade Fair in Bulawayo. Whilst wandering around during a lunch break he struck up a conversation with the woman standing next to him who was admiring the same exhibit. Tommy had finally met the girl he wanted to marry. He lost no time in trying to sweep her off her feet and by the end of the first evening; he had firmly announced that he was going to marry her. Dawn was a sales representative for a company based in Salisbury that produced dog food, cereals and non-alcoholic African beer. She was an English born divorcee with a little boy of 18 months back in Harare. Tommy hadn't really given marriage much thought before, although it had crossed his mind that he would be more likely to stay in one place and not be given all the odd jobs if he was a married man. When he met Dawn he was blown over and his mind was made up. Tom and Dawn were from different cultural backgrounds, but Tommy spent many hours on the phone convincing her that marriage to him would be wonderful. After an enchanting week on one of Tommy's very basic camps in the Midlands she capitulated. He took her out to his sister and brother-in-law's farm at Mayo to meet his side of the family. They were not happy about the fact that Dawn was a divorcee and politely grilled her about her past and her thoughts for the future. After a couple of days, they seemed to accept her and the happy couple began to make plans. They could not see why they should waste any further time, so were married in Salisbury in August the same year.

## Married Life

They set off for their honeymoon at the Victoria Falls and dropped Bryan (Dawn's 18 month old son) with some friends in Bulawayo - who had a little boy of the same age. On the way through Wankie, Tommy introduced Dawn to his great friends Dave and Julienne Rushworth and generally showed her round Wankie. After a wonderful, few days away they arrived back in Bulawayo and soon afterwards, Tommy adopted Bryan as his very own. The newly married couple spent the first 3 months of their life together in a small cottage just outside Bulawayo before being allocated a house at Maleme in the Matopos National Park, where they stayed until Tommy was appointed Warden of Kyle National Park in April 1970. The previous occupants of the house had several pet mongooses and left behind a very active colony of fleas. Spraying was not very effective and after much experiment, Tommy found that only Marigold plants placed against the skirting boards did the trick.

## The Cook

Dawn now inherited Tom's ancient cook/cleaner called Ndhlovu. She was convinced that not only was he too old to work but too blind, to see the dust, which accumulated everywhere. He, on the other hand, was convinced that he only worked for Tommy and that meant keeping the boss's shoes and uniform clean and smart - anything else was done at his convenience, if he felt like it and in his own very slow time. He also believed it was beneath him to work for a woman. Needless to say, this arrangement did not work for long and with legality on her side; Dawn persuaded Tommy that Ndhlovu should be sent off to a well deserved retirement.

## Matopos Baboon

The Matopos National Park abounded with food-stealing monkeys and baboons. Dawn used to go for walks with Bryan amongst the kopjes and they often encountered family groups. These animals were totally unafraid and would only move out of the path when there was only about ten feet left between themselves and the two humans. Dawn felt completely safe and concluded that they did not find human females threatening. Bryan was now a sturdy 2-year-old toddler and used to play by himself in the fenced garden beneath the towering granite rocks. Dawn had planted vegetables and maize in the vegetable garden and the cobs were nearly ready for reaping. She walked out of the kitchen one day to check on Bryan and found him sitting next to a huge dog baboon, both of them with mealies in their hands. As the cobs were too high for Bryan to reach, she realized that the baboon must have picked them and given the little boy one to enjoy alongside him. As she appeared, the baboon took off and jumped onto one of the 20-foot high boulders surrounding the garden. He just sat there obviously waiting for this human to leave so that he could get back to his meal. This was a bit too close for comfort and so the incident was reported to the Warden, Boyd Reece, who decided that it should be shot. Boyd with his rifle tried to sneak clandestinely around the house to get to the animal, but the baboon who was on a rock vanished and he appeared to almost make out that he was cleverer than the humans.

## *Impala Culling*

Whenever Tommy knew he was going to be more than a couple of days in one place he would take Dawn and Bryan with him. So, when he was tasked with culling a large number of impala in the Tuli Block, the family travelled down there and set up home in the D.C.s tiny pole and daga (mud) camp on the west side of the Shashi River. John and Janet Bunce were stationed in the Parks' camp on the other side and the two men not only worked closely together for the duration of the cull, but the families became close friends. Tommy and other field staff members believed this cull was unwarranted, but the Research people had decreed that it was necessary and at that time, their word was law. All the culling was done in the early evening using spotlights. Tommy and his team would shoot as many animals as they could cope with. The next morning they had to complete the skinning and processing of the carcasses before the heat of the day was upon them. Tommy took Dawn to the open-air butchery the first morning to show her how this work was done. This was the first time that she had seen a number of dead animals hanging from a pole and she was totally unprepared for the smell of the blood and the offal. After explaining everything, Tommy cut some kidneys from one of the dead beasts, laid them on the fire and announced that breakfast would be ready in a jiffy. The smell of the freshly slaughtered meat cooking on the fire was too much for Dawn who was in the early stages of pregnancy and prone to morning sickness – it made her feel quite ill! During this culling operation, they also captured some impala to restock a number of game ranches. Just behind the little camp where Tommy and Dawn

*Tom on the hunt!*

were staying, a ten-foot high boma was erected to keep the animals in while they awaited transportation. It was a small area and they were amazed to see a couple of impala leap straight over the top from a 'standing' start. Apart from the cull itself, this was a very happy interlude for the new family. Tuli is full of history and they spent many hours combing the site of the pioneer fort trying to find reminders of the occupation. The most dramatic incident was a nightlong cacophony of incredible sounds when two hyenas fought to the death and the carcass of the loser was found the next day not far from camp.

## *Tsessebe*

Alan Sparrow remembers Tom on a tsessebe capture in about 1970, at the same time Tom was doing a survey/game count on Essexvale Ranch. They were catching tsessebe to restock Lonestar Ranch and Tom was there to make sure everything ran well. Tom was checking on the animals and put his hand into one of the pens and promptly got a horn thrust at his hand. He was ragged about this for a while afterwards. Dawn was with him and remembers being asked to dinner by the Ranch manager. They found themselves sitting down to a formal dinner at a table beautifully decorated with silver candles and accessories while several waiters hovered in the background dressed in their whites. It was like being in a movie set back in the 1930s.

## *John Posselt*

John Posselt was a great friend of Tom's and had done some valuable work in the domestication of eland at Doddieburn Ranch. When Dawn and Tom went to visit him there, they arrived with their dogs and the chickens on the roof rack of the cruiser (for fresh eggs) and stayed with him at the DA's camp. The Government had decided that the eland should be moved to Kyle – a move that John was not happy with, because the habitat was so very different. However, when they did move they settled down well. A wild bull joined the semi-domesticated herd and allowed himself to be handled and sprayed in the crush with the other animals.

## *Warden Kyle*

In April 1970 Tommy was appointed as Warden of the 12 000 acre Kyle National Park. Tom was to stay here for two years in a busy place that was competing with Main Camp in the size of its staff complement. The regional headquarters were situated in the same office complex, with Doug Newmarch as the Regional Warden; Paul Reid the Senior Ranger and Colin Singleton was there for a short time in charge of Problem Animal Control. Some of the rangers who passed through during this period included Richard Peak, Howard Shackleton, Ian Salt and Glen Tatham, while Spud Ludbrook & Bob Norris were with fisheries. Tony Ferrar was the research officer who worked with Tom in helping to consolidate the Park. They prepared a scientific burning and stocking rate plan and set up a monitoring programme to work out the best species mix, for this mostly open, grassland park. Kyle was now a well-organized and well-run National Park with beautiful facilities for tourists, a handsome office complex and good staff housing. Tommy found it rather tame compared to his time there in the early days, but was very proud of the progress that had been made. Tony had an unusual bit of bad luck once, while going for a walk with his dog and a girlfriend in one of Rhodesia's parks. His dog went up to an elephant and barked at it. When the elephant turned on it, the dog decided to run back to its master (Tony) for protection. The elephant followed and Tony ended up with a fractured pelvis. All seemed to end well as while he was immobile in hospital he was said to have met his young wife Suzie. Kyle was also doing research on crocodiles breeding in captivity. There was also the introduction of buffalo, tsessebe from Portuguese East Africa and warthog from the Sengwa. On arrival, some of the warthog ran into the lake, a common reaction for animals brought to Kyle.

## *Home Front*

On the home front, the family settled in well, with the Tilley lamps burning at night and the foxies, Rookie and Muffy keeping them company. They inherited a ground hornbill that attached itself firmly to Dawn. If she was inside it used to peck on the door until she paid it some attention. Eventually it became jealous and aggressive if anyone else went near her. They were fearful it would attack Bryan and go for his eyes, so another home was found for it with the Sparrows in the Lowveld.

## *Paddy*

Thomas Patrick Junior (Paddy) announced that his arrival was imminent very early in the morning of 21st August 1970 when Dawn's waters burst. He was two weeks early which was most inconvenient, as Tommy and Dawn had been given complimentary tickets for the following evening to the Des Lindbergh and Dawn Silver show (a momentous occasion in the small town of Fort Victoria). Dawn quickly dressed Bryan and placed him in the car with her small suitcase. Tommy however took his time to get dressed in an orderly fashion. By the time they got going, Dawn was in hard labour and worried about producing the baby in the car. As one particularly bad contraction took hold of her, the vehicle hit a jackal. Tommy insisted on stopping the car and (again) took his time, making sure it was dead and then moving it off the road. When they arrived at the nursing home in Fort Victoria, the Sister in Charge was not ready for an imminent delivery and Dawn was told to "Wait – no pushing". Luckily, everything was ready when the doctor arrived 10 minutes later. However, as the two of them were good friends, he chatted to Tommy for another 5 minutes or so before going to look at the patient. By this time Dawn was desperate and when now allowed to push, gave a couple of heaves and out popped Paddy. "Well done my girl" said the doctor. "Oh great, we have a girl?" from the new mother. "No it's a bull calf," said the doctor.

## *Catering*

Being a warden's wife meant you had to entertain people, often at short notice. At first Dawn was unprepared for this. One day Tom phoned her at 12.45 with the news that he was bringing six people up for lunch. Dawn had grown up in a home, where these things had to be planned properly and as she had only planned a sandwich for Tommy's own lunch, she was horrified and let him know it. When she had finished Tommy said, "I have been holding the phone so that the visitors heard everything you said and they will now not be coming to lunch!" Dawn learnt her lesson and after that always made sure she had sufficient emergency rations or tins to open should people arrive unexpectedly. She realized that it was the company that mattered and not the food.

*Party*
Initially Tommy thought his wife would be quite happy staying at home. He and Dawn did not socialize much with the other members of staff as they rarely drank anything other than tea or coffee. They seldom went anywhere unless visiting Dawn's parents in Salisbury, or dropping into the Mitchell or Pringle families on their way back home from Fort Victoria. Kyle being very central had become the focal point of Parks' meetings and New Year parties. The Lowveld rangers joined the Midlands crowd and they would congregate at the Zimbabwe Ruins Hotel. So when Paddy was about a year old there was great excitement that the annual staff party was going to be held at the Hotel. They went across the lake in the ferry and Dawn decided she was going to enjoy herself. She let other people buy her drinks; she had a ball and drank too much. Tom was not impressed. She woke up the next day with a throbbing headache and Tom would not talk to her for about three days. She told him off and after that at parties, he danced with her, bought her drinks and was a charming gentleman.

*Responsibility*
Tom's responsibility at Kyle stretched across parts of the Lowveld and the Middle Sabi area. Rob Austen was an honouree warden working jointly for the "Middle Sabi Estates, Sabi Limpopo Authority" and the then "Rhodesia Game Association," and was directed by Tommy in his duties. Rob was to work with Tinkey Haslam and John Jarvis in trying to deal with severe poaching and Hippo/buffalo crop raiding outbreaks in the Middle Sabi Estates. They were directed by Tommy to eradicate all the buffalo, including many wounded ones from the Sabi River Islands, on the boundary of the estates. These men had many hair-raising experiences, but many laughs as well. Tommy would look at them with a blank face, stare them down and then comment that, if they were not up to it, he would gladly delegate to them one of his trackers, to show them how to get the job done. On noticing their indignation, he would then admit that they had a huge job on their hands and would break into a smile, commenting that if he were not so busy, he would love to partake in a

little action. Tom was the 'Boss', efficient, no-nonsense, helpful, ready to listen and always ready to have a good yarn. While Tom was at Kyle, the government was out to cull buffalo in the country; to eradicate the foot and mouth disease, and Tom was not happy with this.

## *T & S*
Tommy's relationships with Head Office in Salisbury were not always that friendly. When he did not receive his travel and subsistence allowance for several months, he let them know of his displeasure. He made such a fuss that they eventually made out a cheque for him and he went to collect it when he was next in Salisbury. He was still so angry that he tore it up in front of the official accounts clerk and threw it out the window. He said, "Now you can start the process all over again, you messed me around for three months". The accounts clerk complained that he would now have difficulties closing his books. Tom's response was, "toughies, you should have paid me in the first place".

## *Kyle Rangers*
Tommy was a tremendous character, with a great sense of humour and fully dedicated to conservation and National Parks as a whole. He was also very hospitable and would give you the shirt off his back. You could also rely on him when you got into trouble. Many of the rangers were young and inexperienced, gaining from his experience and were captivated by his stories. Tom taught Ian Salt how to bass fish and made sure that Ian's head was shaved regularly on the front veranda, as he didn't like men having long hair. Any sign of hair reaching Ian's ears, brought out the scissors! When Charlie Mackie came through Kyle on his way to his first Parks' posting in the Gonare-Zhou, he bumped into Tom. Charlie arrived in standard uniform, but because he was a new recruit, he did not have the usual tailor made shorts. Tom was adamant that he should not be seen with non-regulation shorts, went home, brought back two pairs of his and gave them to Charlie. Those shorts lasted twenty years or more. Being generous does not always help. It was about 1971 that Tom lent his .505 Gibbs rifle to Bruce Couper, convincing Bruce to borrow his weapon for some hunting in the Bumboosie area. Bruce was left-handed, the stock was high and so when he fired the thing, he lost a tooth. Bruce described it as a cannon on wheels and speedily gave it

back to Tom.

## *Coke & Buns*

Kyle was often referred to as a coke and buns station, as it had no lion and elephant and much of your time was spent dealing with people. Tom preferred the wilder places of Wankie, Mana Pools, Kariba and the Sabi Valley (in their wild days) and most of all the Gona-re-Zhou. Kyle was within half a day's drive of Salisbury and only a short distance from Fort Victoria on the main road to South Africa. The beauty of the surroundings and abundance of wildlife in the park attracted many tourists and tour operators. The lake had been stocked with bass and became a fisherman's paradise. The fishing at Kyle was good or awful, depending on who you spoke to! The appointment of a tourist officer helped take some stress off Tom. He could now concentrate on his fieldwork in the bush with his animals or undertake necessary repairs at the workshop. Tommy had a total belief in the power of Redex (fuel additive), with which he would periodically dose his Toyota. After a good dose, you would see clouds of fumes billowing out of the Kyle workshop. He was a good mechanic and both the vehicles under his immediate control and his own land cruiser were very well looked after and always reliable.

## *Exotic*

Kyle became a haven for crows. They were noisy irritating birds and the rangers hated them. A unanimous decision was taken to brand them with the title of 'non indigenous'. One Sunday morning a major offensive was undertaken against these avian creatures. It was like a foretaste of the gulf war. There were .303 rifles; shotguns, .22's and .458 rifles firing away as every able-bodied male were trying to shoot the crows. Nobody is saying, but the crows probably won. One non-indigenous species that had arrived earlier in Kyle were the Blesbok that Bruce Austen had brought in from South Africa. These attractive animals were thriving and were a great attraction in the Park. However, the Research Department, backed by Archie Fraser, decided they must go because they were not indigenous to Southern Rhodesia. Although Tommy was the Warden in charge of the Park, he was not given the responsibility for the capture operation. He believed that darting them would be the best option to avoid unnecessary stress and tried to put his views across. However, the authorities knew better and sent in a team which set up very high capture nets. Then, with much

*Dawn feeding Salty at Kyle*

noise and lots of action, the animals were rounded up and funnelled into the nets. They panicked and tried to jump out. It was a total fiasco, the animals were badly stressed and half of them died. It was heartbreaking to watch and Tommy was extremely upset and very angry. It was particularly galling that they were sent to the ranch of one of the most powerful politicians in the country.

## *White Rhino*

The white rhino Tom had brought in were doing well with calves being born, and for the first time two adult rhinos broke out of the game area, following a fight and had to be recaptured. The rhino used the road signs and telephone poles as rubbing posts, with predictable results. Fiona Wilmot, who was a schoolteacher, saw Tom at Kyle in this period, when she took a group of children there. She was amazed that when she asked Tom at the office where the rhinos might be, he told her the exact place they would be and the exact time, and even the tree or rock they would be rubbing on. She had been expecting a rough direction. When Brian Sherry was horse riding with Tom, they located the rhinos and Tom, ever the showman, had them dismount and approach the rhinos. He talked to them in soft, high-pitched tones, got right up to the big bull of the group and gently scratched the side of the white rhino. It was good old Ngazana again, Tom's favourite rhino.

*Salty*

In 1970 41 black rhinos were translocated to Gona-re-Zhou, from heavily poached areas in the north and this operation continued into 1971. Rhino catching is not an easy job and ranger Richard Peak was caught in the pens by a semi drugged bull. The horn pushed right through his lower leg and he received 29 stitches at Mt. Darwin. On a trip from Umi to Chipinda Pools, one of three trucks carrying the rhino left the road and overturned seven miles from Fort Victoria. Ian Salt was called out from Kyle and had to shoot the badly injured mother whose small bull calf was wandering around crying but unhurt. Kerry Kay was the patrol officer who attended the accident and as it was late in the afternoon, she took the calf to the Police station. She put it in a cell for the night and made it comfortable with her own blankets, etc. Tommy collected it the next day from the Police Station and always told people afterwards that he felt sure it had received better treatment than any prisoner ever had there. The baby was named Salty after Ian and settled in well at Kyle where he became a great attraction. He was hand reared by Dawn and the first ten days or so were very worrying. No one had ever raised a baby rhino in captivity before and therefore there were no guidelines as to what formula to use. He contracted diarrhoea and everyone feared the worst. However, Tommy went through his veterinary and wild life library and found that the slime from over boiling rice could be very effective. So Salty was given a mixture of rice slime, fat free powdered milk, glucose and Vidaylin. He soon recovered and a suitable formula was concocted on which he thrived. He tamed very quickly and became very lovable and playful. Because Dawn spent so much time with him, he grew up preferring women and men risked getting horned. One day Fat Boy got into the rhino pen for some reason. Salty was stronger than he realized and Fat Boy was soon being pushed by Salty against the side of the enclosure. There was lots of screaming and "it's killing me," as Fat Boy was convinced he was going to die, but he managed to slip out. After a couple of months, another young rhino of much the same size joined Salty. In the middle of Kyle, they had a prison for short-term offenders and they used to work in the park. The inmates were used as labourers both within the Park and around the houses and offices when necessary. One time the prisoners were trying to strengthen the rhino pen when the two young rhino decided to chase them. Salty decided that he wanted to play and took off with the other youngster hot on his heels and started to chase the prisoners around and round the stockade. Within minutes, the trees were festooned with very frightened white-garbed jailbirds. Those who could not find a tree managed to keep just ahead of their pursuers until Dawn and Tommy restored order. The two babies thought this was a great game. Salty was eventually sent to a zoo in Chicago where he continued to favour the ladies!

*Hartebeest at Kyle National Park*

*Shangaan poachers with game scouts Giyane, Phineas?, Timoti, at Mabalauta*

## CHAPTER 14
# MABALAUTA 1972-1976

### To Mabalauta
After two quiet and uneventful years at Kyle, Tommy was delighted when he was told of his appointment as Warden of the Mabalauta section of the 5000 square kilometre Gona-re-Zhou National Park. Kyle had become the National Parks regional centre and was very civilized. Tommy longed to get back to the bush and real wilderness. The family happily packed their belongings and set off to this beautiful unspoilt paradise in 1972. The warden and ranger's houses were built on the banks of the Nuanetsi River under huge Cordyla and Mahogany trees with lawns rolling down to the river itself. There were no fences and at night, the animals took full advantage of the greenery in the garden. During the hot summer nights, Tom and Dawn

*Tim Braybrooke with Dawn at Mabalauta*

slept outside on the patio under mosquito nets and often awoke to crunching noises. On a moonlit night there is nothing more awe inspiring than to sit quietly watching elephant, buffalo or hippo grazing within a few feet of you, or to lie awake listening to the lions roaring close by (One of the resident male lions that patrolled the area had a wheezy roar and was nicknamed 'Vicks'). During the day animals came down to the river pools to drink and there was always some activity either in the river bed itself or across on the other side in Buffalo Bend. The bird life was varied and colourful and the abundance of butterflies soon had Dawn and Tom setting traps and running around with nets in pursuit of their new hobby.

## *Base*

Tim Braybrooke had developed the staff housing, offices, a well equipped workshop at Mabalauta and installed a swimming pool that provided great relief during those steamy days when the temperatures soared over 100 degrees Fahrenheit. The houses were built out of prefabricated concrete sections and even though they were shaded for much of the day, the insides became extremely hot and everyone was very appreciative when a large generator arrived, accompanied by some air conditioners for the bedrooms. All the houses were wired for electricity and the generator was run every evening until nine o'clock. Not only did this eliminate the need for lamps but also the few hours of air conditioning in the bedrooms made a huge difference to the night's comfort. Down the road there was a beautiful tourist camp named Simuwini. This rest camp was habitually visited by a pride of lions. The hosepipes would be chewed and the lions would lap at the birdbaths and persuade the tourists to keep their windows closed.

## *Work*

Tom quickly got down to the business of organizing the routine of running this large area with his Ranger, initially Mike Bromwich. He always brought a touch of extra spit and polish to his postings and Mabalauta was no exception. Everything had to be immaculate and even the garden taps were highly polished. He was very proud of his game scouts who were a smart and disciplined unit. They would nearly knock out their teeth, when their knees came together, in standing to attention. He also demanded a high degree of professionalism from all his staff and had no time for shirkers. Needless to say he clashed with the odd youngster who had more relaxed ideas. There was still a lot of development work to be done in the southern end of this huge Park and during Tommy's four years, he made steady progress extending and enhancing the road network. Every year all the roads had to be graded and adequate drains cleared. Large concrete 'elephant proof' signs were erected at many intersections. On one occasion, Tom had a shortage of paintbrushes to paint a sign, but with some humour soon solved this problem. One of his rangers, Hans Van der Heiden had long hair and Tom did not approve of long curls, so Hans was ordered to cut his mane off and this was then used to make a paintbrush! As the Park was now receiving more and more tourists, the interior of the tourist office was given a face-lift with Jenny Fynn (Ranger Mike's wife) adding some fine art work. The bushfires sweeping in from Mozambique, were not normally a problem, as Tom had as usual, put in good firebreaks.

## *Office*

The postbag at Mabalauta would be taken to and collected at Nyala siding. A cyclist would peddle the twenty kilometres and ran the risk of an elephant or lion attack. On one occasion the postal attendant Mafira, was treed near Simuwini rest camp by a lioness and three cubs near the Mumunyo drift. He had been cycling back from Nyala siding with the mailbag. The lions ripped apart the mailbag and scattered the letters all over the place. A very white looking Mafira was found by the other staff hanging in a Tamboti tree, with the lions patiently waiting for dinner nearby. Phoning someone here was not easy as one had to go some distance to Chikombedzi. Tom partly solved the problem by having the keys to the railway phones. Most of the communication was done using radios. Tom was intimidating, cheeky and made his staff nervous or angry on occasions. Regarding authority, Tom had a saying that, 'the dog must wag the tail and not the tail wag the dog'. One of Tom's visitors was so furious with him at Mabalauta that the man tried to thump the table with his fist. His hand came down on some paper hiding a long steel, paper spike. As you can imagine there was lots of pain. In dealing with his adversaries or challengers at the office, Tom had a well mapped out strategy. He used to have a higher chair than his visitors and their chair was put in the corner, where there was little room. If he wanted to intimidate his junior or a visitor, he would gradually push the table until the man was squashed in the corner. Sometimes the trapped man would have his circulation threatened and he would be cowed into submission.

## *Red Tape*

During the years in Parks, Tom had a forthright way of telling people off, for things that were not really their fault. There were also those who probably needed a verbal tirade. Tom was straight up front, there being no grey areas and there were no half measures. Government officials in Salisbury could regret having stepped on his toes. One of his tricks was to send mail 'postage to be paid' to those who troubled him. One government official demanded an account for every bullet fired and requested that the cartridge cases should be given back. This was an almost impossible task, as it was often hard to find cartridge cases strewn across the veld after a hunt. Tom had to just ignore the order. At Gona-re-Zhou Tom once had a problem with a lost cent, as his books showed he had a cent too much. There was turmoil in headquarters, with the auditors getting involved and they were convinced there must have been corruption somewhere. The auditors spent more than 30 dollars in postage (about 30 British pounds), in trying to deal with the problem, which was a lot of money in those days. Eventually Tom got hold of his brother Ken and asked him for help, seeing that Ken worked for a bank and knew how to deal with these things. Ken painstakingly went through the books, to find that there had been two, half-cent deposits at the bank. The bank had rounded up these two deposits and this had led to the extra cent on the books.

## *Pets*

Tom had a huge vegetable garden that was for the benefit of the black game scouts and the white staff could harvest any surplus. Tom had his pigs, chickens, donkeys, dogs and cats, tame ostriches and a wild cheetah that eventually went to the RLI military unit. Then there was the family cockerel that was magnificent in appearance, being a huge, rainbow-coloured, indigenous cock, which would happily and haughtily strut around. Tom decided that as all the cockerels were making too much noise and disturbing the tourists, they had to go. So Tom's big cock was killed and put in the deep freeze. Later the Orfords had some dinner guests and Dawn tried to impress them with some chicken. The cock was cooked with much care, but was as tough as leather and ended up getting its own back, as the guests were not impressed and they showed it. In 1973, Tom and Terry Fenn went to Pashlelas village in Naivasha to organize a patrol. Tom saw a piglet and grabbed it by the back leg. A large domestic pig then came to the rescue and charged the two men. It may have been after this that Tom acquired some of the local pigs to breed for staff rations. Soon there was a famous Black Pig, who used to saunter around with lots of flies buzzing around his smelly body. One day Tom, Mike Fynn and Mac were talking about the strophanthus plant poison that was put on the arrows of the Shangaans. Tom wanted to see how it worked and so they tried an experiment and placed some poison on an arrow and shot one of the pigs. The end result confirmed Tom's view that strophanthus was a deadly poison. Apart from a lovely golden Labrador called Nuchi (who would carry things for you and sit by the bath); Tom had a grumpy female fox terrier. One of the other ranger's dogs was trying to get a bit romantic with Tom's foxy and Tom did not approve. When this ranger went on leave, Tom was left with his dog to look after. Tom grabbed the opportunity and paid a visit to a vet to cut its knackers off. When the ranger got back, he noticed his dog was different and it seemed 'something was missing'. So he asked Tom, "Do you know what happened to my dog?" Tom replied, "Sure it was trying to get into my dog, so I took it to the vet to take its balls off".

## *Donkeys*

Donkey or horse patrols were popular with some and not with others.

Ollie Coltman was one of those who showed little enthusiasm for horses. When doing a mounted horse patrol at Kyle, he decided he would rather run the route in the time given, than ride the horse. The horse was summarily tied up and Ollie and the game scout ran the patrol. Some folk in Parks liked using donkeys, while others preferred to skim around in land rovers. Most rangers did not like it at first, but later on, they changed their minds, when they got used to it. Tim Braybrooke was convinced that mounted patrols were better for antipoaching than land rovers. When Braybrooke went back to Main Camp as the warden, he re-established mounted patrols. The donkey cartel included the likes of Tim Braybrooke, Bruce Austen and Tom. At one stage, these three were said to have had a donkey programme in the Gwaai district. The plan was to help the black folk get better harnesses for donkeys and they even got some made up in Wankie town for them. The mule packsaddles at Mabalauta had been used by Edward Dyker and had been left in a storehouse on Nuanetsi Ranch. Tim Braybrooke bought four that had been left over there and took them to the Gona-re-Zhou. In the years following, donkey and mounted patrols were done enthusiastically by many, including the fun loving Tinkey Haslam, while Richard Harland loved donkey patrols and instead of doing two weeks, would go out for three weeks. Horses were more difficult to look after than donkeys. Tinkey Haslam once had a beautiful black mare down in the Gona-re-Zhou. It escaped and ran around for a while, with Richard Peek trying to catch it, but he failed to get her. He tried to dart her from horseback using a crossbow, but had no success and about a week later, she was found dead. Tinkey had a horse (possibly the same one) that got a government pay cheque every month as a game scout. This happened, as finance was needed to look after the horse. Richard Peek found mounted patrols useful to hunt elephants over the rough terrain in the Gona-re-Zhou. He would go ahead and sort out the problem elephants and the donkeys would bring up the supplies.

*Donkey trails*

Tom was keen to get safari trails going in the Mabalauta area and donkeys were the best way to carry supplies. Natal Parks had already tried out this novel adventure-safari scheme. Tom approached Graham Child with the idea and with persistence and patience, head office gave the go ahead. Head office had to first do the pricing and logistics. When the plan came together, it was intended to have been

*Donkeys resting on Trail by Nuanetsi*

between 1-5 people, with no children, but teenagers could come. Before they did donkey patrols, campsites were organized and donkey bomas built, so the donkeys could be protected from lions. Hans van der Heiden started doing walking patrols with Tom on set routes. Tom would send Hans off with the clients and the route was often spied out beforehand, so he could direct Hans to any interesting animal activity. The donkeys would be carrying the jerry cans, stores, pots, biltong etc. The pack donkeys carried the parties' loads in saddlebags to the base camps, while the trekkers carried out their daily explorations. Before a walk started, Tom would instruct his clients on the dangers of snakes and big game and how he would signal if need be. By 1975, Tom was doing 17 wilderness trails in the year along the Nuanetsi. The wilderness leadership school of South Africa was sponsoring these, while the trails lasted three days and two fly camps were used. The donkey trails were tremendously successful and remembered years later with nostalgia by those who went. They were a howling success and so many requests came from South Africa that they could not take them all.

## *Trail Dangers*

Tom led the trails with his monster .505 rifle and he was on the ready

*Elephant shot in self defence by Tom on trail, being viewed by Brian Wilson and Tom at Mabalauta PHOTO in Lowdown by Mike Roscoe*

for any elephants, defiant buffalo and lion trouble makers. With the trusty Shlupo armed with a .375 rifle or some of the other reliable game scouts, they were ready for almost anything. The Nuanetsi provided great camping sites and nice pools to swim in, but one always had to select a crocodile free stretch of water. Gona-re-Zhou trails produced their white-knuckle incidents and twice Tom had to put down dangerous elephant on these wilderness trails. On the one instance, he was on a single trail with some porters behind him, when all of a sudden an elephant bull charged down the path. Tom raised his .505 Gibbs rifle, flicked the safety and fired from the hip. The animal fell a rifle length away from him. He also shot a female cow when she endangered the lives of his clients. This aggressive mother of two calves came in for the kill, in dense combretum bush and fell dead 12 feet from him. On one of Tom's trails along the Nuanetsi, Tom had a troublesome lady with him, when he shot a charging buffalo. She said, "What did you shoot that poor animal for?" Then she asked, "Were you afraid?" He replied, "Madam, if you want to know how afraid I was, stand down wind and my underpants will tell you." There was the occasion when he told everyone to freeze. They did not know why – they only heard from him afterwards, on how a huge black mamba had slithered almost across their feet. Tom in addition stood on a black mamba and when he took his foot off, it came rearing up to look him in the eye. He said that he nearly wet his pants.

## *Home Life*
In Parks, the rangers' wives often ran clinics for the black staff. Dawn did her duty at Mabalauta and was involved with the running of the rest camp. Her other duties included dealing with screaming kids, snakes, loneliness and broken items she couldn't fix, while Tom was away. Tom once gave Dawn a super pellet gun for shooting snakes. At times, she felt she was getting bush happy while Tom was in the army and would have to visit friends to deal with the pressures. If Bryan and Paddy were not trying to drown the cats in the swimming pool, they were probably hitting each other over the head. Both Bryan and Paddy were home schooled, but Paddy was better behaved than Bryan. Bryan would escape the schooling by running around the house and hiding from Dawn. Both kids had their umfaan or older boy to look after them. Tom wanted Paddy to speak the Shona language, so he instructed the staff to only speak in the local lingo. The result was that Paddy spoke fluent Shona. On one occasion, she had a problem in getting Paddy to pee at the right time on a long trip. She eventually turned to Sergeant Patrick and asked him for help and he told her the Shona code words for having a pee. And presto! She could now get him to pee at the right time and from then on, she never had a problem with Paddy. Later when Paddy went to school, he stopped speaking Shona as it was not taught at school. Tom used to put the two kids to sleep with African stories of 'tsuro' and other wild animals in a make believe world.

## *Neighbours*
The nearest place of civilization to Mabalauta was Chikombedzi, which was some 35 kilometres distance. Here one could buy booze and petrol and a there was a mission station close by. At one time, there was a good doctor working there by the name of Paul Deimbrie. A poacher hit a game scout on the head and the scout's head caved in. With the help of a friend, he was taken to the mission station. Paul cut around the damaged area, took out the skull and then stitched it back

again and four weeks later, the man was working. There were very few people in a huge area and only a handful of white people. One of the residents in the area was old man George Palfrey who owned a store on an exposed hill. The Palfreys, like many of the old-sensible folk, built their house on a hill where it could catch the breeze. Palfrey had the bedrooms and bathroom at one end and the kitchen at the other side. The breeze would come right through the house. They were a delightful old couple and Dawn and Tom ended up with much of their furniture when they finished living there. Mr. Palfrey worked with the Wenela labour system and would take new recruits down for the South African mines. Dawn and Tom also went across the Limpopo to visit ranger Mike English at Pafuri in South Africa. Tom simply drove across the river avoiding all border formalities. Paul Bosman was advertising in Joburg when he decided to run a bush lodge. He and his wife built up a Morocco style lodge at Malapati and Paul started painting as a hobby. He sent 20 paintings down to his Mother in South Africa to be framed. The gallery where they were framed was so impressed that they wanted to buy them. His Mom sold the paintings and he was not happy with what his Mom did, but was convinced by the gallery to have an exhibition. His painting career took off; he moved to Hartebeest Poort dam and became a famous wildlife painter.

## *Good Times*

Tom had the ability to tell stories and had an absolute enthusiasm for the bush and animals. He could have everyone mesmerized for hours and he made the best boerewors. Dawn was attractive and both were a lot of fun. Mabalauta was a happy time, with braais, friends, the odd party or a visit to Manjinji pan, or one of the beautiful places on the river. Tom was like a walking workshop, with an incredible knife (Swiss army I guess), but it was huge and had a tool of every description one could ever want. If you needed something in a hurry, he had it right there somewhere. One day Tom and others were driving on their way down to Manjinji pan. Somehow, a box of matches in Mike Fynn's pocket caught alight and he jumped out the vehicle. He ripped his burning pants off in front of all the ladies and there was a rapid and desperate, beating of the flames. Mike then looked up to see Tom armed with a fire extinguisher and he said to Tom, "Where did you get that from?" The fire was soon out. When Tom flew around Gona-re-Zhou, he was also normally very prepared,

*Orphaned elephant calves arriving at the pens, Mabalauta 1970's*

with his survival kit of a .22 rifle, two knives and all the rest, just in case of an accident. There were always visitors at Gona-re-Zhou, including government people, police and the like. An interesting buffalo researcher, by the name of J. Mloszewski came down and spent some twenty or so days living with buffalo. His trick was to sneak into the middle of a buffalo herd and get within 3-4 metres of them and they would be indifferent to him. He had more problems from the elephant on his jaunts. A nervous Tom was able to participate in one of these buffalo adventures with him.

## *Vila Salazar*

The police post at Vila Salazar was great fun and with any excuse, the Parks' rangers would be there for parties at the Gonna Stagga inn with the police. Tom used various code words with the police on the radio, to talk about beers and meat, while they were organizing the odd party. There was also the nearby Portuguese town of Malvernia. Malvernia had nice, tiled buildings, a hotel and railway café. At Malvernia one evening, they had a huge party and Dawn took her nice, soft leather jacket. The men were getting drunk out of their minds and they started to throw mealie meal over each other and then beer. With the mealie meal and beer everywhere, Dawn took her jacket off and

*Dawn and Paddy at Mabalauta*

they later left as it got totally out of hand. She never saw her jacket again, as she had left it behind. Some SAS soldiers were helping with the Parks' culling operations and joined the Parks' rangers for a jaunt across to Malvernia to Chico's bar. Richard Smith and Ian Salt were there, led by Howard Shackleton and followed later in the day by Basil Williamson, Mike Bromwich and Tinkey. In Portuguese East Africa, they got up to lots of nonsense by chasing a football around with a land rover and a whole lot of other stuff. Much to Tom's horror, they were interfering with protocol and messing up his public relations exercise with the Portuguese. It was Portugal day there and the Rhodesians were soon thrown out of the country for being too drunk. Tom was not happy, as after this they had to use passports to go across.

## *Culling*

The Rhodesian Parks were quite busy in this era, culling various animals such as hippo, elephant, impala and even porcupine in the Gona-re-Zhou. At Mabalauta Tom was involved with impala culls in which they killed a couple of hundred in a few days. Impala were common and were eating so much vegetation that they were compared to goats. They made a few mistakes in the night cull, when some nyala were killed by mistake and one of the culling rangers knocked himself out on a branch of a tree. The porcupines at Mabalauta were also a problem given that they were ring barking the beautiful Wild Mango trees. Tom had them caught alive and had a whole herd of them stuffed in a storeroom. Later he told Hans and others that they should eat the porcupines, as they were good meat and so they did. In the period Tom was based at Mabalauta there were over a thousand

*Dawn and kids with game scouts and Harold and Edna Fridjhon at Nyala siding Gona-re-Zhou*

elephant culled in the park. Tom desperately loved his wildlife and would probably have preferred humans to be culled than his beloved elephants. Being a dedicated wildlife man, a true conservationist, he like others felt it was a necessity and had to be done. The culling in the Nuanetsi part of the park was under his jurisdiction, but he could not participate and was tied to office duties. Ron Thomson ran the cull from a camp near Simuwini, while Tom continued with the day-to-day running of the region. Tom would often turn up to see what was going on with his equipment and himself in immaculate order. Most of the animals were shot using teams of hunters, supported by helicopters and fixed wing aircraft. The carcasses were sold mainly to Ian and Alan Henderson and Paul Grobler. These contractors used some SAS troops to help when they were off duty, as they were reliable and knew the bush well. Some farmers who bought meat from the culls lost quite a bit, as the black staff on the back of the trucks would throw the meat off the moving trucks into the bushes for later collection. Some of the carcasses were buried in an attempt to stop anthrax. This did not work that well, as the massive elephant stomachs expanded and bloated and grew to make a little hill, which popped up in the air. Later they used a machine excavator to punch holes in the stomachs to prevent expansion. Mike Bromwich was a dynamic, hard working ranger and a good thinker. He built the bomas at Gona-re-Zhou in which the baby elephants were placed. Some of these calves were kept up to six months, before Delfs of Windhoek shipped most of them out. One of the penned elephant calves nearly killed a Mr. Jagger, while Tom was also given a work over, being crushed against the side fence by the same animal. The Sparrow family ended up with many of the baby elephant from the Lowveld and other parts of the country.

## *Poachers*
Gona-re-Zhou will go down in history as the most controversial and dramatic of Zimbabwe's parks. It has produced a crop of famous black and white poachers. The Chipinda pools side in particular, has had its drama and many National Parks' staff have not been immune to the poaching bug. There were some regular poachers at Mabalauta and some had files on their crimes. When Mike Bromwich took over as warden at Mabalauta, he used spies to report on the poaching and the whereabouts of firearms. These informers were paid off, either by a visiting game scout, or when they came around to his office. Probably the most famous poacher in this period was Shadrack, although there was possibly more than one Shadrack. One of the 'Shadracks' was said to have been a coloured man and the son of the famous white poacher named Barnard. At one time Shadrack was nearly shot by Charlie Mackie, but Charlie had a misfire and Shadrack managed to escape. After this incident, many black folk thought that Shadrack had magic protecting him. The Shangaans used bows, arrows and muzzleloaders, but hardly ever used snares. Nick Gregory was a ranger under Tom at Mabalauta and had a dramatic first week there while on patrol at Nyala pan. He came across six Mozambique poachers armed with two rifles and some bows and arrows. These men fired on Nick who returned fire and he killed one of them.

## *Elephant*
The elephant at Gona-re-Zhou were very aggressive and Tom had to shoot a cow at close range in thick bush, when it attacked his vehicle. Mike Bromwich had his unattended vehicle at Lipakwa pan damaged and in May 1975, a bull elephant charged Tom for nearly 500 metres and he was in reverse gear all the way. When Mike Bromwich was at Mabalauta with Tom, the elephants were so bad that Mike used to drive at night with his lights off, so he could see their silhouettes on the sides of the roads, stopping the tunnel vision. He did this with Tom one night and Tom was not impressed. Tom ordered, "Switch

*Sergeant Mac. and Tom at Mabalauta*

your lights on, put your lights on." Once when Dawn was with Kerry Kay and Kerry's brother, they were driving down the road with Bryan in the back. Some elephants charged and they stopped to time how fast the charge was. In the back of the truck, young Bryan started to eat his hat. Sometimes one could have a good laugh at the aggressive nature of these animals, when you got away, but some did not. Tom was to witness a black-pregnant woman, with a baby on her back, skewed by an elephant. Tom went to help but was too late.

## *Elephant Damage*

An oil salesman paid a visit to ranger Tony Osborne at Beitbridge. He was going to go to Fort Victoria and wanted to go via the Nuanetsi and Mabalauta. Tony told him it was not a good idea because of the elephants. The man however insisted, as he said he had good experience with Wankie and Kruger elephants. Tony nonetheless warned him about going along the Nuanetsi. The man ignored Tony's advice and set off for Mabalauta. Tony radioed Tom at Mabalauta to tell him about the travelling salesman. Tom waited for the man to arrive and next morning he was still missing, so Tom checked with Tony on the radio. Tom decided to go and investigate and off he went along the Nuanetsi. Here Tom, found a big terrified man, stuck up in a large mopane tree. What had happened was that he had taken his Peugeot station wagon along, where he was warned not to go and had come across some elephants. An elephant bull then came down the road towards him in a menacing manner. He put on reverse and high tailed it backwards. His reversing not being up to the occasion, he went into a mopane tree. The elephant then hooked itself against the front of the vehicle and crumpled it up into a V shape against the tree. The poor man watched as his company car began to be destroyed and the elephant punctured the radiator. When the boiling water came out the radiator, the elephant decided to push off. The shaken man at that moment climbed out of the wreck and found a convenient mopane tree to take refuge in. During the night he spent there, two more herds of elephants came along and further damaged the car and rolled it around, until it was almost in the river. It was about 50 meters away from him and totally wrecked, when they had finished with it. For the salesman things got only worse later on, when his boss fired him for damaging the car. Dawn was warned by Tom of a stony area on the road to Chikombedzi, which could damage the Cortina. However, when she went down the road, she was not really thinking and went into the rocks and hit the fuel tank with a nice plunk and the fuel gauge started to creep down. She looked up to see an elephant bull appear and menacingly amble down the road to her. She had two kids in the back and a rapidly diminishing fuel supply, while the elephant continued his approach. The sides of the road here were sandy from the grading and she reversed into the bank and broke the exhaust. With the aggressive elephant still coming, she managed to turn around and escape to base. Tom had a few comments and then took a spoon and measured how much fuel was left in the tank. There was only one spoonful left.

## *Crop Raiders*
Elephant crop raiders continually raided the villagers around Mabalauta. The villagers were in turn, often guilty of poaching. When the poaching started, Tom would go to the village elders and tell them straight, that they could poach, but when the time of year comes for the villagers to enjoy their crops – he would not come and kill the elephants eating their maize. He got their co-operation. Tom believed that shooting should only be done when necessary and the novelty of hunting had worn off him by this time in his life. Occasionally he would go off and sort an elephant or lion out, or shoot for rations, but

*Tom on trail in Gona-re-Zhou with Doug Newmarch at back of group*

normally he would send out his rangers. Once Tom was in a nearby village area, where elephants had been raiding crops, where there was a black farmer with lots of watermelon and who used to drive a tractor. Tom was with Sergeant Mashlavana (Mac) who was an ex poacher, an excellent tracker and who always had a sharp axe ready. Tom was having his tea early in the morning, when a report came in of recent elephant damage. He said, "Just watch my tea" and off he went. They spent the rest of the day chasing the elephants. In very thick bush, Tom then shot and wounded an elephant that he then tracked with Mac. Soon he was crawling through low, thick, bushes, which thinned out, as they got higher. All of a sudden, he felt something wet dripping on him. Having a look, he noticed that it was blood. His eyes wandered upwards and there was something large and grey, with its trunk up like a periscope, smelling and trying to locate its human foes. Tom carefully aimed his .505 rifle skywards and fired, killing the elephant. Tom scurried away as the elephant almost fell on top of him. Not far off, Mac stood and laughed at the proceedings. Tom had shot the elephant so close that the rifle shot had left powder marks on the elephant's skin.

### *Terry*
Terry Fenn was there in 1972 for less than a year and spent most of

his time in the bush. He would come in from his patrols, do his reports and stay a few days. While back at base, he would get revved left, right and centre by Tom and then he would head back into the bush with his short wheelbase. In Tom's office there was a quality .470 double rifle that many a hunter would like to get his hands on. Occasionally Terry Fenn would be allowed the privilege of seeing it. This was normally done with great ceremony, as tea was ordered first. This would happen only when Tom was in a good mood. A member of staff would be given the privilege of accessing Tom's huge bunch of keys and then be ordered to bring the rifle out. The Parks' weapon then had to be assembled. While Terry was on his patrols, he used to dream about shooting it. One day another warden Johnny Bunce came by and asked Terry, "Have you shot an elephant yet?" He replied, "No". Johnny stated, "What you haven't shot an elephant. I'll sort this out" and off he went to get permission from Tom to shoot an elephant. Terry was called to the office the next day and Johnny said, "Right we are going to shoot this elephant." Terry asked, "What are we going to shoot it with?" Johnny said, "This" and pulled out the double. Terry was elated and Tom was there, seemingly indifferent to all that was going on. They drove off and shot a young bull on the boundary of the Malapati Game Reserve and a tractor with staff came to clean up the carcass. Terry brought it down with no problems and his dream had come true.

## *100 Pounder*

While Tom was away, Mike Fynn was in charge at Mabalauta and the District Commissioner came around and asked Parks to shoot some crop raiding elephant in the Sengwe. The rains were on and so were the juicy crops. In those days, Parks' staff would normally wait about two years, before being allowed to shoot an elephant, after having first accompanied experienced hunters. Tom was cautious and was wary of allowing young rangers to hunt elephant. Mike Fynn and some other rangers though, jumped at the opportunity to get experience, even though they did not really have the go ahead. Mike Fynn went to see Mac and said, "Mac what's the story with hunting elephant. Is it really that complicated?" Mac's reply was "no, let's go" and Mac taught Mike how to shoot elephants. Soon Mike was busy in the Sengwe TTL and was joined by Mike Bromwich, Angus Anthony and Brian Sherry, who came along for the ride. Things took a turn for the worse, when Brian shot a large 100 and 110 pound tusked elephant by mistake. Over 30 bulls had been shot and Ron Thompson, Doug Newmarch and Tim Paulet (who had experience with elephant) put a stop to it. When Tom got back, he had to do a lot of fiddling at this point, to protect the rangers from getting into trouble.

## Sherry

Brian Sherry had this to say about hunting with Tom. "I did go on one elephant hunt with Tom - crop raiding was a perennial problem in the Gonakudzingwa Purchase area and on one occasion, I went along on one of the 'control' sorties. But nothing remarkable transpired - we picked up spoor on the edge of some lands, followed a small group of bulls into some fairly dense woodland and shot a few of them; wounding one which led us on a long follow-up back into the Park; where we eventually caught up with the wounded animal and dispatched it. No real drama, but I always remember the excellent bushcraft and tracking ability of some of the scouts. Sergeant Mac (Matchovana) was one of these - quite old by that time, but a really seasoned campaigner of Tsetse Ops and Parks. Mac was a tall, wiry, distinguished old fellow; excellent in the bush! The thing I remember perhaps most clearly is Mac and his axe. He always took a small hand axe when hunting - kept razor sharp with a piece of cylindrical rock core from some drilling operation. Mac was amazingly quick at hacking into an elephant with his axe, cutting out the heart in short time and very soon after a kill, he would have strips of heart cooking over an open fire. He carried a small bag of course salt for this operation... I'm almost getting emotional at the memory of the texture, smell and taste of that mixture of rare to scorched elephant meat, washed down from the canvas water bag, to round out a successful hunt!"

*Feeding the orphaned elephant calves Mabalauta 1970's*

*Tom with Sgt. Mervyn Pannell in 1968 on TCU training on the Lundi River, PHOTO Dave Scott-Donelan*

## CHAPTER 15
# COMBAT 1961 – 1979

*Army*
The Rhodesian Armed Forces had a proud history and tradition. During the late 50's and 60's, the Territorial Army, made up of civilians, was reputed to be second only to the Israeli army in efficiency and readiness. All young white males had to do an initial period of military training, which was then followed by a short call up every year. They were always on standby should there be any need to deal with riots or uprising. The British South Africa Police (B.S.A.P.) was also a dedicated and legendary force that attracted recruits from around the world, although mainly from the British Isles. Tommy was brought up to be proud of this heritage. He started his national service at Nkomo Barracks where he joined the 5th Royal Rhodesia Regiment. He embraced army life with enthusiasm and became very military minded, particularly enjoying his training with the new automatic weapons. Like so many other young men of the time, he did not realize what horrors war would later bring to everyone. When the

*Alan Savory, Tom's friend in the Game Dept. research section*

Joshua Nkomo nationalists first started problems for the Rhodesian government, Tom was chafing at the bit, wanting to get in on the act. Tom did some military service in Nyasaland (Malawi) in the early 60's, when they had some political troubles up there.

## *Training*
During his initial training, Tom was punished for not cleaning his kit properly. His unit was temporarily camped in the bush and his punishment was to 'dig' a pit latrine or long drop for the officers. However, the ground where he and his mates had to dig was extremely hard and stony. They could do little more than scrape a very shallow hollow where the toilet had to go. So they ingeniously 'built' up with two stone walls, rather than 'dig' down. This latrine had to be 'straddled' and could not be 'sat on' as one would normally. All went well until sometime later the commanding officer arrived for a visit early one evening and immediately went off to the toilet. No one remembered to tell him that there was anything different about the amenities. Naturally, he reversed his rear end to the structure in the usual fashion, sat down and promptly fell in because the wall was so narrow – not the normal seat! There was a cry and the soldiers ran to rescue their stinking superior. The poor man had to wash himself off in the river and Tom received further punishment by a demotion.

## *The Soldier*
Crawford Nish of Fort Victoria remembers Tom rocking up to see him in 1960 in a short wheel base land rover, which was kitted out with a machine gun placement on the back, manned by a warlike tracker. Tom was festooned with knives and army webbing across the chest and elsewhere. He looked as if he belonged to the long-range desert group (Special Forces of WW2). Tom was convinced there were going to be problems – and he was right. It was not long before they started, with a notable event at the Umkondo copper mine. A whole lot of men were called out at 3 am. to rescue the white population there, who were convinced that they were under siege. They had fortified the sports club, with the bar equipped as the final stronghold, which they were then going to defend to the last man.

## *Bush War*
Alan Savory often stayed with Tom at Kyle in the old farmhouse. To pass the time they used to fire a pellet gun at a lemon tree in the garden for target practice. Alan was trying to keep tough for the army and in the middle of winter would sleep on the veranda covered only in a parachute, much to Tom's amusement. Alan's home over the years was Tom's home and vice versa. Tom and his good friend Alan Savory were very interested in unconventional bush warfare and shared many evenings around campfires enthusiastically discussing this subject. They read a lot and kept abreast of what was happening in other parts of the world, particularly the Far East. Tom had struck up a relationship with Sir Roy Welensky (Prime Minister of the Federation of Rhodesia and Nyasaland) while he was working on Operation Noah. Now possibly encouraged by others, Tom decided to put the whole concept of a bush warfare unit on paper and then pay the Prime Minister a visit. Sir Roy loved dogs and had shown an interest in some of Tom's fox terriers. So off Tom went with a basketful of baby fox terriers and his letter to see the Prime Minister in Salisbury. When he arrived at Sir Roy's office in his bush clothes, the guard refused to let him in - dressed as he was, saying, "you can't go in there like that", and Tom replied, "Yes I can, he told me to come." Sir Roy then called Tom in, even though they were having a parliament meeting. In the room, there was a plush red carpet. Roy said to Tom in front of all the men present, "Put them out on the carpet." Tom said, "they'll sh*t and pee on the carpet." Roy said, "No put them out." Tom then placed the puppies on the carpet and the first

thing they did was to mess up the carpet, leaving a puddle. Roy chose one saying, "That's the one I want," and then said to Tom, "I know you Tommy, you don't give me something without wanting something in return." Tom then said, "Here you go" and gave him the letter. Three weeks later, the beginning of a bush warfare unit began. I have the letter from Roy thanking Tom for the dog, which was called Bobby. The letter was dated 12th Oct 1961. This secret tracking, training, bush craft school, trained blacks and whites in G.A.T.U teams (G.A.T.U stood for Guerrilla Anti Terrorist Unit). Special Forces, S.A.S, Police Special Branch and C.I.D were taught various techniques of bush warfare. Alan Savory was largely responsible for this training. It was in 1962 that Alan Savory first introduced tracking to the Rhodesian S.A.S when he gave an address to the whole squadron at the Air Force base in Salisbury. After the break-up of the Federation and around 1965 Alan did some training of S.A.S operators in Gona-re-Zhou. Some of those were TC Woods, Andre Rabie, Stretch Franklin and Brian Robinson. Due to police and army differences, the police broke away to form P.A.T.U (Police Anti Terrorist Unit) and to develop their own techniques.

## *Congo*

We will go a little north now to the Congo, where Tom paid a brief visit in 1964 as a mercenary. Here a revolt took place following the withdrawal of Belgian colonial rule and the country was in constant turmoil. On August 5, Simba rebels seized control of the city of Stanleyville and took over 1600 foreign hostages. The Congo government with the help of western nations and mercenaries did a counterattack to rescue the captives in Stanleyville and surrounding areas. Tom probably became a mercenary after hearing stories from his friends or he might have been sent up with the help of the Rhodesian government. Down near Birchenough he often visited an elderly Italian grandmother living with her family at Chibuwe. She used to spend her time sitting in a rocker knitting and whenever Tom stopped by for a meal, cup of tea or to reciprocate in some way, he used to try and shock her by saying that he was going to resign from Parks and become a mercenary in the Congo. She was very fond of Tommy and was always worried that he would take off for the Congo! Nevertheless, Tom did try his hand as a mercenary. He took sick leave and probably proceeded to the Copper Belt of Northern Rhodesia in his land rover and enlisted with the mercenaries, or went up with the

Rhodesian government's secret support. He joined Mike Hoare's mix of professionals and novices. He appears to have been flown in just as Stanleyville was taken. There is a possibility that he went up more than once. He remembered seeing the Butcher of Stanleyville, as he called the one rebel leader, naked and dead after the battle for the city. The mercenaries had to liberate captives throughout the eastern part of the Congo and it was sometimes too late when they arrived.

## *Mercenary*

As a novice, Tom was ordered to approach a mission building with wire mesh. It was very quiet apart from the buzzing of the flesh loving blowflies. He carefully came in view to find seven nuns who had been sawed in half by rebels with band saws and hung up on meat hooks. Then there was the time when some jeeps were in a clearing. These jeeps were mounted with machine guns. Suddenly a swarm of people came out of the thick bush with their magic talismans around their necks. Soon the men were faced with a barrage of poisoned arrows, spears, primitive guns and everything. The machine guns opened up and Tom had to hold the ammunition belt. He spent most of his time jumping and hopping around as the hot cartridge cases landed on him. On this occasion they got about 200 kills (This may have been the action at the Stanleyville airport). Tom with others came across some cannibals eating what he said was an American pilot who probably died in a plane crash or who was killed after landing. The cannibals were busy cooking up a good meal, with the victim slung up conveniently nearby to help remove the meat. The cannibals offered the mercenaries some of the meat and a discussion followed. They told the mercenaries that they liked human flesh, because it bounced around in the pot when boiled and so they called it 'happy meat'. The French-speaking mercenaries were not impressed. They blindfolded these cannibals and then shot them. Tom found this mercenary job had few benefits and could have proved hazardous for his health and so he decided to stick to wildlife.

## *Communists*

Rhodesia came under attack by what the government then called terrorists. These were mostly black fighters, fighting for black supremacy; communism and they often followed spirit mediums. The Rhodesian government fought for white supremacy and a westernized life, which included democratic ideals and Christian views. In the

**PERSONAL.**  12th October, 1961.

my dear Tom,

I would like you to know just how much my wife and I appreciate your kindness in giving us the puppy. He has been called Bobby, and really is a delightful creature. He has very swiftly endeared himself to both my wife and myself and all the members of the family, including the grandchildren. Naturally he has one or two idiosyncracies as yet, but I have no doubt that these will be eradicated in the fullness of time, and that he will be persuaded that the garden, and not the house is the appropriate place! All the other dogs have accepted him, except for the elder Ridgeback.

Once again our thanks,

Sincerely,

Roy Welensky

Mr. T. Orford,
c/o The Southern Rhodesia Game Department,
P.O. Box 8054,
Causeway,
SALISBURY.

*Letter from Prime Minister Roy Welensky to Tom with reference to Bobby*

confusion of this war, there were all sorts of motives and bad eggs on both sides. One wonders if the war was necessary and if it ever did anything good for the country. The terrorists as they were then called, I will refer to as communist fighters.

## *Infiltration*

1966 was the year when many of the communist fighters really started coming into Rhodesia. Large and small groups began to enter from Zambia and later on also from Mozambique. In the Mana Pools area, Jackie Myburg remembers an early incursion, with hundreds of men crossing over at night. Luckily for her, they did not pay a visit to the tented camp and were interested in other targets. The crowd of men left quite a trail and it looked like a herd of buffalo had moved through. Later on, those working with Parks would come across what looked like pieces of twisted tree-trunks. These were the communist fighters, who had died of starvation in the harsh Zambezi valley, when they ran out of food and water. They would have an identification tag, AK rifle and equipment. These men had a rough time, with some trying to gnaw bark to survive in the inhospitable valley. This incursion may have been the large 1968 crossing that took place in the Zambezi Valley along the Chewore River. One hundred and twenty three communist fighters, crossed over in a period of weeks. Their presence was undetected because of heavy rains that year and patrolling in that area was sparse. The communist fighters were able to establish a chain of bases, stretching from the Zambezi River and through the valley towards the escarpment. Their intention was to proceed into the European farming areas, recruit and train within Rhodesia. It had little chance of success, as game ranger Dave Scammel, who was an excellent tracker, was on a routine patrol. He detected the "four-lane" highway created by this large number of men, moving backwards and forwards, as they conveyed supplies inland. A large-scale military operation was mounted and within a matter of weeks 69 communist fighters had been killed and a large number captured. The Rhodesian war added a dangerous new twist to the life of a game ranger. Sometimes you did not know if you were following poachers or communist fighters, although boot patterns often helped to identify the communists. After the fall of Portuguese East Africa Russell Williams was killed, doing a Parks follow up on what they thought were poachers and many more were to fall victim over the years.

## *Bush Craft*
With these incursions, the Rhodesian government turned to National Parks, to help train the army in bush craft courses. These bush craft and survival courses, were done in Wankie and the Controlled Hunting Area, where they lasted for about ten days. Tom was said to have done the first general-army, bush course at Wankie near Mandavu dam. It involved teaching the army various things about the bush foods, tracking and the like. Some on this first guinea pig course were officers and were to spend most of the time doing practical stuff with Tom in the bush. Tom had no rank and was simply a lecturer from Parks. One day these men did a game drive with Tom. On the

drive, they were seeing everything, to the point where Tom began to complain that he wished he had real tourists, to appreciate what they were seeing. As they were enjoying the big five and some other good game, Tom was pointing everything out to them and then the word 'duck' was spoken. One of the army staff looked up to see where the duck was. As he did, he was nearly truncated by the branch of a tree. Other Parks' rangers and game scouts were roped in to teach the army, one being Dave Rushworth, who later started a good work in running bush courses for children. Willie de Beer did many of the tracking courses and they often tracked poachers to make it more realistic.

## *Wankie Incursion*
In the first half of 1967, some small incursions took place west and east of Lake Kariba, all of which were easily dealt with. However, in August 1967 a group of about 90 communist fighters, comprising half ZAPU and half South African ANC, entered Rhodesia East of Victoria Falls. Their intention was to move into the Tjolotjo Tribal Trust Land (TTL) and establish bases for the recruiting and training of communist fighters within Rhodesia. Once the Rhodesian element was secured, the South African fighters intended to move through Botswana and head for Soweto. However, their presence was speedily detected. One of them got tired and he jumped on a train. A black conductor found him without a ticket and so he was taken off at Dett. The communist fighter drew a revolver, shot the conductor in the groin and absconded on a bicycle. After this, he took Ivor Palferman's car and raced down the Dett vlei, stopping at the Gwaai. Here he bought sandwiches and drinks and gave Harold Bloomberg five pounds and told him to keep the change. He managed to get through roadblocks and into the Figtree area. Here he was shot on a farm through a glass door. Following the Dett arrest, a patrol of Rhodesian African Rifles with some police drove overnight to the area where the communists were hiding. A battle soon took place near Inyantue after a spotter plane sighted the enemy. Soon there were bullets flying and ambushes and two black Rhodesian soldiers were killed. The Algerian trained enemy fought well and the battle continued through the day into the night. When the sun rose over the harsh bushveld the next morning, the enemy had slipped away. They had lost five to the Rhodesia's two, while four Rhodesians had been wounded. One of the enemy had died in the night and had tried to slake his thirst by drinking urine from his Russian water bottle. After this, further

skirmishes took place, the enemy dispersed, with more being killed and some tribesmen helped capture others. Many filtered through Wankie National Park and Warden Hatton did not know whether to close the Park or not. Already ranger Don Stott had been shot in the stomach in an ambush, as he came back from Shumba and some tourists had also been shot at. This had been hushed up, a seriously injured Don was placed in hospital and it was blamed on a zebra accident. The security situation meant less Parks' patrols were done in some months and large parts of Wankie Park were closed for security purposes. Due to the communist fighters, Main Camp and Shapi airstrips were used as airbases. Tom had to stop his game capture operations due to all the activity. In his diary he records, "Building holding pens Makololo, check area for game, very little game of any kind, very few wildebeest etc. C/ranger Hodierne arrived to collect rations. 2130 ranger Hill, ranger Hodierne and Ray Field arrived to move us back to Main Camp due to terrorist activity. 2300 leave Makololo, call Kennedy siding to phone police."

*Detection*

In the first major operation of the war, 47 of that group that moved through the Wankie area were killed within the first three weeks. In excess of 20 were captured and the remnants, many of whom were wounded, escaped into Botswana where they were imprisoned and subsequently released to Zambia. Some of the communists reached Manga vlei where white rhino had been introduced into pens. Here they asked for food from the pump boys, who later reported them. The presence of the communists meant increased military activity in the park. Tom wanted to join in the action and John Hatton did not want him to. However, when the police drove down the road, there was a very enthusiastic Tom, waiting and wanting to go to war, armed with his small .22 rifle. Tom jumped into the back of the truck and off they went, but they failed to make contact with the communists. John often had a handful with the likes of Tom working under him. The police warned some Parks' staff working in the culling unit of the presence of the communists in the area and of the general direction they were taking. They were shown the boot pattern and told to be cautious. It was not long afterwards that the police heard a gunshot at Nehimba springs. They went to investigate and found a dead communist fighter. What had happened was that the culling staff had seen the man hiding by the side of the bush road and continued on, pretending they had not seen him. They carried on driving, but Ronnie van Heerden jumped out and sneaked back. The communist then went back onto the road, but was shot by Ronnie with a heavy calibre elephant gun. During the war, Parks' staff made it a habit of ambushing communist fighters at waterholes.

## *Battle*

Down at Sibanini some pump boys were walking 60km in for their pay and off time. They found communist fighter spoor, which they followed into the Linkwasha valley. They heard three shots and then ran off and reported at Main Camp. Using helicopters, the South African Police and Rhodesian military, with Parks, went down to where they found a dead white rhino. All the trackers at Main Camp had disappeared and were probably too afraid to get involved. Tom wrote in his diary about going down, "3/9/67 Sunday. Main Camp sorting kit, chopper arrived, R/W and ranger Wright proceed to show police, army area. Find shot rhino, three shots Linkwasha vlei, no mileage." The army took up the chase and they followed the figure of 8 boots. The communists were found a few miles away the following day and were killed with napalm and the veld burnt for weeks after that. In the fighting, it seems an enemy fighter jumped up, grenade in hand and pulled the pin with his teeth. Something went wrong, his head disappeared with the blast and the dried out bush caught fire. Screams could be heard as the fire swept through the dry bush and Russian and Chinese ammunition exploded adding to the early morning inferno. Later on there were burned-out metal weapons and burnt men left in the veld. Contacts took place all the way down to the Nyamandhlovu TTL where a white policeman was killed and a radio stolen. Eventually most of the communists were killed and some of their bodies taken to Shapi. The South African police were also involved, as many of the communists were South African and trying to infiltrate into South Africa. The South African communists were yellowish in colour and some were captured. The Rhodesians did not have a high opinion of the South African police as fighters. Most of them were in a foreign country and probably did not take the fighting seriously. They would often spend their time sun bathing and taking life very easy. They were well fed and better supplied than their poorer Rhodesian counterparts, who often scrounged material items left over by the South Africans. The Wankie campaign was a disaster for the ANC and Joshua Nkomo's ZAPU party. Without the help of

Parks' staff, pump attendants and trackers, the operations would not have been that successful. The tourist industry continued unsuspectingly.

## *The Range*
The Wankie home front was threatened and Tom decided to teach Pat Wright the art of war. Tom was always dramatic and Peter Wright came home to find his wife in hysterics. They had bought an auto pistol for her use and had mentioned this to Tom. Tom immediately decided to train Pat in the correct use of handguns and how to use them in self-protection, according to the "G" man of the FBI. The instruction followed all the action as per the movies, pirouetting along a wall to peep around the corner, then emerging with arm outstretched and the gun clutched or clasped in both hands, pointing in the direction of the villain. She was taught to drop to the knee and shoot, while the left hand was held upwards with the hand and fingers outstretched as a distraction. This went on for the best part of the day. They exhausted themselves with the pantomime and Tom left well satisfied and very seriously hoping that Pat had grasped everything.

## *TCU*
Alan Savory had been busy training the SAS and army, but realized that some of the best trackers and bush soldiers were in civilian life. So civilians (many in National Parks) were recruited and Alan was chosen to run what was to become the Tracker Combat Unit in 1968. Some of the men were good and some mediocre in the original group, of what was to become known as the dirty dozen. Tom was chosen for his expert medical skills, his practical bush experience and his sense of humour. Being a self taught medic, he became the unofficial medic for the unit and he had a good capacity for learning and a retentive mind. When the unit was being formed, Tom was very involved in some enthusiastic recruiting.

## *Chitove*
The men seemed to have done a large part of their training in the Gona-re-Zhou area at the Chitove pools. Training in bush craft and survival skills was complemented with jungle range shooting, stealth tactics with hand movements and dog whistles. Tom remembers wading through the croc and hippo-invested Lundi River at night. In the TCU one of the training methods used, was to set an ambush for

the tracker team and they used live fire on occasions, to stimulate a contact. To make it even more realistic, they used catapults. Tom remembers being hammered hard by a rock from a catapult in his shoulder blades. Gordon Cormack comments saying, "Tommy's more serious attitude to our training and his quiet sense of humour helped mollify the more volatile elements of our motley band as we tracked and ambushed each other, using live ammunition to add reality to our exercise, over the next few weeks. The fact that this live ammunition was aimed and used in impromptu ambushes and was never on fixed firing lines led to some close (deliberate?) misses and frequent altercations. Tommy was a fine rifle shot and very careful and thoughtful about it, as in all he did, cleaning and putting away everything correctly. He noticed me watching and said, 'Ones life might depend on the smallest thing, so take care at all times.'" Dave Scott-Donelan recalls, "After a training segment which taught them how to cover their own tracks and avoid detection, the trainees were ready for the final tactical exercise: a competition between three four man teams. Wearing only shirts, shorts, boots and hats, each team member was given rations consisting of four tea bags and a four ounce packet of shelled rice. They were assigned a series of map coordinates to follow over a seven-day period. The exercise was planned so that routes would cross and the objective was for each team to track and hunt down the other two groups. The rules were simple. If a team caught another team, they were allowed to confiscate anything from their prisoners. It was not unusual to see naked trackers slinking through the bush in pursuit of their confiscated uniforms." In one of the firearm drills Tom was very embarrassed when he left his rifle behind somewhere and had to go and look for it. To make them tough Tom's superior poured the little water they had on the ground, to make them suffer in training and to learn to go without water. When the man did this, Tom said, "This is very hard!" and it was.

### *Character*
While on training for the TCU, Tom was regarded as being a talkative and mischievous chap, an interesting character, often at the receiving side of some pretty nasty practical jokes, but he always gave as good as he got and had an incredibly acerbic tongue. Tom always took something with, 'just in case'. He had everything, everywhere, fishhooks and you name it. Each time the men went off on operations the soldiers had a 'noise check', as absolute silence was necessary.

The way they checked the men, was to get them to jump up and down. Invariably Tom would fail the test, as he was like a Christmas tree with all his armaments. Things had to be tight and close to the body, with nothing on the sides and no half filled water bottles. When Tom jumped up and down, there would be a clattering, as all his kit made a noise, with the medical kit, armaments etc. They would then take tons of stuff off him to make him a bit quieter and everyone would have a good laugh. Tom was the original gadget man on the Tracker Combat Unit operations with his acquisitions in the way of knives, compasses, freeze dried rations and the like. You learned not to get too enthusiastic about any particular item, because he would insist on giving it to you. There was a man in the TCU that decided to bully Tom. This man came up to Tom and kicked the log Tom was sitting on by the fire and tapped him on the back of the head. He then challenged Tom to come and fight. Tom looked up at his larger and stronger adversary and in front of everyone pointed to a log on the fire and said, "If you want to hit me, hit me, but you better hit me pretty well, because I tell you what... you see that log. When you are asleep you will get that on the back of your head." The guy chickened out, but was still a problem. While they were creeping through the bush doing their various exercises, the man came past a tree. Suddenly a hand came out behind the tree and the barrel of a handgun rested against his head. He was told in a polite manner that in future he should desist in making trouble.

## *Day Off*

Gordan Cormack recalls, "Towards the end of our course Alan rewarded us with a day off, to do as we wished, as a reward for our diligent efforts. We could take the Land Rover and visit some native saloon, as long as we came back that same day. Being miles away in the bush this meant a drive of at least 60 miles on a dreadful track to get to the nearest Rhodesian waterhole, so, using the initiative that we were sure our C.O. would approve of, it did not take long for the Bunces, Cooke and King to convince us to go to Mozambique for the day. They argued that we would find a closer, better stocked and salubrious bar and that it would be more adventurous. Malcolm King smiled, in his disarming fashion, when Tommy suggested rather bluntly that it was more likely that they sought salaciousness than salubriousness. Jannie Denecke, looking puzzled, said, 'I don't know what you are arguing about as we just want beer and sex?' Early in the morning I, as the youngest, convinced Tommy to come along as a more sobering influence and, leaving two of the fainter hearted behind, nine of us clambered on the L/R, as rank as chacmas (baboons) in our sweat stained combat attire. After a short drive we crossed the Sabi and not long after were at the border fence on a barely visible, little used track. There was an old rusted gate with an even older, massive rusted lock on it that did not look as though it had been unlocked in years. Jannie Denecke blew the lock off with one shot from his FN, with an insouciance instilled by years of illegal entry and poaching, and with cries of 'Vinho' and 'Cerveja' we went to meet our allies! Some thirty miles inland, after enquiring of astonished natives, we found a saloon, a bawa, run by a delighted mulatto who quickly arranged food, drinks and music. He had ice in his paraffin run deep freeze and we set down to assuage our three weeks old thirst. At last, the copious quantities of vinho verde and cerveja had a soporific effect on our volatile band and as the sun dropped towards the horizon, silhouetting the leafless mopane's, some of our deeper thinkers debated the manner of our return to camp. 'Has it occurred to any of you', said Tommy 'that we will have to replace the lock on the border gate?'"

### *Call Up*
Military call up kept men busy from the 1960's through to the 1970's and Tom like many men at the time was called up for military service. There was lots of pressure on the TCU and Tom was involved in follow-ups, but did not see a lot of action. He would go away for months on tracking operations. In one operation up in the North West of the country, Tom was in a stick (group of soldiers), waiting at a particular point for the enemy. It was pouring with rain and another group of men passed by. One of them was Alan Elliot, who noticed Tom cheerful as ever, in the pouring rain, even though he had no poncho. He seemed quite happy and content with life. This was just before Operation Teak. The unit was involved in some actions together and then they were seconded out to other army units as trackers. The TCU operated in teams of about four men. There was a tracker, two wings and a controller. These worked in an inverted V shape and they would walk in front of the army soldiers. Using hand signals, the controller would work with the three other TCU soldiers and communicate with the army officer behind. The army would normally be in an extended line behind the TCU ready for action.

*Paul Coetsee
PHOTO Jackie Pringle*

Tracking was not only dangerous, but also difficult, as many of the enemy hid their tracks well.

## *Op Teak*

At the end of 1969, Operation Teak took place, starting up near the Victoria Falls and continuing into the next year through the teak forests. In Operation Teak, the TCU men were dished out as trackers to the RLI, RAR, SAS and KAR military units. These army units would call in the nearest trackers in the rear and the TCU were involved with lots of kills. Tom was in a group that tracked for two days on the trail of some of these communist fighters. They had hit the Victoria Falls airport and it seems that they shot out some windows. Tom remembers missiles left near the airport, which had not been fired. This may have been on Operation Teak or on another occasion. These were to be fired at the aircraft, but they failed, as the batteries were not connected properly, or possibly had run out of water. The communists shot up the South African police camp at Kasikili and blew up the railway at Mubiya siding. All the 20 or so communists were eventually killed, with 4 by the TCU as they were arguing in rainy weather and others in the Matetsi area. Two heard the Rhodesian soldiers and escaped to Botswana.

## *Disintegration*

It was also up at the Falls that the TCU was to begin to fall apart on Operation Teak. The TCU men had no food and their shoes had holes in them. The unit was small and did not even have a quartermaster, but it was flexible enough to operate anywhere in the country. The men felt that even though survival skills were necessary; if food was available, why spend all your time foraging for bush food. Their commander's idea was that they would be macho and live off the land. However, after 2 or 4 days of no supplies, it was hard for the men to operate. They had bandoliers strapped around them, small pouches, hats, t-shirts, caps and very little other kit. There was a time when Tom was starving in the TCU and only had some peanuts left. Tom made all sorts of little meals with these precious peanuts, as he battled to survive. On one occasion the RLI had a plane drop of canisters with supplies, which scattered all over the bush and some broke open. Barry Duckworth began to help himself and his superior told him off, as this was not the roughing, he was expected to go through. One night they were freezing because of the cold and in line with macho standards, had not been supplied with blankets. When Mike Bunce found the newly arrived commander in the bush next to a small fire, this did not go down well. The commander had expected the others to rough it, but now he had a fire in a combat area. The men also took exception to him arriving in a helicopter to check on them, clean-shaven and well fed and smelling of eau de cologne. Soon the commander had a rebellion on his hands. While on the operations there, an RAR soldier was lying on his back and he looked up at the TCU commander and said, "the loneliness of command sir", as the commander battled with his rebellious men. The rigorous, tough and often ridiculous conditions caused many, including Tom to leave the TCU. It was also found to be impractical to have a unit, which was working most of the time and then suddenly called up.

*VTU*

It was about 1973 that the military leadership (including Don Price mentioned later) got together. They decided to create the Selous Scouts and so the TCU in 1974 was absorbed into the new Selous Scouts and the VTU. Many of those who had been in the TCU joined the Selous Scouts, but others like Tom were to work in the Volunteer Tracker Unit (VTU), which was to be controlled by National Parks. The Selous Scouts were an Army Unit like the RLI, SAS, Grey Scouts (the mounted unit) and Armoured Cars. There was much rivalry between the Scouts and SAS, as both units had selection criteria to be achieved before appointment. There was also a unit called the leopards that used to look like the black communist fighters and were said to be as effective in this work as the Selous Scouts. The Rhodesian army was to also use the tracking skills of the Tsholotsho bushman and of the Shangaan tribesmen. Dogs were often used in the war for tracking, not always successfully. One dog up near Wankie followed communists for two days and was later honoured with a monument.

## *Parks Trackers*

After leaving the TCU, Tom joined the Volunteer Tracker Unit (VTU) or Parks Tracker Unit, which was made up of Parks' staff and was a voluntary irregular unit. The VTU really started in the very late '60s, when Paul Coetsee volunteered his services to the Police in the Sinoia area to track some criminals. Paul was the Provincial Warden of Mashonaland North Province. With the first influx of communist fighters and the murders in the Hartley area in the early '70s, Paul immediately volunteered the services of trackers. Thus the Volunteer Tracker Unit, as an entity was born. Initially the VTU was formed to operate in the Operation Hurricane area. As the unit met with so much success, the calls for their services became more and more frequent and the work load and administration, all being undertaken from Sinoia, became too much. Tom was involved in the unit and recalled a bus with a whole lot of people being blown up by a mine in this area and he was in the follow up. Then with the incursions along the Eastern border by ZANLA communist fighters; the Army requested the VTU to extend their area of operations beyond the Operation Hurricane area. By 1976, the VTU had three sticks of men in the field, 365 days a year. Barry Ball and Roy Killick were to play an important part in running the daily operations of the unit.

## *Tactics*

Paul's private army, as the VTU was sometimes called, was different from the TCU in that it was made up of teams of both white and black soldiers. These men would be posted to hot areas of the country using a roster system. There were normally at least two teams working in the country at any one time. You would go out every few months for about two weeks. The maximum duration of a call out would be about three weeks, as it was physically and mentally demanding work, especially for the trackers. The men used army kit, but were allowed more flexibility than other soldiers. Tom used his semi automatic military carbine in the war. Some of the 'hot' Parks' stations like Gona-re-Zhou, Chirisa, Mana and others, would have their staff excused from military service towards the end of the war. These men were not called up, as their stations were so dangerous. The principal purpose of the Unit was to track and locate communist fighters for the accompanying army squad. Normally the men would work in pairs, a white ranger and his game scout tracker. If the white rangers did not have their own trackers, they could pick trackers up at head office or in the bush. In this, it was best to go to war with your own game scout. One ranger was given a research game scout, who did not know how to track and the two were choppered into a 'hot zone' (dangerous area). When they came across a vehicle damaged by a landmine, the game scout's eyes were as wide as saucers. It turned out the game scout could hardly walk, let alone track.

### *Tracking*
The army commanding officer would call in the VTU trackers who were on standby at the army bases, for any work to be done. The VTU stick (as it was known) was composed of two black and two white soldiers, all National Parks' staff. The stick, together with the army patrol would proceed in 'arrow head' formation. While the black Scouts followed the spoor, the Rangers looked for the enemy and protected the scouts. As soon as they found the quarry, the VTU team would back off and leave the army to do most of the shooting. This backing out by the VTU was a trackers' privilege, as they were normally the first to be shot at in ambushes and were normally very tired after the tracking. It was not their function to engage the enemy, but they did this whenever possible and with considerable success. There was one occasion in 1978, when a game scout had an enemy in sight, but the Ranger could not see him. After much pointing and whispering, the Ranger told the Scout to shoot the enemy and he (the Ranger) would shoot the communist as soon as he broke cover. With that the Scout fired, hit a grenade on the enemies body and the Ranger never had to fire a bullet. On one occasion, a Parks' member accounted for 9 out of 11 of the enemy, when he suddenly came across them having lunch.

### *Exceptional*
One little story is certainly worth mentioning and that is the time a stick was on the track of five of the enemy that had infiltrated from Zambia. The leading tracker casually mentioned to the Army Sgt. i/c of the patrol that there were five communists; all wearing hockey boot, type footwear and two were in bell-bottom trousers. Naturally, the Sgt. expressed his amazement and sure enough, when the patrol

caught up to and killed the five communists two days later, all five were wearing hockey boots and two were in bell-bottom trousers. This story spread through the army and gave the Unit some respect. The longest tracking recorded was by a team, which included Barry Ball. They tracked the communist fighters a few hundred kilometres from the Zambezi valley to Tsholotsho. In the years before Fire Force and the Selous Scouts began to take their heavy toll on the enemy, the Parks' tracker teams were involved in most of the kills. In the early years, they helped account for as much as 90% of the kills, through their outstanding abilities. The Parks' units continued right to the end of the war, being particularly effective in the South and West of the country. Parks' rangers killed in tracking operations included Richard Smith, Norman Payne and Nick Gregory.

### *Nick*

Nick Gregory was one of the rangers that worked under Tom at Mabalauta. He appears to have had an unstable childhood and had to fight his way through life. Nick had already survived landmines up at Marongora. He was a loner and loved going into the bush. Having grown up with black friends, he was able to speak Shona, Ndebele and Nyanja. Nick would go to the SPCA and get about 20 dogs, which were used for hunting. The dogs would get the best life any dog could want, as long as they were obedient and killed baboons. All those dogs that were cowards were killed. The baboons killed were turned into biltong and fed to the dogs. Nick did not drink. At a function in Salisbury, the Veterinary staff (Nick had been in Veterinary), were together having a drink and he ordered tea at the Park Lane hotel. The waiter serving walked off and scoffed about Nick drinking only tea. After the waiter cleared off, Nick got up quietly and went into the kitchen and there was a war. There was plenty of noise and the cooks and waiters were coming out of the windows, as he gave them a sound hiding. Nick was tracking for the National Parks' Volunteer tracking unit, doing a follow up, when they caught up to the enemy in a riverbed. The communists were killed and Nick went down to the river to fill his water bottle as the sun was setting. Hidden in the reeds was a wounded communist fighter, who fired and shot Nick in the neck. The man in the reeds was shot soon after, but Nick died of his wounds.

*Rhodesian army helping remove snares towards end of war at Umfurudzi, PHOTO Chronicle*

## Dirty War

When Tom resigned from Parks, he was no longer eligible to be a member of the VTU, which was a strictly Departmental Unit. He now spent time doing convoy work, possibly guarding farms and working with intelligence. Much of Tom's military career is a mystery, as he and others of his time, have not spoken due to fear of victimization. His later war activities seem even more shrouded in mystery, but he may have been busy doing lots of lone ranger stuff. It was said that he was used as a spy in the rural areas, collecting information from villagers on the activities of the communist fighters. Tom also mentioned a spy ring along the Zambezi. Here spies in Zambia would radio through with information on hunting and animals, like 21 guinea fowl etc. These coded hunting conversations would reveal the numbers and movement of the enemy. When the communists crossed the Zambezi using ropes and were half way across, they would find the Rhodesian army waiting for them. War is not clean, there are often no rules and Tom used to feel guilty later in his life, about the people he was involved in killing. In the Rhodesian war, he and his fellows found a terribly murdered and mutilated family. They tracked down the four communists responsible. After capturing the communists, they tied them together and bound them inside an old jeep, with a load of explosives on the dashboard and a timer clock-detonator attached. Tom and his comrades then proceeded to picnic about 200 meters away, while the assassins cried and watched their lives tick away. When Tom was flown into operations, he and others would ride on a helicopter. He travelled differently though by going under the helicopter, where there was often a big net for carrying dead bodies. Tom preferred to ride in this (without the dead bodies), as he could get fresh air and was not cramped up inside with the others.

## *Home Guard*
After Parks, Tom did convoy work on the Beitbridge-Bulawayo route and in the Eastern Highlands. He was not happy with this type of army/police work and wanted to pack it up once, when another convoy person he knew was killed. Tom's job was to sit in the back of a truck with a machine gun and deal with any communist fighters in ambushes. In the Eastern districts, he had a few narrow escapes. He was once based up at a farm somewhere near Centenary and was guarding the house when it came under attack. The farmhouse was armed with a homemade cannon, loaded with all and sundry. With all the bullets and tracers flying around, Tom decided to put this cannon to effect, hoping to put an end to the attack. With the cannon aimed at what he thought was the enemy, he fired and waited with a satisfied expectation to see the outcome. Well there was a huge explosion, as he scored a direct hit, not on the enemy, but on the tobacco barn's boiler. The almighty explosion put the fear into everyone for miles around. The enemy fled and the farmer was to return later on to find his barn terminated.

*In the TCU 1968 Tom, Ollie Coltman and Hans Otto, PHOTO Dave Scott-Donelan*

*Picture of the Original Tracker Combat Unit 1968 - L to R - Top Row - Allan Savory, Bruce Cook, Mike Bunce, Johnny Denecker, Dave Scott-Donelan, Hans Otto, Charlie Williams, Malcolm King and Ollie Coltman, Bottom Row - crouched - Johnny Bunce, Paul Coetsee, Gordan Cormack and Tom Orford*

*One of Simuwini lodges at Mabalauta*

## CHAPTER 16
# THE WHEELS FALL OFF 1976 – 1978

### War
With the collapse of Portuguese East Africa, the new communist state of Mozambique began and Rhodesia now had a hostile neighbour. It was not long before the communists began to start infiltrating Rhodesia from the South East and Mabalauta became a hot territory. Tom was one of the first to observe the presence of communist fighters in the area, as his spy network told him of their activities. When he notified the authorities in Salisbury, his superiors sent a letter and rebuked him for being an alarmist. Tom was always willing to help the police and army during the war and provided Shangaan trackers to PATU sticks and other security units when the war reached the South East. As the war heated up he was continually off on army call-ups, for weeks at a time. At Mabalauta, he was to grow more safety conscious and slept with a revolver in case nocturnal raiders turned up. The respectful Sergeant Mac was like a father to Tom and would protect Dawn while Tom was away. Mac would sleep at the

back of the house and on one occasion, nearly clouted Tom when Tom returned back home at night. Military matters were out of Tom's control and he was to spend more time in the office. Soon the donkey patrols ended as things got too dangerous. Army units began to use the camping ground at Mabalauta as their base and some of these units included the SAS and the Grey Scouts.

## *Are You Poaching?*
Tom worked a great deal with the police and army, but was inflexible when it came to the army or police poaching. Tom and Ron Thompson classified Police and Veterinary staff as poachers and the enemy! Often the vet guys were simply known as poachers, yet many were innocent, while others were passionate about hunting and were caught poaching by Tom. The police at Vila Salazar had permission to crop a certain amount of animals for food, but some would overdo it. Tom would send his game scouts to try to catch them and it ended up with a game of hide and seek to see if he could apprehend them. Tom had good reason to eye out the police and he foiled the attempt of one white policeman that was snooping around for elephant. Tom having outwitted him, they were to then remain good friends afterwards. Other white poachers operated in the Gonakudzingwa area using airplanes and other means. One of these poachers was caught and was so upset at being on the wrong side of the law, that he went around trying to get people to sign a petition on his behalf. One of Tom's scouts reported that an impala had been shot in the park. Tom roared off in his trustee land cruiser, leapt out at the South African police camp, saw the impala carcass hanging there and promptly threatened to arrest the entire police contingent for poaching. The only thing that may have discouraged him was the thought of an international incident. "What the h**** is that?" the reply "an impala". "You are not b*** allowed to shoot my **** impalas and I will have you up ******." They had to back off. He told them if there were to be any shooting for the pot, he would do it.

## *Dangers*
Tom began to teach Dawn shooting techniques with the military carbine and an FN rifle, in standing, sitting and lying positions and with point and shoot. In 1976, the Park became a subject of abuse, with continual military contacts, in a Vietnam type war. There were roaring aircraft and the firing of light and heavy weapons, almost

daily. It was surprising that the Communist fighters did not launch an all out attack on a soft target like the National Parks Warden's camp. Mines restricted movement and there were uncontrolled fires, due to the fighting and poaching by both sides in the conflict. Mines were a hazard and at least three rangers in Parks, were to have their legs blown off in the war. In Mabalauta landmines were detonated all around, posing a threat for Parks, the Veterinary Department and the army. Some of the rangers lost their kit after land mines blew up transport vehicles and the furniture transport companies became reluctant to enter the area. Mines were particularly dangerous to the big Parks' trucks, as they were not mine proofed and they sometimes had to carry fuel drums on these vehicles. Artillery fire and mortars went off across the Nuanetsi River from the camp, while they were having their braais and they realized they were living in a surreal world.

## *Leaving Parks*

Tom had been considering leaving Parks for a while and wanted to go cattle ranching. It was a huge mistake to leave Parks, as his many years in the Game Department and Parks, had been his happiest and he was to later regret this move. Mabalauta was 120 miles from the nearest small town and as there was soon a ban on the movement of private vehicles, it meant Tom and Dawn could not get their furniture out. This ban was due to several landmines going off and there had been ambushes, so all vehicles had to go in protected convoys. The only way to evacuate Dawn now was by plane. Through the generosity of a ranger named Graham Hall, Dawn was flown out of war torn Mabalauta in April 1976 and dropped off at Rutenga. Dawn fitted into the back seat of his Super Cub with Paddy and their bare essentials in the little baggage compartment behind. After Tom and Dawn had left Mabalauta, the new warden Willie de Beer bought the pigs at Mabalauta and later when he left, he took them to Ruwa. Some of the pigs he sold to Ozzie Bristow. Dave Winnel shot two lions that climbed into the pig pens once. When Willie came back, he was furious with his ranger, as he felt the use of thunder flashes was more appropriate. Willie ended up with a 24-hour guard over those pigs to protect them from lions. Willie got rid of the donkeys and gave them to the staff. After releasing the donkeys, one of the females came back to the station and took up residence on the airstrip. She was not looked after, but went habitually to her pen daily, even though she was

*Mabalauta, Tom and ranger Nevin Lees-May with Fat Boy, Shlupo, Serg. Mac, unknown*

forgotten.

## *Lawlessness*

After Tom had left Mabalauta, the lawlessness got worse, with Gona-re-Zhou being abused by many people into the late 70's and right through into the 80's. While Willie was there, the Selous Scouts took over Simuwini camp, which they then damaged. There was one particular man named sergeant M, who not only used the camp as a base without asking, but also blew up Willie's Parks' supply store at Vila Salazar. The supplies used to come down by rail and were locked up in the store by the train driver. Willie complained to Butch Swart, the leader in the area and to Reid Daly about this problem. They did not have to deal with him though, as a few weeks later sergeant M died in an accident in South Africa. Some Parks' staff were to take to poaching at the end of the war in the Gona-re-Zhou and in other Parks for a quick buck. These men felt there was no future in the country and they tried to make the most of the situation. It was rumoured that some individuals worked with a few soldiers to move ivory out of the Gona-re-Zhou area. They shot big bulls and stacks of ivory were shipped out using military transport and then helicopters flew the ivory out. A few wild and dangerous men in the Selous Scouts were involved with these shady activities. These Selous Scouts were active at Groot vlei just outside the Park, where there was an airstrip to help move the ivory out. One of their own leaked information to someone in army intelligence in Salisbury. The Selous Scouts involved wanted to eliminate this fellow soldier, but he was given protection. The whole thing was silenced, with politicians and the army dealing with this sensitive, poaching matter.

## *Later Dangers*

Willie and Graham Hall were involved with the collaring of big elephant in the Gona-re-Zhou as a means to protect them. As there were many communist fighters coming in from Mozambique, it was dangerous on patrols. Willie was lucky that his friends in the army and air force helped move him around. The army helped with antipoaching and he would give them the odd impala for ration meat in thanks. Networks of minefields were placed along the border to stop the entry of the enemy, but these were still blowing up elephants twenty-five years later. Mike Bromwich looked after Mabalauta in the war years and would often patrol these minefields. This was dangerous work, they often saw where the wire was cut and the human spoor told them the communists had crossed. Every so often staff from more comfortable zones would bring in good food and luxuries for those rangers stuck in these remote and tough stations, which had little comforts. Land mines and ambushes kept you on edge. One of the game scouts left behind by Tom at Mabalauta, named Giyane, was tracking with the security forces, when he was injured in a vehicle ambush and shot in the leg.

## *Savory*

Alan Savory was a plausible, charming and controversial politician. He was born in 1935 in Rhodesia, where his father was a big-time dam builder. Alan had his successes and failures and tried sugar farming, ecology, the military and politics. Alan went into cattle/game ranching on his own land in 1964 and later added another cattle ranch. He had controversial ideas in both politics and ecology. In 1973, he was voted Rhodesia's most popular person and was an active politician in Ian Smith's Rhodesia Front. Soon after, he was to cross the floor to start a new party called the Rhodesia Party, which made him probably the most unpopular person in the white community. Alan became a liberal as he opposed the hard line stance of the Smith government, saying it was not going to work and a new approach was needed. Tom supported Alan and was to clash with Sheilagh his sister, who was pro Smith. At one stage, brother and sister were not talking to each other. Sheilagh later on became a member of parliament after independence in Smith's party. After the war Alan was to become good friends with President Robert Mugabe, who he would occasionally visit. Alan Savory had a ranch in the Matopos called Gumela and approached Tom about it. Tom was warned by his friends about this business venture, as unknown to Alan and Tom, they had both over estimated the livestock carrying capacity of this farm. With the war also warming up, Tom did not know what further risks he was going to face on the farm. Tom made the deal with Alan, without listening to his friends or consulting Dawn, who was sick at the time. He was about to make one of the biggest mistakes of his life.

## *Gumela*

Gumela farm is nestled in some beautiful granite country in the Southern Matopos, just south of Bulawayo. The farm had an excellent assortment of bushman paintings and one rhino painting in particular, was particularly good. There was a huge secret cave with a low entrance with grain storage bins and the farm was great for walks in the rocky hills. Tom and Dawn found many interesting places and never finished exploring the farm. It was a triangular shape, with most of the north of the farm being very rocky. There was a central water point and very few roads on the property. A wagon-wheel, paddock system, seemed the cheapest way for Tom to do the fencing. This system enabled cattle from different paddocks to drink at a central point. Alan Savory noticed the benefits of this scheme, combined it with the high-impact, short-duration grazing system and later promoted it around the world. This Kezi area had been the home of many pioneer farmers and their graves could be found scattered around the district. Many of these had been Afrikaans farmers. Tom seldom saw the local white community here and this was normally only at the Van Vuurens store, where the RMS trucks halted. Due to Alan's politics and the unpopular Short Duration grazing scheme, the community was split into two camps and some did not trust Tom, as he was working with Alan. Tom was classed by some of the white community as being liberal, although he never got involved with politics. At one time, this had been a close and happy community, with a nice church built by the farmers at the Van Vuurens' place. This was later abandoned and then pulled down. There had also been a school, which was closed and it became a reformatory run by a major Blunt. One of the punishments for the kids there was to get in the boxing ring with the master and they would then be pummelled. The white community once celebrated Christmas at Kezi, while Tom was at Gumela. Father Christmas arrived in a donkey cart. While all the adults celebrated together late at night, the kids slept together in one room. Things got worse after the war, as the North Korean trained 5th brigade moved in and killed some of the farmers and threatening others, caused them to leave the district. Eventually only a few of the original white community were left.

## *Attacked*

With the war heating up and reaching into the Matopos, Tom constructed an impregnable fortified turret out of the chimney, which was used as a gun turret. The house was built on a rock dwala (huge rock) and did not have a security fence. Tom surrounded it with loose wire and glass to discourage intruders, but it was not sufficient to stop a determined enemy. Wire screens were used to stop hand grenades being lobbed through windows. When three communist fighters did try and attack, Tom climbed up the chimney and used this to fire at the intruders, while Dawn went and sat in the kid's room. These three men managed to get behind the back of the house near the kitchen and after being fired on by Tom, did a strategic retreat. They went down to the workers compound where a few shots were fired. The farm mechanic had meanwhile hidden himself to avoid being shot. ZIPRA (one of the armed groups) were told that Tom was a good man and after this, they left him alone. Tom always got on well with black folk and knew their culture. Kamchacha (Tom) was said to talk too much, but was a good chap and treated his staff well with food and assisted the locals. Dawn would cook sadza for the 22 staff and they were supplied with meat, even though many of them were not working properly. As ZIPRA had a policy of not killing all whites, he was never shot and while Bryan and Paddy played in their exposed positions around the house, they never fired on the children. Some of the fighters active on the farm were Lookout Masuku, Dumiso

Dabengwa and Misheck. It also turned out that Douglas Dube (Khumalo), who was working for Tom, was Dumiso's brother in law and that probably helped. After the war, Tom and Dumiso became friends and Dumiso showed Tom in his diary the times he could have shot at the family. Later in the war Dumiso had to leave the country and go into Botswana as the Rhodesian security forces were hot on his trail. The Khumalo family was the royal family of Mzilikazi and of the Matabele people. Douglas was a direct descendant of Mzilikazi and his son Nkulumani. Nkulumani the rightful heir, had gone down to South Africa, but was scared to come back due to the competition over the kingship, although he did come back briefly. Douglas was to hunt with Tom into the 1980's and both men helped each other through the war. When Tom was broke at one time, he even borrowed money from Douglas in those hard years.

*Neighbours*
Mrs. Grobler was a lovely old lady (in her 70's) and was very kind to the local people. Her husband though was not liked and regarded as being disrespectful. He had an affair with a local girl and produced a coloured child, which made him an unpopular person and this was probably his death sentence. Tom and Dawn were down in the Transkei on holiday. Mrs. Grobler had been sick and decided to go out with her husband after a long absence from the farm. It seems one of the reasons they went out to the farm, was to collect or sort out Tom's dogs. The couple was ambushed close to their house as they drove near a termite mound and were killed outright. She had her hair and her feet cut off by the ZIPRA fighters, possibly for witchcraft purposes. The Van Vuurens saw the smoke going up in the distance and assumed it was a communist fighter attack. They contacted the police and the member in charge. He did not realize the danger and went in his private vehicle, but turned around when he saw the carnage in the distance. After this the District Commissioner told Dawn that she couldn't stay there on her own anymore and she then moved into Bulawayo with the kids.

*Bankruptcy*
It took Dawn some time to discover what the paperwork and farm deal involved. The first nine months or so at Gumela had seemed to be okay, until the reality of what they had entered into became a bit clearer. Even after trying to revise the paper work, they still found

themselves heading for bankruptcy. Alan had become a staunch believer in the controversial Short Duration grazing method of ranching. It involved the use of large amounts of animals grazing on a piece of land and these were to have a high impact on the soil, before being moved to a new piece of ground. This works well in some areas, but unbeknown to Alan and Tom, was not suitable in some parts of Zimbabwe. Many tried it and went out of business and Tom was one of these. Tom's problems on the small farm were compounded with foot and mouth disease, thefts by the communal people, someone letting him down financially and the war. The farm collapsed quickly and the cattle that were left were sold to recover some of the debt. There were escalating security problems and death lurked around every corner on the farm. The war took its toll and Tom had a nervous breakdown and at one time could hardly talk. He fell to pieces as everything came apart and at times became suicidal, putting unrealistic pressure on Dawn. Fat Boy felt his life was in danger from the ZIPRA fighters and left to rejoin Parks. The army was to use Gumela as a temporary base and eventually the Gumela house was to become a ruin. Twenty-six years after Tom left the farm, the place was a mess. The bridges to the farm were washed away; the roads overgrown with sickle bushes, as were the lands that had once been clear of trees. The farmhouse can only be found now by searching 'lost city' style. It and all the farm building are now hidden away, forgotten, with a few stray cows going by. Gumela has a strange …what you would call a spiritual feel to it. Nearby is the famous mountain and cave called Njelele. This is probably the most important religious site in the country and the home of the Mwari god. On one occasion, Tom and someone else (a reliable witness) were travelling towards the farm, when they saw what they believed to be a UFO. They saw a green-lighted thing going across and around in the sky a couple of hundred meters away. It was nothing like normal and travelled towards Gumela. They still felt safe as they were in the armoured land cruiser, considering it as being secure, as one could only climb in through the top of the vehicle. Tom had this long wheel base cruiser armour plated (proofed) for land mines and bullets. Did this object in the sky have something to do with the mountain? In later years, Christian groups went to pray at the mountain shrine, some at night. After they prayed mysterious fires and lightning, hit the shrine, the surroundings and the shrine buildings were burnt. Soon after this, strife broke out between the locals and the guardians of the shrine and one of the guardians died. Tom's big stone welcome sign still stands at the Gumela farm entrance, as a reminder of better times and broken dreams.

## *Bulawayo*

Alan Savory had been under intense pressure. The CID came to his house and told him they would lock him up on a treason charge, because he had given an interview and released some information. Alan decided to pack his bags that night and he was out of the country within 24 hours. It was a low point in his life, as he flew to the Cayman Islands and was to restart his life in the USA, while his wife stayed behind to receive abusive phone calls. Due to problems at Gumela, Tom moved off and managed Mhlahlandhlela farm in the Matopos for a few months, but it became very dangerous. He soon moved into the safety of Bulawayo where he was to live in various flats, including Chilham Court. Here he would often wake up in the night to all the strange town noises, of cars, motorbikes and the incoherent, loud noises of drunks. Once he saw two drunks arguing in the street below. Tom took his catapult, with some steel bearings, took careful aim and hit one of them in the back. The smitten one was furious and turned around to blame his accomplice for hitting him. The two then had a merry fight. Bulawayo was also a great place for Tom to mix with the gun crowd, who were in full swing with the war. Sheilagh his sister came down to visit Tom in Bulawayo, just before he got divorced. He was on a diet at the time. However, when the ice cream man came past and the bell rang, Sheilagh and Tom looked at each other with a knowing look and it was ice cream time. The serious financial stresses and Tom's mental breakdown were too much. Tom had become a victim of the war. Some lost their lives, some their loved ones and friends, while others had their lives left in tatters. Tom was one of the latter and his marriage ended in a divorce, he was broke and at the same time, communist fighters shot his niece Madeline.

## *Parks Again*

Tom tried to return to Parks and came to see Graham Child asking him for a job. They didn't normally rehire staff, but with Tom they decided to make an exception. As there were few jobs available in Parks, they had to send him to the only position existing. He was dropped from a warden to ranger and posted up at

Chimanimani/Melsetter. While he was there, Melsetter was subjected to a communist fighters' attack. Soon after that someone acquired a 20 mm cannon from a Spitfire, mounted it on a gun carriage and tested it at the highest point in Melsetter. Tom was seen there, making sure it was not fired in the vicinity of a herd of eland. Melsetter had cold foul weather, little game, was lonely and was one of the most dangerous places in the country. The little road that went up to the huge house, with little furniture, was the perfect place for an ambush and it was no wonder that four rangers were stationed there in that year and most moved on very quickly. It was not a place for a man just divorced and who had lost almost everything. Tom lasted for about a month before moving on to safer pastures.

*Rhodes Matopos National Park (Matobo) close to Gumela*

*Dale Paas, Tom and trackers with 80 pounder 1979*

## CHAPTER 17
# ADRENALINE TIMES 1978-1982

### *Professional Hunting*
Gumela was a failure for Tom and he had to start professional hunting as early as 1977 to make ends meet. There were few hunting operations in the late 1970's, as professional hunting safaris were still in their infancy in the country and the war made things difficult. Tom was to find himself at odds with some operators he worked with, as they often bent and broke the law, putting him in a sensitive position. He was viewed as being too much of a warden, as he was always trying to go by the book. Tommy became quite a talking point in the hunting fraternity. There was no question of Tommy's competence, but his dislike of hunting in its professional form, for the mere gain of trophies raised some eyebrows. There were also many comments about the painted lotion bottle full of ashes that he had hanging round his neck. Some thought the throwing of ashes up into the air, to see which way the wind was blowing, was unnecessary and bordered on witchcraft. However he did this, as hunters need to be aware at all times of which way the wind is blowing, in order to stay downwind of the game. Tommy often made a client pass up a good trophy, because

he quickly got to know many of the animals in the area and did not relish the best trophies (his friends) adorning someone's wall. Mind you, he was not the only professional hunter to act in this fashion. Tom never bragged about shooting animals. It was part of his work and he did it well, but he never made large amounts of money - as he was always spending it or giving it away. Tom's right hand man and friend on his early hunts was Douglas Khumalo, who later joined the veterinary department with Tom. Tom's trackers regarded him as a brave hunter, as he would get very close to elephants using his .505 and Douglas used a backup .375 rifle. Tommy loved animals and could not bear to shoot things like elephants unless it was absolutely necessary. In the war years they were always kitted out with bandoliers of ammunition, hand grenades, water bottles etc. Mlilo was Tom's tracker on hunts and there was always the scoff (food) box, which was used for picnicking in the bush.

## *Matetsi*

Hunting had started early on in the Matetsi farms, when the farmers shot for the pot and dealt with besieging lions. Some were to start professional hunting before the government took over the area. Several of the rich landholders used their properties as shooting boxes and one farmer was recorded shooting zebras with a machine gun. Many of the Matetsi farms went bankrupt though and the government took them over in 1973. It was decided that the area was more suitable for game than cattle, the landholders were compensated with money, and some were given farms. Alan Savory lost his Kazuma farm and managed to replace it with Waterford near the Victoria Falls. Matetsi was subdivided to form hunting concessions, forestry areas and national park areas. There had been a Parks Controlled Hunting Area along the northern border of the Wankie National Park, with a central camp at an old farmhouse called Bumboosie. This Controlled Hunting Area was leased to a well-known Professional Hunter who ranched in the Mtoroshanga area. The Wankie Controlled Hunting Area was abolished, the fence taken down and the area incorporated into the Matetsi Hunting Area and Deka Safari Area, with Bumboosie becoming part of Wankie National Park. Dan Landrey, Geoff Broom, Lew Games and Fanie Pretorius were some of those who managed to get hunting concessions in the area. 90% of the buildings on the original farms were pulled down and all the fences. Dan ended up hunting on the old Denda ranch and a bit of Parks' land, which made up one of the state hunting areas. There were no cut lines between the concessions and so there was a gentleman's agreement about boundaries. Dan also had a camp in the Chewore, where the young Rusty Labuscagne worked for him for a while. While Tom was working as a professional hunter at Bumboosie Trevor Edwards renewed his acquaintanceship with Tommy. Tom showed him something amazing. They went to the old border where the fence had been for so many years. It had been taken away to encourage the surplus of elephants in the Wankie National Park, to spread into the relatively, far less elephant-populated Matetsi Area. They watched a herd of elephant plod up a gentle slope to the old border. When it reached the border, the herd turned and walked along the perimeter as though the fence was still there.

## *Operators*

Tom was to do freelance work for many operators in the late 70's and early 80's. An Operator was a businessman who ran a hunting operation. Most were very professional, like Peter Johnstone and Dan Landrey. There were also the coke and buns and fly by night operators, but considering the many years Tom worked for them, there was few complaints. Tom was horrified with one operator, as he would cut his toenails in front of the clients. During the war, some Rhodesian soldiers came in from the bush exhausted and stopped over at the camp of this man. He offered them cokes to quench their thirst. When they left, they were given invoices for the drinks they had drunk. In addition, when Tom worked in the butchery of this man, he would often help himself to a little biltong while supervising the processing of the meat and there was lots of it. At the end of the month, he found a biltong deduction fee on his salary cheque, with some money deducted for storage, as he had some of his kit there. Some of the hunters did not like this operator and once when they all had a drink together; they had a little talk to the waiter. After having spent some money on drinks, they all jumped up when the bill arrived and the waiter thrust the bill into the man's hands. Then there was the occasion, when a fellow hunter came over for tea to visit this operator, but when the visitor was leaving, he was presented a bill for one tea. Without making a fuss, the man paid the bill and asked his fellow operator, to come over sometime for a return visit. So Mr. Operator went for a stopover with his wife and enjoying the hospitality, the couple spent the night. The next day when they were about to leave, he was given a bill in US dollars for the daily rate of a client and was charged for having an observer. When a client shoots an animal, the whole carcass normally belongs to the client, but operators often make money out of the skins and the meat, as the clients only want their ivory, horns or trophy skins. To get his own back on one operator, Tom suggested and helped the client to sell the meat and the skin of an elephant they had shot. This took away quite a bit of money from the operator. Later when the operator complained, Tom's response was, "Yah you've lost double. It's your own fault". Professional Hunters also had their bad days. Tom was not impressed by some who he saw one day, as he was driving through a hunting area near Wankie. He noticed the hunters patiently waiting by their vehicle and drove up to ask if they had a problem. In the distance could be seen a zebra in some sort of trouble. After a few questions, Tom found out that these hunters had run out of bullets and were now waiting for the animal to die! Nevertheless, most operators and hunters in Zimbabwe were professional and are highly trained. Maybe some operators had their gripes about Tom. Once Tom refused to eat dinner at one man's camp, saying he was on a diet. The operator's wife was not too happy with this, as Tom had turned down the well-cooked meal, only to walk around later and polish off about a kilogramme of peanuts.

## *Marongora*

In 1978/1979, Tom hunted from Makuti/Marongora going down into the Zambezi valley. It was one of the dangerous areas of the country and they often saw the spoor of Communist fighters. On one occasion, after crossing the Nyakasanga Bridge late in the afternoon, Tom drove over a landmine. They were lucky, as it blew up after they had just passed. To avoid mines they would drive down the tar road until they found the spoor of elephant and buffalo and then walk in. This meant there was less chance of hitting a mine. Rangers such as Ollie Coltman and Mark Butcher would escort the hunters and clients on these hunts for added security. Walking through the cathedral mopane and jesse bush, Tom was continually pestered by tsetse flies. He dealt with these with borax. Sometimes they would sleep under shelters in the valley while hunting. Each man was exposed in this position, but they slept with their weapons and Tom did not bother with guards. The Parks' base at Marongora above the Zambezi Valley had four rooms in a row. Tom was in one, a Parks' ranger called Mike Court in the other and Tom's client, an American colonel in another. This colonel was a well-known gun writer for magazines like Guns and Ammo. While the colonel was cleaning his rifle, it went off. The bullet went through the wall, flashed through Tom's room and took out the mattress under Mike, as he was reading. Tom went ballistic and it was very embarrassing for this famous gun writer. Tom did not care if you were the Queen of England, he would tell you if you had done something wrong.

## *War Ending*

In 1980 the war was basically over, barring a few roaming, gun-toting criminals and Rhodesia was now becoming the new state of Zimbabwe. Tom was now very involved in hunting with Dan Landrey and spent much of his time in the Wankie area. Dan operated at Denda, Chewore, Ntundhla, Sengwa and Makuti. In the war, Dan would air-wing his way over these hunting areas and shoot up any suspicious people with the mounted machine guns on his Cessna gunship (some other pilots did the same). Dan flew much of the time and avoided driving though the extremely dangerous hunting areas. Denda had its fair share of police and army visiting the camp during the war, but Dan did not try to make too much of a big deal about the conflict. There were incidents, but everyone continued with his job. In the Matetsi he was actually quite safe, as the Communist fighters had made it a no go fighting area where he was. They wanted to use the area as a route into the country and never hit Denda, hoping the army would stay away. Dan was also regarded as an operator that treated his black staff better than most. Unbeknown to Dan, the Communist fighters would get food from the staff. Dan was an experienced hunter, having shot hundreds if not thousands of buffalo and other game. Hunting in the Matetsi district had its risks. Eddie Cooper, who was working for Fanie Pretorius, hit a mine with his clients and seriously damaged his legs, the veld caught fire and the land rover was a write off. Another hunter working for Fanie, named Edwards, was ambushed along the old main Kazungula road and shot in his stomach and he died with his tracker. It actually got so bad that some operators gave up hunting. Later when the war was over many of the ZIPRA communist fighters were in the process of being disbanded. These men, whose leader was Joshua Nkomo stayed at the Gwaai copper mine, which had previously closed down due to the low world copper prices. While Tom was in the area he had trouble when there

*Gerhard Bolt with 65 pounder and Douglas Khumalo on right*
*PHOTO Bolt family*

was an attempt to call in ZIPRA to shoot him, Douglas and his other worker named Kastel. They had been labelled sell outs and the situation needed to be defused. Douglas got help from Dabengwa who was high up in ZIPRA and he came down and told them to leave the old man alone. Many of these men were not happy with the Mugabe run government and approached Tom, asking him to help them overthrow the government, but Tom told them it was not a good idea.

## Gerhard Bolt

Gerhard was in the South African navy and was doing some work on the sunken ferry at Kazungula, which went between Botswana and Zambia. This ferry was sunk in the Rhodesian war and Kazungula was the spot where four countries met and was quite a sizzling spot for military activity. Don Price was in the Rhodesian army on the Rhodesian side and on active duty there, looking for communists to snipe at with his 30.06 rifle. He saw Gerhard on the just raised ferry in his diving gear, after having just come up. Gerhard looked like an East German and Don had him in his scope sights and was about to shoot him, when Gerhard went back under the water. Later Tom met Gerhard, Johan and Oupa (Gerhard's father) when they came up to hunt in the Matetsi and Tom was the pro hunter. They were to hunt at Ngamo, where they shot a 65-pound elephant. In 1979 Tom was to take a large 80-pound tusked elephant, while hunting with another client in the Zambezi valley. Anyway, one day, down near Mana Pools in the lower Zambezi, Tom was hunting with Gerhard, Johan and Oupa. They came across a land cruiser parked in the road, obviously in trouble and stopped to help Don Price and his client. Don recognized Gerhard as the man he nearly shot at Kazungula and the two, now meeting for the first time, struck up a great friendship. While Gerhard was hunting in the valley, he walked off to do a sit down toilet in an animal pathway, while the tracker ambled out of range down the path. Gerhard pulled down his overalls to his feet and settled down to relieve himself. Suddenly the tracker came fleeing past with a black rhino after him. Gerhard had little time to escape and from his relaxing position, lurched into a small tree, naked and with his overalls around his heels. The rhino thundered down the path, ran straight through his toilet and splattered it all over Gerhard's beautiful .470 Westley Richards rifle.

## *The Gwaai*

While Tom hunted in the Gwaai valley, he mixed with Stuart Campbell (who Tom stayed with for awhile), Tom Fulton and Clive Lennox. Stuart had the habit of walking around in nothing but his underpants. Tom had two apprentices working under him at the time, this being the bearded Ian Lennox and Paddy Curtis who was called Bloodnut (because of his hair colour). The youngsters had to spend their time in the bush all day and really wanted to sneak away for the weekend to civilization, to enjoy themselves. Tom would not allow it and they had to go and learn about animal tracks etc. They were told to stay in the camp and pay attention and listen to him, which was not really to their liking. While Tom was at Intundhla one of them went off to buy veggies for the hunting camp. Instead of doing the shopping though, he had wonderful booze up on the money and had a great time. Tom was furious when his appy returned with no money and no supplies. Paddy's casual character was seen at the Gwaai pub when he was seen without shoes and asked, "Where have you been?" He answered, "I have just been chasing elephants. I had slops on and lost them in the hunt." Ian and Paddy were said to have also shot a kudu at Ngamo and by chance, both shot a horn off the animal with their two shots. On one occasion Clive Lennox, Trevor Lane and Ian Lennox were bogged down in the mud flats at Ngamo. They managed to get filthy while trying to get their vehicle out. Later they came to the railway line and hitched a ride on one of the little railway trolleys. As they were heading down the railway line, they saw Tom driving down one of the firebreak roads with his two clients. All three men jumped off the trolley, looking really dirty, scruffy and armed to the teeth. They then burst through the long thatching grass by the road and jumped into the road, waving Tom down with their guns. The two clients' eyes went wide as saucers, as it appeared that some armed rebels were on the rampage. Tom's diary comments were, "Ian, Clive, Trevor bogged on flats. Submarine needed".

*Forestry*
Tom did not like the look of the scruffy young hunters who worked in the area. He used to reprimand the Forestry Commission youngsters for drinking and having a wild time, and his advice was, "don't be drinking beers and smoking cigarettes in the bars", which they obviously ignored. The Waterbucks Head pub at Main Camp was one of the drinking holes in the district and was frequented by the likes of Barney O'Hara, the pilot with nine lives and Mark Butcher. Some of the youngsters caused havoc here once, when they drank too many beers and stripped off their clothes. The Forestry guys were a wild young bunch and they contrasted to Tom's older regimental disciplined way of life. They would go to the Gwaai Hotel and drink for days. Two of the young men in the district once got really drunk and went down the main road. It appears one wanted to visit a really good looking girl down the way. On route they decided to have a rest and bedded down on the tarmac. A big truck ran over one of them and he groaned in agony, but was lucky to still be alive. His accomplice panicked, thinking his friend was being attacked by a lion. He took refuge in a tree and stayed there the night, while his mate moaned nearby. Many of these men worked hard in the introduction of game to the Forestry areas and worked hand in hand with Trevor Lane in bringing the game back to the Gwaai valley. Trevor Lane was an unrecognized hero of wildlife, converting the extensive forest areas of Sikumi and Ngamo to wildlife land. Nothing used to get into these areas before, as Parks and Forestry would shoot anything that came along the borders. A gentleman Forester named Farquar, brought Trevor Lane to Buck de Vries when Trevor was a young man. He told Buck, "I am hoping to make this guy the game manager in Forestry"

and Trevor lived up to expectations a few years later. He did a great deal of wheeling and dealing, as did many of the Forestry staff, to get water into areas where there wasn't any. New boreholes and pumps were installed, with the key to Trevor's wildlife plan being water and game capture. Trevor was responsible for bringing in a tremendous amount of game and white rhino were introduced, with many other species of large game. Animals also moved into Forestry from neighbouring farms. The intention was to use these areas for hunting and Trevor built up Ngamo safaris, which was to become one of the biggest hunting operators in the country.

### *Buck*

Buck de Vries who was ranching in the Gwaai, used to buy most of the game caught in Wankie in later years and most of the young elephants. Those were the days of Willie de Beer, Norman Payne, Cliff Freeman, Clem Coetsee and Willie Koen. Over many years, Buck exported about 1800 elephant babies to places like Dallas Fort Worth, Germany and as far as Russia and Brazil. The main buyers were the Hunt brothers - wealthy men, who at one time tried to buy up all the silver in the world, but the price of silver dropped. These men had an international wildlife park at Grand Prairie in Texas. Forty to Sixty elephant at a time would be sent there. Arthur Jones, who was well known for his nautilus exercise machinery, also bought about 80 elephant at one time. More than half the elephant in the Presidential herd around Sikumi came from Buck. They were too big to load on the plane to fly out of Africa and were, as a result, released. Almost every year for about 27 years, they released elephant that later made up a part of the 'tamish' Presidential herd, who would often touch people on game drives. The antelopes Buck bought were to restock his shot out property. He bought sable caught at Tshabalala and the Matopos, which were all skin and bones and covered with ticks. Some folk in Parks were not impressed with Buck having brought in these sables, as they thought they might contaminate the genes of the local sable and reduce the horn size. However, Buck was not concerned by the argument for long horned sable, half sables or thoroughbred sables. It turned out that many of the sable in the Matopos had originally been brought down from Wankie years before. Impala were brought from Mana and the Gona-re-Zhou; Buffalo came from Wankie and some from Buffalo Range. In the 1960's, the Buffalo Range buffalo were removed due to the foot and

*Hunters dining in camp, Gerhard Bolt, Tom, Don Price, Litty Price, Oupa Bolt*

mouth disease and were in a designated red zone. Buck bought the buffalo, which in later years built up into the thousands. Tom was to do some work for Buck (African name was Chikwatula, the one who beats). Buck was also credited for inventing the 'Gwaai clock'. One day his workers asked him what time they could knock off work, as it was going to be dark soon. Buck threw a stone up in the air and told them that when they threw a stone up and could not see the stone anymore at the top of its flight, then it was time to stop work!

## *Odd Clients*
Tom was freelancing with Peter Johnstone in the war years near the Victoria Falls. Peter had a beautiful hunting camp, with barbwire and an electric fence to keep out the communists. Many of the clients were not aware of the dangers before coming out to hunt. You had to be in camp by 5pm for safety and wear a pistol when you went to the toilet. One day while Peter took a client hunting, Tom took the two daughters out. Now these two ladies were extremely fat and obese. When they arrived back at camp to everyone's surprise, they both made a mad sprint for the toilet. They had been too scared to go to the toilet while out in the bush. Hunting clients come in all shapes and

sizes, nationalities and characters. Hunting elephant in the Gwaai, Tom had his 85 year old 'slow shot' client and then he had the ones shaking with fear. On one instance, Tom had a rich young American come out to hunt with him and this man did not seem to have everything together. One day they were out in the bush and Tom was admiring the scenery. The man commented, "You have nice grass here". Tom replied, "Yes I suppose we have", thinking the man was talking about ecological things. The man then went into a talk on the niceties of marijuana from this part of Africa, grass being another word for the drug. Tom eventually worked out what the man was saying and gave the youngster a stern dressing down. It was some time later that Tom met this same American hunter. He had taken Tom's advice, was now cleaned up and had a nice girlfriend. While Tom hunted at Intundhla at the Gwaai, Trevor Lane remembers him doing a 21-day warthog hunt. The client had a crook in his head and was drinking double vodka from 5.30 in the morning. In this whole period, he only shot one warthog along the railway line. In the same area, Tom left his vehicle and went off with his client to hunt on foot on the Ngamo flats. He left Betty, the client's wife, in the vehicle. Just as they were stalking a herd of sable and about to shoot a good bull, she fired a shot with Tom's revolver, to call them back (Tom's emergency signal). The men ran back to find her weeping, as she was afraid of being alone and she had to be left in camp after that. Some clients are trigger-happy and are more dangerous than the wild animals and you might even find them shooting you in their excitement. Tom found a sable bull, which his clients insisted was good. The very excited Rudolfo shot and wounded it and his father Ortica snatched the rifle from him. Soon there was an argument as to who would shoot next and after lots of shooting, the animal finally collapsed and the horns were only a small 37.5 inches a side.

## *Baboon Dung*

Tom enjoyed telling a story of a particular leopard hunt. A professional hunter built this beautiful tree platform, like they do in India for shooting a leopard. It was a well-prepared masterpiece, with its screened sided and exposed roof and it was against the side of a big tree. The Professional Hunter and client sat there for two nights with no luck. On the third night, a troop of baboons had roosted in the tree above them, which is normal, as they often change places. In the early morning as the sun was lighting things up, the leopard came and the client fired his rifle. The loud gunshot was surprisingly followed by sounds in the big tree above them. The noises increased and the volume went up, as the baboons panicked. When this happens baboons can begin to excrete a brown liquid and on this occasion it came raining down on the surprised humans, who vacated at great speed and little ceremony. I am not sure if they ever got the leopard.

## *Dangers*

Many clients did not like working and walking for their elephants and it was at times dangerous. This was shown when Tim Wellington was killed in October 1979. He was a senior ranger and was tracking a wounded elephant with Clem Coetsee, when they were separated. The elephant enraged by its wounds it had received from safari hunters, suddenly ambushed and charged Tim. Tim managed to fire two shots with his rifle before the elephant seized him. The elephant then threw him on the ground and crushed his chest. Clem arrived a few minutes later and followed the elephant, which he then killed. Buffalos are often regarded as being the most dangerous animals to hunt. Tom's client Phillip shot one 12 times at Chirundu and Tom finally put the buffalo down a few feet from him. At Ngamo, it took Tom and his client 10 rounds to bring one down due to bad reloads. There was a hunt, which I think took place in the Zambezi valley or Chirisa. I am not sure if Tom was involved, but he used to talk about how this particular hunt went wrong. The buffalo bull charged over the client who ended up underneath and in passing over the man, the bull's crown jewels smashed the man's spectacles.

## *Herman*

I will take you on a quick buffalo hunt with Tom and Herman the German (real name). Tommy would normally go through a ritual when he took a client to the firing range. He would put up a target and then have the client fill the magazine and shoot as fast as he could at the target. The client did not have to hit it as Tom only wanted to see if the magazine jammed, or if the rifle action worked smoothly. Herman the German had a brand new 9.3 by 74 Mahillon, with gold engraving. It was a beautiful rifle and the German knew how to use it. He had hunted in East Africa and so already had some good trophies. Tommy was so enamoured with the rifle that he forgot to go through the usual ritual with the client. They went after buffalo that day and started to track down three bulls. They finally caught up with these tough old

*Tom after hyena hunt during war years*

bulls and followed them across a dry riverbed to the other side. The tracks went into some thick grass under an albida thorn tree and the men were sure that the buffalo were in there. Tommy set the client up to shoot should anything good come out of the grass, and then walked to the side and threw a stick into the tall grass. A black rhino exploded out of the grass and charged straight for them. The client and Tommy were in a wild panic, jumped over a four-foot embankment and hid in the riverbed. The rhino was mad and frustrated and was horning the ground above their heads, making strange noises. It was so close that when the rhino looked across the sandy riverbed, they could see into its nostrils, only feet above their heads. After this drama they continued on until they caught up with the bulls, which by this time were grazing up a steep hill, covered with small pebbles. They circled around and as the buffalos came over the top of the hill, the German shot the one bull through the shoulder and lunged it. Tom took a shot and was to also belt it in the lungs. It turned and came charging down the hill towards them without a moment's hesitation. Herman and the gang took to their heels as Herman's weapon had a jam. Tommy heard a gun being thrown onto the ground behind him and many German expletives. He heard some shattering, but he had his hands full with a charging buffalo. With his .458 Winchester, Tom coolly and calmly put another four rounds into the chest of the buffalo, before it fell only paces away. The German had lost all his ammo when he had tried to reload quickly, as the magazine had fallen open. He was cursing and telling Tommy, how he was going to go back to Belgium and wrap this Mahillon around the manufacturer's neck. Tom's response was, "No, no. It's not the manufacturers fault... it's my fault. I should have had you do some quick shooting... like I usually do, but I was foxed by the beauty of the gun."

## *Honeymoon*

Tom worked in a managerial position for Ian Piercy of Zambezi Hunters in the Zambezi Valley and was accompanied by Paddy Curtis and Ian Lennox. They were all based at D Camp, where Tommy and his young Professional Hunters were entertaining an Italian couple on their honeymoon, plus a young German booking agent. Tommy, I believe was looking after the agent, while Paddy and Ian were hunting the honeymooners. Ian Piercy was very efficient in the recovery and usage of the carcasses from hunts and there was little wastage. Tommy and the German had shot a big buffalo and in an attempt to protect the meat from staff and hyenas, Tommy hung the entire buffalo in the centre of the camp. After everyone retired to bed and things were progressing in the honeymoon tent, a pride of lion arrived, attracted by the buffalo carcass. Of course, the noise was horrendous and the Italians and the German agent were terrified half to death. Tommy jumped into his vehicle and with Ian and Paddy, tried desperately to chase the lions from the camp, but to no avail. The Italian woman screamed most of the night, as she thought she was surely going to be eaten by the lions. Early the following morning, when the lions had departed, a very irate husband demanded that he and his young bride be taken to Makuti, so Ian Piercy could take them away, as Africa was far too dangerous a place for a honeymoon! On one of Tom's hunts, his client shot a 21-inch impala. Three lionesses unexpectedly appeared, caught the wounded animal and disputed the kill with them. After eating half of the trophy, the lions left Tom and his client with the other half for stew.

## *Baboon Biltong*

While Tom was hunting in the Zambezi valley, he would shake his head at times when he saw what his apprentices got up to. If they were not chasing elephants between concession areas, they were up to something else. One day one of them shot a kudu, but it was technically illegal, as it was shot in the Nyakasanga instead of the Sapi hunting area. When Tom found out, he got to work on the meat making some biltong. About a week later a group of about six white and black policemen and Parks' staff, turned up in a boat from Chirundu, with the intention of getting them in trouble. Tom was very hospitable and welcomed them all with a box full of biltong and they were happy saying, "nice, nice" They asked, "What type of biltong is that one?" Tom's reply, "It's mixed up man." He took photos of them gladly receiving the biltong. Later back at their base, they had been eating for a few days and reached the bottom of the biltong box to see a picture of a baboon (Tom had mixed baboon biltong in with the kudu). They asked Tom about the baboon biltong and Tom said, "There's no problem. You can eat it, it is nice." Later when the police were asked, "Where is your evidence?" they replied that they did not have any, as they had eaten it. Not only this, but Tom had photographed them in the act of receiving stolen goods, so they had to drop the case. Tom was not always nasty to the police. In the late 1970's near Wankie, a policeman became a bit too tipsy and crashed his vehicle. Tom being the first on the scene felt sorry for him and doctored the vehicle so that it looked like a mechanical, rather than a human cause and kept him from getting into trouble.

*Zambezi Valley tuskless cow in full charge PHOTO Zack Moore*

*Richard de Angelo with 26+ lion 1986, PHOTO Richard de Angelo*

## CHAPTER 18
# THE QUIET YEARS 1982-1986

*Veterinary*

In 1982, Tom went to work for the Veterinary department in Bulawayo as an inspector and transport officer. Later he moved to Harare (which he didn't like), where he looked after cattle and sheep and got hooked on full cream milk. Tom was a capable handyman and did a variety of tasks in veterinary, from building dips, to collecting small carnivores for rabies tests. Tom had a reputation as a poisoner of predators in veterinary and helped Chris Foggin a great deal, when Chris was doing his PhD on rabies in the early 80's. Tom gave him information and the kit to make his own "coyote-getter" cartridges as they called it and details on how to make "smelly bait". The staff he worked with were abusing the transport in veterinary at this time, with drums of fuel disappearing and vehicles doing only 2 miles a gallon. When Tom tried to stop this, he became very unpopular and there were accusations of racial abuse thrown at him. With a fellow worker Alan Shaw, he found they could build cattle dips on the Shashi, five times cheaper than the contractors were charging the government. The corruption and the racial situation were too much for Tom, who started

*13'4" crocodile lower Zambezi with James Lapinsky*

to look for work elsewhere.

### Dissident

It was about 1983 that Alan Savory sold his Gumela farm. After the war Tom had represented Savory and leased out Gumela farm to ZIPRA nationalist leaders. In early 1982, security forces raided four farms occupied by former ZIPRA (i.e., ZAPU guerrilla army) fighters, where arms caches containing rifles, machine guns, mortars, rocket-propelled grenades and cases of ammunition were found. One of the farms on which arms caches were found was Gumela, where four drums of AK bullets had been hidden near the sheep shed. The result of this was the sacking of Joshua Nkomo from the government in February 1982, with all of his ZAPU allies. This was Zimbabwe's first treason trial, in which Tom had to be a witness and nearly found himself in serious trouble. ZAPU leaders Dumiso Dabengwa, the Chief of Intelligence and the Deputy Commander of the newly established Zimbabwe National Army (ZNA) (who Tom regarded as a friend), and Lieutenant-General Lookout Masuku, were arrested and charged with treason. They were later acquitted, but rearrested and detained without charge until 1986. It was said that Lookout never came out of prison. Hundreds, if not thousands of ZIPRA fighters took to the bush and for many people this was the start of the 'Dissident' era. These fighters fought a guerrilla war in which tens of thousands died. Most were innocent victims of a ruthless genocide, perpetrated by some in the government. Tom saw the horrors of this genocide when visiting the Tsholotsho district in the rainy season. He found murdered babies washed out of termite mounds, where they had been previously deposited. On one occasion some men looking like dissidents knocked on Tom's door. Being possible trouble, Tom pointed his pistol at them and asked what they wanted. They said Joshua Nkomo wanted to borrow his cruiser and there was also a message from Joshua, asking if Tom could provide some white lion skins. It was in the Gukurundi (genocide era) and Tom had to be cautious. Tom being hard up at the time thought about it and then told them that if Joshua would supply 2 helicopters and 5 million, he would sort it out. Tom decided to do a reconnaissance in South Africa and went to look for the white lions there. After seeing the security used to protect these animals, Tom's response was, "yeee I will die here" and came back home. His plan had been to kill the lions and then tie them with ropes to the two helicopters. The choppers would then fly back to Zimbabwe with two lions dangling underneath on ropes. Nkomo had wanted the skins for magical or cultural reasons.

## *Liebigs*

In 1983, Tom spent some time working under Bob Gawler at section 8, on the huge Liebigs (Lemco) ranch near West Nicholson. Lemco was a fine ranch with its bushveld country and the odd towering, granite kopjes. The ranch was big enough to boast its own golf course and had a large complement of staff. The Brahman cattle were fine specimens and Tom used to feed some of the calves up at his house. Most of his ranch employment was with cattle, but there was still a little antipoaching work. Lemco still had a large amount of plains game and a good population of leopard. There were rumours that the managers hid some buffalo for a while, before they were discovered and then removed by the government for foot and mouth reasons. To help deal with poachers here; Tom used a necklace of sorts to scare some of the locals with his 'magic'.

## *Keeper & Jessie*

Keeper was a loving, big, half-breed, ridgeback dog. You could be sure that baboons would get chased away from the house, while the fox terrier gave a supporting yap. Keeper would always try and climb on Tom's double bed and pretend he was one of the smaller fox terriers and in the process he would almost push you off the bed. He had one trade trick in his younger days at Lemco. This was to pee on people. Every morning he would go around and pee on various objects to mark his territory. If there were any newcomers he would walk up behind them, cock his leg and pee on their legs. All the staff used to keep quiet and wait for newcomers to be peed on, so they could have

*Tom and client with scoff box*

a good laugh. On one occasion one of the big bosses came over from the UK. This man was given the same treatment as everyone else, much to Tom's embarrassment. The man took it well with a stiff upper lip and refused to show any emotion. While visiting Harare (Salisbury) at one time, Tom left his fox terrier Jessie in his cruiser. The window was left open so the dog could get some air. Some money was left on the seat. Unbeknown to a loitering thief, who happened to look in at the money, there was also a dog there. The thief placed his hand through the window and his groping fingers were mauled. The man made a strategic retreat to a nearby alleyway. When Tom came back he could see that there had been an attempted robbery and called a nearby policeman. They then followed the blood trail into the alleyway, where the policeman grabbed the thief. The thief was unceremoniously brought back to the scene of the crime. The policeman then shoved the man's face against the window opening and the man was bitten on his nose. Not a good day for the criminal.

## *Medicine*
Being into non-conventional medicines Tom used to stop at Milbrow in Bulawayo for medicines and talk over a cup of tea. Tom used their veterinary medicines for himself, the dogs and his staff. Tom often told the delightful story of how he saved a man from snakebite

poisoning. He used a cattle prodder on a man who was suffering from snakebite. Tommy pulled down his pants, placed it on his behind and gave him a large zap of electricity. The man ascended into a vertical and running position with much sound and did not stop until he was way down the road. Tom had used this treatment on various occasions and found it extremely successful. He also treated a man who claimed to be sick, but who was just trying to get off work. The guy didn't want to work and so Tom gave him a jolt, which helped him to recover. Another common treatment was to give people simple pain killing disprins for what they thought were major problems. They would soon recover showing a lot of it was only in the mind. Speaking to Clem Coetsee in a letter in later years after Clem's success in moving whole herds of elephant, he says, "Congratulations on your world record! Glad my "snake bite" prodder arrived to be of some help. Please put it into your box of tricks for future use! The heat must have been hell! Very hot up here too."

## *West Nic*

In 1983, the Lowveld was hit by a bad drought. Lemco had to sell their cattle and Tom was laid off as a manager on section 8. Tom now spent much of the early to mid 1980's working in the West Nicholson area, which he used as a hunting base with a little ranching on the side. He worked with various folk and on different ranches over these years, with Ralph Ferreira, Sam Levy, Dudley Rogers, Basil Steyn, Ken Drummond and Clive Lennox. One of the ranchers asked Tom to move on, as Tom was critical of his senseless slaughter of wild animals for fun. With Ralph, Tom lived at Highway ranch, where he had a good pot of stew for any visitors coming around. His hunting trips took him up to his old haunts of the Matetsi and the Gwaai. Tom spent a lot of time on Tshabezi, which was owned by Dudley and bordered on the timeless Todd's hotel. At one time at Todd's hotel there was a terrible drought and Mary Richardson left a paraffin tin out for the tame giraffe. The giraffe came to drink the water in it and caught the tin on its head. A tourist from South Africa helped Mary to get the tin off the giraffe's head. When his boss heard this story of a giraffe with a tin on its head, he thought his employee was going insane and nearly fired him. Tom often visited this hotel for a cup of tea or the odd party. At one time it was a popular stop over for South African travellers.

## *Kitted Out*

From West Nicholson Tom began to roam far and wide as a freelance professional hunter. Tommy was a notorious perfectionist and paid much attention to detail. Before heading out on a hunt or anywhere, he was armed to the teeth with spares, tools and gadgets. He had special chucks, a stump that he put under the axle in case the jack lets go and a whole tyre patching kit with tyre irons and all. Using the hilift jack, tyres were dismantled, repaired and put back together in no time. The vehicle would be checked every day methodically, oil, water, tyre pressure and he would be habitually under his cruiser greasing all the nipples or draining oil. Guns were oiled and I would say caressed at the end of a day's use. On the hunts, there were noise proof water bottles and a daypack with a garden spray bottle (in case the client gets too hot and needs cooling off), a first aid kit, towel, a skinning knife and a bottle of wood ash. Tom was a firm believer in ash and shooting sticks and he wouldn't hunt without them. When the wind is blowing steadily, it swirls and when you are getting in close to an elephant, you have to know when it's going to turn, to see if it is going to smell you. It was always fun watching which way the wind blowed and it helped one to approach the hunted animal. Kicking the ground or smoking cigarettes Hollywood style, was not Tom's way to see how the wind was blowing. He preferred mopane wood and all ash was sifted, while household powders were a no, no. Metal and wooden padlocked boxes would fill Tom's house and often when opened, there was a list of all the contents pasted on the lid of the box. The toolbox was tightly packed and few knew how to repack the boxes afterwards. If you needed some wire, a bolt or anything, he had it. If you were in the middle of nowhere, he had what you wanted and through experience, he was ready for any breakdown. Tom by this time had reckoned that one had to sleep with an army coat and woollen cap to stop heat loss and he would always be found with a beanie in his bed.

## *Gwaai*

There was very little in the way of tourism in the Gwaai valley until about 1987. Tourism was still recovering from the war and the anti government dissidents were roaming parts of Matabeleland. Some tourists were killed and people used to travel in convoys from the Gwaai hotel in the mid eighties. Tom's advice to the Forestry staff was, "keep your head down and your powder dry". Tom had a little

*Tshabezi ranch West Nicholson 1980's*

.22 pistol that he said was part of his snakebite kit and for 'little devils' in the night. Tom tried his hand at photographic safaris and worked a bit for Chris van Wyk, who ranched at Kana block in the Gwaai valley. Chris was one of the first to start doing safaris in Wankie at this time. Tom told Chris that once you get into the middle of a buffalo herd, they would accept you almost as one of their own. Chris decided he was going to test this idea. Using a termite mound and bushes, he managed to sneak into the middle of a herd. The experiment was very successful as the curious herd of buffalo began to crowd around him and began to stare at him. They were not even running away and they came right up to him. Lying on the ground, Chris found himself within 5-10 meters of the buffalo and he started to get a bit uncomfortable. It ended up with Chris desperately trying to 'shoo', his new found, dangerous friends away. When Richard Amyot was a student, he met Tom in the Gwaai valley at Kana block. Tom would force Rich to carry his Ruger mini 14 around in case of snakes. While here they would sit around a campfire, listen to Tom's stories and have long discussions on the meaning of life.

## *Wankie Tours*
One of Tom's dreams at this stage was to restart donkey safaris, something he was to never repeat. When Rob Hopkins asked Tom

*Crossing Nuanetsi River in 1980's*

about the lions eating the donkeys, Tom replied, "well you've got tourists and they want to see lions!" In the early 80's, Tom brought some clients to Wankie. It seems they had been brought all the way up from Cape Town in his long wheel base land cruiser. Rob Hopkins and his wife arrived at the Ngweshla picnic site and Tom arrived with the clients a few minutes after them. Tom was going to camp for the night with his clients. A very excited camp attendant indicated to them that there had been a lion kill right against the low wire fence, surrounding the small campsite. The Hopkins settled down for a rest, while Tom went about setting up his little camp for his clients. Rob was to go back to Main Camp where he was staying. While Rob was having some lunch with his wife, another safari vehicle turned up with a fresh-faced youngster and some clients, obviously new to this sort of thing. Tom sauntered up to this raw recruit and spoke to him, obviously up to mischief. He told the young man that the best place to camp would be right over there, against the fence. Unknown to the youngster was the presence of the unfinished lion kill, which was only a few metres away. So off the youngster took his American clients and put up his tents against the small fence. Tom had a choice position under some camel thorns a little further away. Next morning Rob saw the youngster at Main Camp. His eyes were wide like saucers and he said to Rob, "I never slept a wink last night; the lions were performing right outside the camp." After this Rob saw Tom and asked him what happened and Tom laughed. The young man had run up to Tom in the night saying, "Mr. Orford the lions are there." Tom replied, "what do you expect man!"

## *Dudley*

Tom worked for and became Dudley Roger's tutor for about two years. He did a few hunts with Dudley who was just starting out. Dudley got some of the highest marks when he did his licence and gave Tom credit. Tom was a good, but reluctant hunter and inflexible when it came to anything close to breaking Parks' rules. This was even to the point of not using spotlights on private land, which he treated like Parks' land and yet it was perfectly legal. He had a strong conscience and did not want to do anything he thought was unethical. He could be difficult and Dudley often felt like grabbing him by the throat, shaking him and saying, "Tommy let go man". He was a dramatic and colourful warden from beginning to end, taking a stand. In trying to teach Dudley one day, he was enthusiastically demonstrating rapid action fire and he kept putting the stock into his shoulder and jabbering away about how it was done. Then in lowering the stock, he tore off his pocket and there was a strong silence. He was trying to demonstrate the superiority of peep sites, something he did manage to convince many people to use over the years.

## *Piers*

Tom hunted with Piers Taylor in the 80's doing a few buffalo hunts. Tom regarded Piers as one of the best and cleanest operators in Africa. Tom was not an easy employee and was not too interested in trophy sizes, very set in his ways and normally wanted things his own way. He always had a jacked up camp and a fox terrier present. He loved using his carbide lamps, which were old miners' lamps. These worked by the addition of carbide and water and produced a surprisingly large amount of light. With Piers Tom insisted on taking his fox terrier on hunts. It did not matter if it was a 10-day hunt or a 3-day hunt, Tom would have his servant and his fox terrier. One client had to put up with the foxy sitting on his lap and peeping out the car window, while they bumbled around looking for game. The client was too polite to complain. After hearing the client's complaint about the fox terrier from Piers, Tom's reply was, "if the client doesn't want my dog he doesn't want me."

## *Buffalo*

Up at Matetsi while working for Piers, Tom's client wounded a buffalo and in the follow up, they shot another by mistake. Unfortunately, one had only one horn and Tom had to explain to Parks what happened. Being a professional hunter it was very embarrassing and it was worse as Parks had to investigate the incident. Trackers were sent to study the crime scene, but liked Tom so much that they went out of their way to prove him innocent in the matter. Meanwhile Tom was squirming as the investigation was going on, as he did not have much money at the time. He had once been the investigator, but now he was on the receiving end. Parks let him off when they realized it was a mistake. Tom had this to say about another one horned buffalo hunt. "I had a doctor from Cairo who I crept up to this fallen mopane tree, with three buffalo bulls on the other side. Two were lying down and the one was standing, but it was missing a horn. I tell him be sure and shoot the one lying down on the right. He is so nervous that I whisper to him to relax. There is no way the buffalo can get us and besides, they didn't even know we were there. Suddenly he shoots and then throws his rifle down and starts to crawl away. My tracker grabs him by the foot and he starts screaming ... the other leg and the two hands are still crawling. 'They are going to kill me!' he is screaming and meanwhile the buffalo have all run away. I see the one bull fall dead and we all go up to look at it. He has managed to shoot the one missing a horn. He threatens to get me fired as I had him shoot the wrong one. He had lost face, a trophy and our respect."

## *Blinds*

Leopard and lion blinds can be a good source of amusement for hunters and then there was always the danger of a hunter being 'kissed' by a leopard. On one occasion, seven people were injured in a leopard hunt in the Gwaai valley, either shooting each other in the melee, or getting a bite or two for their efforts. Tom told a story about some hunters building a lion blind out of thatching grass near Binga. They had killed a warthog and tied it to a tree. During twilight, some bush pigs came and started to eat the warthog. Then a lioness came charging in and tried to catch one of the pigs. The pig she was after took off straight towards the blind with the lioness in hot pursuit. The pig ran straight into the blind and then the lioness came in after it. Two National Parks observers sitting on chairs, a Professional Hunter and the client were all mixed up with a fleeing pig and a lioness. Shots were fired and there were arms, legs and chairs, flying thatch and amazingly, no one was hurt.

## *Officials*

In the early 1980's it often happened that gun toting, half-drunken, government officials, would stop people. Tom often spoke of his tricks in moving things in his vehicle around the country, through the multitude of irritating roadblocks these officials set up. Tom would place things in rabies boxes, which had warning signs on and no one ever wanted to look in there. They would just wave him through, instead of harassing him like they did with other motorists. They would ask Tom the standard questions, "Where are you coming from?" "Cape town" was Tom's reply once. "Where are you going?" "Cairo." Without thinking about it the policeman said, "Have a good journey". Tom loved going to South Africa to see friends and to do his shopping. When he was in a long queue at immigration, there was a protracted wait and to speed things up, he offered to hold a lady's baby. He then gave the baby a painful tweak, which resulted in much howling. The immigration official could not handle the noise and whisked Tom, baby and the mother to the front of the queue, thinking Tom was the father. One of Tom's tricks to get through customs was to cover everything with dirt and oil and as the officials dressed in immaculate whites did not want to get dirty, so they would leave everything unchecked. One of them once tried to inspect and got his beautiful white clothes covered with oils and ended up very angry. In South Africa Tom proved to be a chronic jaywalker. A big white policeman came up to him and asked what he was doing breaking the law. Tom pleaded innocence, saying he was from Zimbabwe and that he did not know what a street light was. The policeman being a real gentleman, then explained to the ignorant Zimbabwean what a streetlight was and how they worked and then let him off.

## *Kobus*

In the 1980's, National Parks was doing a fair amount of elephant culling in Hwange Park and Tom helped with odd jobs at Shumba Camp. Clem Coetsee was the man in charge at the time and he was beginning to earn a reputation with his skill in game capture. Kobus du Toit who was a well-known wild life vet in South Africa had this to say about Tom. "I met Tommy Orford in a bookshop (Van

*Kobus du Toit with black rhino at Umtshibi 1980's PHOTO Kobus du Toit*

Schaik's) in Church Street in Pretoria 1984/5. He was browsing through books at the Wildlife section of the shelf. My first impression was that he was a Zimbabwean. He had a green sweater on with a cheetah if I remember correctly. I was very tempted to start a discussion with him and after about 10 minutes I asked him, 'Are you involved with wildlife in Zimbabwe?' He looked at me and nodded. After about five minutes, we found that we had much in common and went for a cup of coffee across the street. We had a long chat and he missed his lift, so I offered to take him home. He was staying with Gerhard Bolt of Jumbo Jack fame. My first impression of Tommy was that he was a typical management person and had bad experiences with research personnel in the wildlife fraternity. His most used phrase was probably, "Publish or perish". I was a third year veterinary student at Onderstepoort and completed a degree in Wildlife Management. I was then co-author of the book Wildplaasbestuur that was later translated in English. I gave him a copy and was then seen as part of "his camp". He did a lot of reading but his practical experience was remarkable. We became good friends and I went to visit him as a student when he was at West Nicholson. He never boasted about himself and money and material things were not important. Tommy introduced me to two persons that I will always remember; John Condy the well-known wildlife vet in Zimbabwe. He was involved with the moving of white rhinoceros from Natal to Zimbabwe. Tommy was one of the rangers involved in this introduction and was very proud of it. The other person was Clem Coetsee who was well known for his culling of elephant and capture of black rhino in the Zambezi Valley to save them from poachers. We went to visit him in Umtshibi in Wankie. I became very good friends with Clem and did elephant translocations from Gona-re-Zhou to South Africa. We introduced 200 elephants and the total transport distance was 80 000 km (twice around the world). This friendship was due to Tommy Orford and the introduction of adult elephant family groups resulted from my work with Clem."

*Elephant bull at Mana Pools on the Zambezi*

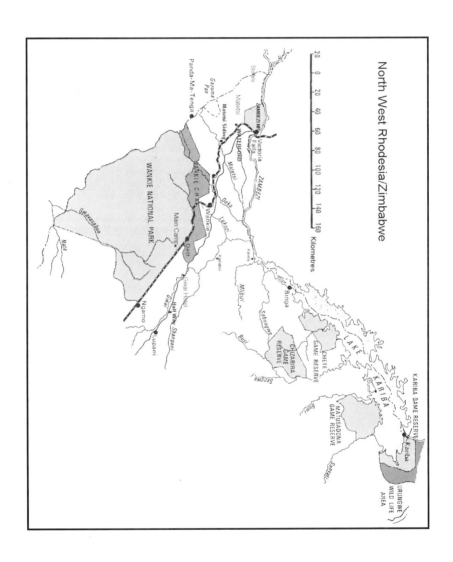

*Chura bull Matusadona*

## CHAPTER 19
# WATERFORD 1987-1994

*Moving North*

Alan Savory had given Tom shares in Waterford ranch close to the Victoria Falls airport and bordering on Fuller Forest. Waterford ranch had been leased out to the Greek Karesselos family of five brothers. On Waterford, they would corral their cattle every night and they would hunt the lions in the day. The Greeks (as many folk called them) got together in business in the 1960's, with garages and other businesses in Wankie town. Then they began to set up cattle ranches along the railway line up to the Falls. They stayed in Wankie and came out on weekends to their farms. Like many others, they were booted off their farms after the millennium. A new settler who arrived on their one farm hacked a back leg off one of their cows and he left it alive, while the cow tried to stand on its remaining three legs. Tom decided to move out from West Nicholson and make a go of Waterford, which needed to be fixed up, as the major shareholders had little interest in it. Before he began to look after the place, Alan

Sparrow, who was working for Forestry, took care of the place. He helped combine the hunting right of Fuller with those of Waterford and with some care; the game began to recover on these properties. Waterford had been overgrazed due to the presence of too many straying cattle from nearby villages and had little game. It took Alan about a year to clear out the cattle and about four years to get the game into a respectable condition. At first, the hunting quota was very small, but this began to grow with larger amounts of animals moving into the area. Waterford's small share of the quota was what Tom was to live on while he was living on the farm.

*New World*
The North West of Zimbabwe has Kalahari sands with forests of Teak, Mchibis, Mukwa and Manketti trees, all looming over small sandy roads that seem to go nowhere. The open vlei lines (a good example being Westwood) were excellent for game drives and bordered by towering camel thorns and elephant-broken Mangwe trees. In parts of Matetsi, thousands of pans are scattered in flats and hollows and some are large like Kazuma, while others dry up in days. In the rains, these pans fill up with water and ducks and are the lifeblood of buffalo, thirsty elephant, elusive leopards and roaming lions. The odd permanent pans often had a faithful, throbbing Lister engine and a tin hut nearby. These little huts would have two pump attendants in the dry season. They would keep each other sane in the middle of nowhere and help each other deal with the dangerous wild animals. Trenches were dug around the pump houses to give protection to the pipes, as elephant loved breaking them to access fresh water. The Matetsi/Deka region has hills and more hills, secret springs, klipspringers and great views (like the one at Sinamatella camp). In winter, there are the morning mists and cold winter nights. Some places see no humans in months and years. Signs are broken and trees are pushed over roads by elephant, until some roads disappear. In the north, the shining Zambezi meanders along, with its hippos, crocs, birds galore, islands, palms, makoros, natural jacuzzis and drinking elephant, down to the Victoria Falls (Falls). The gorges below the Falls have their still valleys and gravesites, limestone caves, sandy beaches and wild rapids. There is the cry of excitement as rafts go by and kayakers glide past and this is soon enveloped again by the daily silence. The Falls itself at this time was a going place and there was money to be made, with new ideas coming out on how to make it

*Steam train passes by Dibangombe homestead*

all the time. There were booze cruises, canoes dodging hippo, game drives, bungi jumping and many dramatic ways to die. There were always planes of various sizes and shapes and the noisy choppers. One old resident wanted to shoot them down, as he hated the noise so much. There were casinos and hotels, with some being glamorous and some gaudy, with the Victoria Falls hotel, Elephant Hills, Makasa, Safari Lodge and the Downtime disco. Then there was Sopers and the Morrisons, nearby the shoddy camping grounds, later fixed up by Rob Gee. Shearwater and Safari Par were in a perpetual war for supremacy, while the little minnow companies and irritating vendors, would try to get the rest of the business. Then there was the multitude of sun-bronzed ivory and ebony hunks in the form of river rafters, kayakers and the odd hunter. Most were either in safari kit or river gear and the Explorers bar was the focal point. The older generation was either at the Spray View or at the Boat Club with their families. Rob Gee was at the croc farm, Rob Francis at Shearwater, Brent Williamson and Clive Bradford on the river and Jay Gopal in his superette. These and many others made the Falls an interesting and dynamic place, before the millennium slump took business away to Zambia. This was Tom's world and after visiting the Falls, he would be off again into the forests and mopane trees, having seen friends, collected supplies and his mail.

## *Tented camp*

When visitors came to Waterford, they would be driven around to look at the hunting camp, springs, beautiful valleys and to admire the Dibangombe River. The hunting camp at Waterford was beautifully situated under some towering Albida trees (same as those at Mana Pools) with their hanging vines. Being on a flood plain it was washed away every rainy season. Thatching and the putting up of tents kept everyone occupied as the months of March and April came around. The bush shower always had its friendly Red Backed Toads hopping at your feet, when the shower was turned on. If you looked the other way, you could see the stars above. Before Tom moved into the old railway house, he spent some time in this camp. One year there was a plague of mice and one of the visitors found a little mouse gnawing through his hair, trying to get at his head as he slept.

## *Home*

Tom fixed up the old railway house at Dibangombie railway siding with its wide verandas. Roads and water points were made operational and the hunting camp kept in fine condition. The house was typical of those built along the railway and similar to his later house at Matetsi siding. It had a phone, but no electricity and used a donkey boiler to heat the water. Every evening as the sun was setting on the hills; the Coleman paraffin pressure lamps were brought out. These would bring light to the rooms and the radio was set up to listen to the daily BBC news broadcasts. Reading on the bed was his main pastime in the evenings and all the dogs would get into a comfortable spot next to him. Early the next morning the day would start with Peter Chauke bringing you tea, while you were still in bed. Good porridge would launch the day and all meals in the day were filling. If there wasn't hunting to do, then there were long antipoaching walks around the ranch, fixing things, relaxing or whatever would take up ones time. In fact it was a hillbilly sort of life and apart from the BBC; you had little contact with other people until you went to Victoria Falls. Tom's adopted son Bryan, spent a year or two with Tom and found himself very bushed and this took some years to wear off. The experience was valuable though and he learnt so much, as did many others who worked under Tom. Tom was often alone at Waterford and his phone was the only way he could share his thoughts and feelings. Chris Foggin remembers getting an excited phone-call unexpectedly from Matetsi. Tom had just been watching some painted dogs at sunset and

*Josiah, Keeper, Muffin, Albert at Matetsi*

talked about how peaceful it all was. It seemed he just wanted to share the experience with someone. When Tom visited a friend in Austria he found it so cold, he never wanted to leave the sublime climes of Africa again, saying, "I am a white African, born and raised in Africa. Africa is all I know. It is my home".

## *The Staff*

Peter was Tom's handyman and able to drive, fix cars, cook, clean, plumb, track, skin, hunt, do leatherwork and do almost anything you wanted him to do. He was from the Shangaan tribe in the south of the country. Tom preferred to employ Shangaans and regarded them as being the best employees amongst the various tribes in the nation. Peter was a skilled hunter in the traditional sense, having killed four leopards, using nothing more than dogs, spears and thorn bushes as shields. Tom had hunted bushpigs with spears and dogs, in a similar manner in his youth. The cheeky cook in the house was called Isaac and he used to get particularly bossy after having a drink. Being of Bushman stock meant he was short and he had a slightly yellowish skin. He was a good cook, making excellent bread and often chased Tom out of the kitchen. When Sue Thomas came to visit Tom, she was unceremonially bundled out of the kitchen by Isaac. He said to Tom, "Take this lady out. If she wants to cook, I will sit down." Sue asked Tom what he was saying. Tom replied to her, "get out, get out". Meat was normally obtainable on the ranch in the form of a Kudu, Warthog or something else. Bryan or Peter would head out and shoot for the pot and the biltong line. Tom did not like predators killing at Waterford, but was proud of the presence of Painted Dogs at the ranch. On one occasion, seven Painted Hunting Dogs killed a Kudu by the old farm buildings across the railway line. Tom ordered everyone to retrieve the carcass and after stealing it from the dogs, it was cut up for everyone to eat.

*Everyday Life*

There were many interesting things about Tom's unique everyday life. To practice shooting wild animals, he used to point and aim repeatedly, while reloading, at pictures in the room. Tom was also very conscious of safety with firearms, whether in a vehicle, building, or anywhere else. Behind the house he would set up at target using a cardboard box, tape and shoot at 25 yards. Shooting and sighting of weapons was very important to him and the dutiful cleaning of them at the end of the day. It was a social highlight at Tom's house to go to the edge of the little hill that the house was on and watch the passenger train as it passed early in the morning or evening. Often a visitor or member of staff would jump off the train. Gail Amyot would frequently pass by on the train on the way to the Falls and almost without fail, as the train wound its way through the hills at Dibangombie, she would see Painted Hunting Dogs running by the train. Tom was a dinosaur already at this time – set in his ways with medicines and the way he did his car. He had old-fashioned habits, but old-fashioned habits that worked. People would laugh, but the last laugh was on him, as he had things worked out.

**The Falls**

When Tom with his short wheel base land cruiser, arrived in town, his friends would often see it and say, "Tom's in town." He would be found walking around with his Zeiss binoculars covered with some leather, which he called a 'snot guard'. He would frequently visit Keith Meadows in Victoria Falls and Keith would enjoy the occasional Bombay Sapphire gin with Tom. Tom sometimes had the occasional whisky, loved poetry and especially the colonial poets like Kipling. Keith was a writer and so they had something in common. On one occasion, a famous actor paid a visit to the Victoria Falls

*Tom hunting in Austria*

(Clint Eastwood or Richard Burton) and he was ambling through the Rain Forest at the Falls. Tom happened to be there at the same time. He walked up to the actor and said, "Dr Livingstone I presume."

## *Travelling*

Tom had his odd jaunts off with his friends around the country. One Christmas the Amyots, Orfords and Harrisons decided to go on holiday together and Gail Amyot told a youngster named Grant, who came along, not to bring any heavy stuff. She did not want to overload the old 'grey lady' 1957 land rover. The trip was through Bumboosie, Sijarira (after getting lost and coming to Chete) and finally to Matusadona. The land rover began to give problems on the long journey. They stopped as it was battling along and Tom investigated to find Grant's weights hidden away in the land rover. Tom did not approve of Grant at this point and gave the good-looking guy, with big muscles a telling off. Grant had the last laugh, as he later became a rich pin-up model, did some acting and was frequently on well-known American magazines. At Matusadona, the walks produced black rhino and the famous Chura bull elephant, which had tusks of about 98 and 92 pounds aside. Tom's diary comment was that "Chura is superb", but the famous bull elephant was later killed in a fight with another bull. Tom also had a trip off to Mark Butcher's wedding in the south of Hwange National Park. This was what you would call a unique, white hunter's wedding. Tom drove the bridesmaids in his land cruiser, while the rough and tough hunting crowd wore their vellies (bush shoes) and bush clothes. One of the guests was well prepared and kept cool with his solar powered fan on his pith helmet. The bride's vehicle got a puncture and then it was found the spare was also flat. The ceremony took place under some magnificent camel thorn trees at Ngamo. While the magistrate gave the solemn words of the ceremony, Tom was taking pictures, tripped over a root and fell in front of everyone. Tom got up and everyone had a good laugh about it. Later just outside the park in the Tshlotsho communal area, at Mark's hunting camp there was a party and wedding speeches. Mark had provided the local villagers with booze and plenty of meat. When the villagers ran out and it was dark, some of them began to hover around the drunken makiwas (white men) like hyenas and began to steal the beers from the metal tubs. One was even trying to take a whole crate, when he was noticed, making it a truly memorable bush wedding.

## *Poachers*

Tom was very involved at times in trying to help fight against the organized poaching of rhino and elephant. He would often feed information to international wildlife groups on what was going on. He tried to get help for Parks to protect the ten or so rhino in the Kazuma area. He was particularly concerned about one particular bull, which had some large horns. When Gail Amyot was chairman of the wildlife society for some time, Tom was often there giving good input. The poaching network involved peoples of all races and included politicians, ex soldiers, businessmen, police and even members of National Parks. It was a murky world, in which some people would have 'accidents.' There was one Parks' warden at Matetsi, who was implicated in the poaching of rhino around the country. Tom decided to scare him and placed some hyena dung on the front seat of his vehicle. It appears he got a fright when he saw the dung as he was driving along and he went off the road and injured himself. Most of the gunmen involved in the actual shooting of the rhino and elephant were ex soldiers, who knew the rhino areas well. Apart from a number of Zimbabwean Nationals, there were also many Zambian poachers. At one time, in the 1980's, there was a virtual war in the country with these poachers and hundreds of people were killed, while many rhino were slaughtered. To help Parks, the Police Support Unit and the army would repeatedly help, using a shoot the poacher policy. While Tom was driving in the Zambezi Park one day, he bumped into one of these poachers, who was a small, bushman-like man, with beady eyes and who was carrying his AK47, bandolier and some hand grenades. Tom stopped to talk to him and offered him a lift, which the man declined. Tom later went and organized an ambush with a game scout, but was too late, as the man with about five others, escaped to Zambia in his blue rubber dinghy.

## *Contact*

A group of three poachers had been in Hwange Park for about a month poaching rhino. In a shootout, one poacher was shot and two escaped via Sinamatella, towards Zambia. After another contact, a poacher was wounded and was later killed near Pandamatenga. This left one who travelled up the railway line towards Victoria Falls. This armed poacher visited the pump attendant at Kalala in Fuller forest. Using his AK47, he relieved the man of his 5 kg roller meal, a black pot and lid. The pump boy ran across country 11 km to report to his headquarters. The police and Forest Protection Unit then began the search for the man and this was to take three days. They tracked the poacher close to the Waterford homestead through the rocky hills, until Peter and Albert Chauke, who were doing a recce, happened to see him. They saw the man carrying a load on his head and his weapon slung, muzzle down, under his arm. The two Chaukes pretended to be tracking and the poacher probably thought they were also poachers. Later on in the day, some police came out and Tom accompanied the three police in tracking the man down. Policeman Bhebe tracked the man at speed, with Tom by his side and the other policemen nearby. They tracked through the tall dense grass and brush for about 600 meters to some Mfuti trees, along the Dibangombie River. Bhebe saw the man in the shade and before he could do anything, the poacher started firing on automatic from about 20 meters. They were miraculously missed, a bullet hitting Bhebe's wooden butt and missing Tom by inches. About 10 bullets passed between Tom and Bhebe, in a space of about 6 inches over and around them. In the shooting that followed, the poacher ran, while Bhebe and Tom stood up. Tom had his rifle sights lined up on the middle of the man's back, but held his fire, as in the confusion he noticed the man had the same colour clothing as the police and Tom wasn't sure if it was a policeman or not. The professional poacher escaped and left 10 rhino horns behind, including those of a small calf. An air force helicopter (which Tom called a cyclone) left Binga to come and help, but went to Sinamatella by mistake. The poacher headed home to Zambia and was later picked up when he checked into a hospital in Vic Falls. A covered cockle-craft was found near Colin Lowe's farm in the Chundu loop area, which was probably the poacher's boat. In the court case, they lost all the exhibits, rhino horn etc. When the poacher was sentenced, he saluted Tom and asked him to tell Joshua Nkomo that he was there, showing he had some military background.

## *Campfire*

Tom made some money doing photographic safaris and the selling of captured sable and waterbuck antelope, but most of his income on Waterford was from hunting. Clem Coetsee was involved in the capture and the sables were so tame that they refused to be spooked by the helicopter. In Tom's diary we read, "Phone Clem about sable capture. Wickus at Nyamandhlovu. Clem injured shoulder by eland in crate." Tom also worked for a short period for Zimtrust in the Hwange district in the CAMPFIRE programme. Part of his job was dealing with problem animals. This involved dealing with crop raiding elephant, lions, porcupines, baboon, warthog and man-eating crocodiles. He was not too complimentary when someone from Parks tried to shoot a crop raiding elephant with 16 shots of an AK rifle. On one occasion, he did not want to shoot a large 60-pound elephant in a group of three bulls. Using his catapult, he chased the three bulls back into Hwange National Park. Tom would pay the odd visit to his old haunts in Hwange (Wankie) National Park and commented on the deterioration, the potholes and lack of dedication amongst some staff. A visit to Main Camp produced many complaints from him of roosters, trucks making noise and shooting. In his diary he says, "Terribly noisy, too many roosters, dogs yapping, noise from staff". When he spoke to the staff, they told a dismayed Tom that the roosters were their relish. On another occasion when visiting Main Camp he happily commented in his diary, "No roosters!" Parks were not the only government organization he went to war with. Tom was always in combat with the telephone companies and the railways. The phone could be down for days, while the snorting steam trains, would burn

*Tom, Steve Sitter's daughter, Big Boy, Peter PHOTO Steve Sitter*

half of Matetsi, as they rolled past. Tom once had to clear his vehicle with the Vehicle Inspection Department (V.I.D). In his diary he comments, "Arrange for V.I.D inspection 1400. All well, fat slug of senior vid asks if I drink (bribe!). Told him I have water, if he is thirsty. Another one says he would like to visit me at home. I asked why. What else but to scrounge meat."

## *Hunting*

When you arrived at the Falls airport to hunt with Tom, he and his trackers, Peter and Big Boy, would all appear and greet you with smiles, bear hugs and handshakes. The gear was loaded onto the short wheelbase land cruiser and you would be whisked off to the best sable-hunting region in Africa. After a brief stop in camp, it was time to hunt, with no time for a drink or a snack, as Tom said, "you ate on the plane and that should suffice till dinner." If you saw a good trophy on a rock-strewn hillside, after the trackers had thumped the back of the truck, it was time to scan with your binoculars. It could either get a thumb down, or some whistles and an excited talk in Ndebele. The stalk would be on with gear on backs, camera, rifles, shooting stick and water bottles. After an afternoon hunt, it was back to camp to a warm shower, dinner and the first of many long, fireside discussions. The talk would continue over the following days and be on all matter of things, through the long sunny days and late into the starry nights. There were the great debates mounted on all sides on proper bullet placement, bullet construction, hunts of the past and the future, philosophy and so on. There was not a subject or problem known to man that was not discussed with great oratorical splendour and passion. In the morning, you may be lucky to be awoken to tea laced with honey. The mornings were cold and so they ate breakfast by the fire. The guinea fowl were literally in herds, but proved to be very difficult to flush when hunting. The hunters would look like bird-bedecked Christmas trees, as they struggled back to camp with birds hanging on them. Tom was not the smack em, stack em, Toyota, safari type of Pro hunter that had become the norm. You did not hunt from a vehicle with him, but on foot. You did not ever think of shooting near or over water where game might drink. Moreover, please whatever you did, do not pull that trigger on any animal without letting him check and double check the animal. As a professional hunter, he was meticulous. Everything about the camp and vehicle had to be 100%, or he would bellow like a bull until it was done right. There was his way and then there was his way. He had done it all and he knew it all. He had a way with his words, a roguish Irish charm. When hunting with him, he was the boss and please, make no mistake about that. When the trail got too long, or maybe you lost your faith that the gap between the hunter and prey would not be breached, Tom would sense it. He would notice your failing spirit and one of his amazing stories of the old days would spew forth. These would never fail in renewing ones energies and spirit, leaving you with a smile. You could not help but be charmed and won over by him.

## *Trophies*

Wayne Grant did a bit of hunting at Waterford and found Tom did not like hunting and that he did it simply to earn money. Tom would rather look after the game than shoot them and Waterford was well run under his control, providing good hunting. On one 5-day hunt a 44-inch sable; 30-inch waterbuck and 42-inch buffalo were shot. Tom met Steve Sitter from Alaska and would hunt 14-day hunts with him and on one of these hunts with Steve; he appears to have shot only one buffalo. The men spent most of their time talking, eating, cleaning

Tom's truck and making biltong. When Martin Nel came to hunt at Waterford, Tom would say, "Where's the meat?" As soon as Martin shot a buffalo, he would then complain, "Why are you shooting my buffalo?" You could not win with Tom. On the ranch, Tom had a beautiful sable bull and contacted a hunter friend to come out to shoot it. As the client was all ready to come out, a lion came along and ate the sable. Tom was disappointed, but not defeated and got hold of a hunter friend who was interested in a lion. Just as the man was about to come out and everything was ready for the hunt, the lion was run over by a train. Trains were always hazardous to animals and porcupines were the main victims, as they tried to scurry along the line.

## *Lion*

One of Tom's later sayings was, "there are many old pilots, but there are very few old, bold pilots". If a lion were wounded on a hunt and hidden in thick bush, Tom would use a catapult and ball bearings to get it out. It was normally too dangerous to go in and the ball bearings or any item that made a good whirring noise, helped locate or flush the beasts. If a lion charged Tom, he preferred to wait for it in a kneeling position and would shoot it when it was about three meters away. Tom also believed in shooting charging buffalo close up. On lion hunting he said, "You must be brave" and he did not think building blinds was good lion hunting. He thought it was better to track them down and thought that most people were not brave enough to hunt lion. He told the trackers, "The lion must see you, so it is a proper war. Tom disliked the use of live baits for the hunting of the big cats. Tom told one young hunter, who was using live donkeys for lion up at Matetsi, it was not right and to please Tom, the youngster gave up on the idea. These donkeys at the end of the hunting season (that is those that hadn't been eaten) were released and would rush back to the communal lands. Back to Jambesi they would go, with relief that they had survived the hunting period. When Tom set up his lion and leopard baits of warthog or other meat, it was slung up to the right height on a tree and a blind was built nearby. Those who do not hunt, may not appreciate the technical detail and work that goes into, 'ambushing' big cats. Once everything is set up, the hunter and his client would often sit for hours, freezing and twiddling their thumbs, while mosquitoes like Marabou Storks gorged themselves with blood. To make life more interesting in these long waits, Tom would leave little bits of meat around to attract mongooses and small scavengers. One of his tricks to get a more enthusiastic cat at the bait was to use catnip oil, which he kept in a shampoo bottle. One night he had three baits hit by lion, after putting this attractant near the bait sites.

## *The Blind*
Tom had a wonderful way of telling stories about himself and making himself the object of the laughter. One of his stories he told was about when he set up a leopard blind and waited in the tree for the cat to arrive. His client sat quietly next to him. When the innocent looking leopard finally arrived, the client fired and missed the animal. The man got all excited and lifting his arms shoved Tom backwards. Tom promptly fell backwards out of the elevated blind, landing roughly on the ground. Sitting up he saw the surprised leopard staring at him not far away. Luckily the leopard bounded away, leaving the short, white hunter, lying on his back winded. On one incident, Tom was hunting with James Lapinsky and his tracker Peter. They placed bait for the lion up in a tree. The following morning he went with James and his staff to see if the lion had taken the bait. There were tracks of both hyena and lion. The men were happy to see the tracks and they waited in the hide that night. The lion turned up at about 7 pm and with Albert lighting the spotlight, Tom and the client fired at the lion. The client's shot went a little below the lung; while Tom's shot, which came shortly afterwards, was a complete miss. The lion made his departure and then went and hid in the long grass. Everyone then went to sleep with the intention of finishing the lion off in the morning. At the crack of dawn, Tom took all the keys, including his car keys and gave them to Peter. He said to Peter, "Before we track this lion... maybe I am going to die. Peter you must get everything, including the car". Then they left the camp and went back to the place where they had shot the lion. They took some time trying to find the blood trail, but after half an hour were on its tracks. They found the lion dead and everyone was happy. Tom said to Peter, "Bring all the keys, including the car keys. Now I am not dead. The lion is now dead." The black staff thought this was amusing.

## *Mamba*
Tom was driving from the tented camp with James Lapinsky to check on a lion bait. As they drove through a burnt out area, with open doorways, they were looking down for lion tracks. Peter and Josiah

were on the back. Suddenly Tom yelled "s... a mamba". James immediately jerked his head back inside the truck. Tom seemed to stare through James at the snake, while in the back the boys were bailing out at speed. James got his M70 .375 rifle on his lap loaded. He thrust it out at the 9 foot black mamba, only 6 feet away. It had its mouth agape and hood flamed and was standing head height. James fired and missed, but the blast disoriented the snake. When it hit the ground, James fired two more times, but the snake escaped and went down into its hole. The men took up the chase and Tom grabbed a 10-foot mopane limb, while James got his rifle ready. Tom rammed the pole down the hole and forced it to come out and it retreated to a tree, where it was to finally receive a bullet. At the end of the hunt the trophy fees included; buffalo 1200 US, hyena 200 US, baboon 25 US and a black mamba 10 US.

### *Difficult Clients*

Tom had some hunting clients who either did not listen or who plainly needed a psychiatrist and not a trophy buffalo to boost their ego. One of his clients brought the wrong shoes and Tom offered him tackies, but the man refused and suffered later on. Tom stated, "My type of hunting is to walk and not sit in the vehicle." There was the client who left him after a steam train started a bush fire in the hunting area and he objected that Tom had spent valuable time fire fighting. Tom took one of his clients to Olive Beadle on the Zambezi River and as they trawled up and down for tiger fish, his drunken client abused the burly fisherman on the bank, much to Tom's irritation. Tom had this to say about one hunt he did down at Malapati. "A good hunting season for me is when I collect good trophies, I don't have to compromise my ethics and I haven't had to fire one shot. I do have trouble sometimes with the clients listening however. I had a Frenchman who was after the impossible and so everything we saw after that, I told him it was too small. I almost had a mutiny on my hands from the trackers, as they don't get their tips, if we don't shoot game. In the end, we had words and I handed him over to Clive. Within twenty minutes they had shot a forty-five inch buffalo that we had already passed up a few times." Tom had taken this rich Frenchman hunting all over the Malapati and Naivasha areas in the Gona-re-Zhou region. He was a high-powered man, working for a French brandy company and was very difficult. The man had shot a 27-inch waterbuck and continuously whinged, moaned and wanted to

*Clive Lennox crosses the Nuanetsi (Mwenezi)*

pay Clive Lennox for a bigger waterbuck head hanging on the wall of the camp. This attitude and the fact that he had shot a 100-pounder elephant near Crooks Corner, just before Tom arrived, did not go down well with Tom. The tusks from the elephant were about 105 and 103 pounds a side and it was said to be a bull from the Kruger. Tom took him out hunting and they shot a klipspringer, which the man wounded and it made many pitiful bleats as it died. The client did not have the stomach to deal with this. Tom did not respect a man simply because he had wealth and decided that this man did not deserve to get a good-sized bull buffalo.

## *Buffalo*

Tom would play "buffalo tag" with his clients. This was a fun filled game, which could get a bit sticky if played wrong. It was played in the long elephant or thatching grass. Elephant grass rose to 12 feet tall and was usually very dense. The trick was to locate one or two daga boys (old buffalo bulls) in this thick stuff. Once this was done, the fun begins. Using the wind and stealth, you would stalk up as close as you could to the buffalo and check out his headgear. Consider though to really check out his headgear properly, you had to get within a few yards, because of the thick grass. This did wonders in the erecting of the short hairs on the back of a client's neck and the intensity of this was almost indescribable. After creeping in to check him out, you either pumped him or turned him down and went back the way you came in quickly! Richard D'Angelo was trying to shoot his first buffalo with Tommy in the Fuller Forest. They needed to get closer to their quarry and this required a careful stalk on hands and knees. Soon Richard was close behind Tom, inching towards some trees and the buffalo. Richard tensely moved forward and in mid crawl looked up to see where he was going. He saw something that made him want to either laugh or cry, but it certainly relieved his tension. The seam in Tom's shorts had split and of course, he had no underwear, so you can guess where Richard was looking! He had to look down as he couldn't bear the sight, but still had to look up anyway in case he crashed into the back of Tom!

*100 pounder at Mabalauta, Bryan on left, Peter centre and Godfrey Clive's tracker*

*Ross Johnson on left helps others handle ostrich at Samanyanga*

## CHAPTER 20
# THE OLD DAGA BOY 1995-2004

### *Matetsi Siding*
Being a minority shareholder at Waterford meant Tom had no choice but to hand over his shares if he wanted to enjoy certain lifelong benefits there. Needing a job he then worked with the new organization, which was experimenting with an interesting mix of socialism and ecology. There was a 'land war' between some of the landholders in the district and Tom felt himself being drawn into this conflict and wanted out. He was also a strong character and had different ideas to the foreign managers on how Waterford was to be run. This led to Tom having to look for work elsewhere and he moved to a new home down the road. This was a railway house at Matetsi siding. It was now harder for him as he had no land and the country was beginning to look politically unstable, but he had to find some work.

## *Samanyanga*

Tom refused to work for Wilderness Safaris in the South of Hwange National Park, as he was not allowed to take his dog there. Working on a ranch seemed more suitable to him and Tom landed a job down on the Samanyanga conservancy near West Nicholson. In the 1980's and 1990's, large ranching areas like Samanyanga (part of Lemco) in Zimbabwe were being turned over to create private game parks. Tom was now working for a multi billionaire named Ralph Soldan who had good taste. Ralph was a fine horseman and a first-class shot with his beautiful engraved expensive .470 Holland and Holland rifle. If Ralph needed to fix the fridge, he would just fly to Bulawayo in his helicopter to collect a fridge mechanic. The airstrip he built was said to be big enough to land a 737 aircraft. Ralph chose a couple of old Daga Boys (name given to older ex Parks staff) to work for him, as he knew they were the best in the business to get the wildlife ranch going. Tom's immediate boss was the energetic, restless, creative, hard working, generous Howard Shackleton. Other members of the team included Richard Aylward who was busy amongst other things on a 35-kilometre electrical, elephant proof, game fence. Richard had lost one leg in a land mine explosion in the Zambezi valley during the war. There was also Stan Elliot and many experienced youngsters to help. Tom was busy on fences, filling in cattle dips, doing water points, pipes and pans and there were roads to work on. He set up his tented camp miles away from anyone in the bush for privacy. Spotty his dog was often carried around; as Tom was afraid the resident leopard would make a meal of him. When he had some visitors, Tom insisted on sleeping near the entrance so that if the leopard took anyone it would be him. Richard would often come around and Tom would show him his gadgets and bring out the scoff box for tea. Once Peter Chauke went on leave and a novice cook was employed and was asked by Tom, "Can you make tea?" "Yes boss" he replied. The aspiring chef then put the tea bags, milk and sugar together in the pot and then boiled it. When Tom drank his tea, he was not impressed.

## *Construction*

In the 1990's, the game populations were recovering in this district on some of the ranches. The Bubiana conservancy was nearby and had a population of about 150 rhino, beautiful scenery and some nice big dams. Over a thousand eland were seen in a herd and there were now other huge herds of antelope. With Samanyanga, Bubiana, Charley

*Tom's camp at Samanyanga*

Davey's place and other wild areas in this area, some wanted to make a fantastic wild area stretching down towards the Gona-re-Zhou. With the removal of the cattle the ecology had improved and some defiant elephants moved in (possibly from the Gona-re-Zhou). They walked along the fence borders and back through the break in point. It seems some of these intruders settled, while others were captured and released on the ranch, with other newcomers like sable and ostrich. While Richard was building a fence across the Bubi River, he had to dig large holes for the pipes. One afternoon Tom took an afternoon drive in his short wheelbase Cruiser with Spotty his Jack Russell. He came to the Bubi, looked left and then right, saw the nice dry river, drove on and plunged into this massive hole. The momentum carried him almost through it, with the front of the Cruiser finishing pointing vertically into the sky, like a rocket that was about to take off. Tom got on the radio and spoke, "bleep bleep, who put this tank trap in the river". Eventually Richard arrived with some labourers to help Tom get his vehicle out of the hole. Tom was embarrassed and walked up to Richard and gave him a sweet from the bag he used to carry around and said, "Please don't tell anyone".

### *River Ranch*
When Tom moved back up to Matetsi, he worked quite a bit as a

ranger on Matetsi River Ranch. There were two girls working at Matetsi river ranch at the Sizimba lodge. One day they were bored and did not know what to do. One of the girls then spoke up saying to her listeners, "what we have decided to do is now... every day, we are going to do something dangerous to make the day interesting." The other girl said, "But we started from this morning." The first girl replied, "Yes we have. What did we do that was so dangerous?" The second girl replied, "We had tea this morning with Tommy Orford!" These two girls became great friends of Toms. While Tom was here he saw some kids running around with socks and shoes, while nearby someone else's kid ran around stark naked. Tom pointed out the naked kid and said, "That is how they should be brought up." Roger Whittal was kind enough to give Tom work, but Tom was now doing less hunting. He would frequently not finish his hunts and would try to hand the clients over to others. He felt he could not get the desired trophies on the place and even though the client was not interested in a world record, Tom still felt bad about it. Being in his sixties meant work was not always easy to find. He was also romancing a Bulawayo schoolteacher helping her financially, when he himself needed support. He was chasing many unfulfilled dreams and tried to set up an anti poaching task force, kids' camps, donkey patrols and wanted another marriage.

## *Youngsters*

Tom often regarded that professionalism had gone out of hunting and was keen to impart knowledge to young hunters. The first time Gary Hopkins met Tom was at Matetsi River Ranch. Gary walked into the house unshaven and Tom seeing him asked, "How old are you?" Gary mumbled back his young age. Tom then asked if his boss paid him enough. Gary continued, "Yes he does". Tom remarked, "Well obviously not enough because you can't buy a razor blade." If you were willing to put up with Tom's cheekiness, you could learn a lot. Gary would go and sit with Tom for hours and talk. Tom would give him the sweet tea, which on certain special days had condensed milk in. You could never go to his house without him giving you something and so Gary used to take something to give him. Gary would help feed Tom's dog Spotty with bits of meat he got hold of. On one hot month in October, Tom came to Matetsi River ranch. He walked in with his hat and zeiss binoculars, knocked on Gary Hopkin's door and walked straight into Gary's room. He said, "Young man I've got some good news and some bad news, what do you want first?" Gary said, "Mr. Orford I want the bad news first." Tom gave him a run down with, "Right you've been reported driving down the Pandamatenga road at a very dangerous speed and hooting at travellers and this and that." After Gary explained it had been an emergency, which had led to this behaviour, Tom said, "all right that explains that... now let's go and fire my .505." Gary was putting his shirt on with enthusiasm when Tom said, "it's got a hang fire problem". Gary said, "Whoa" as a bullet delaying going off in the rifle is nasty and sometimes dangerous. Tom continued, "If you are young and stupid enough, you can fire it." They went down to the quarries where Tom said, "Gary you fire first". When he fired the Rolls Royce .505 elephant rifle, there was a click and then a delay of a few seconds, followed by a mighty bellow. Gary said, "Give me another one" and the second did the same. Tom interjected, "young man you're flinching, you're flinching!"

## *Politics*

Rob Hopkins (Gary's father) had a conversation with Tom on the Pandamatenga road in Matetsi about 2001. Talking about what was going on in the country Tom said, "That this would never have happened in our day." Rob replied, "Tom let's hand it over now, we lost the war, now it's done." Tom looked back with a faraway look on his face, shook his head, walked off and said, "I dunno." He was probably hoping things would come right. The political state of the country had taken a turn for the worse and many people in the opposition MDC party were dying. Tom was not optimistic about Africa's future and stated, "One of the world's great losses is that Nelson Mandela was not younger and is not still in power. This other guy Mbeki?" He said "our mob here are typical of all ex communists and socialists, corrupt thieves etc. who only care about themselves." In the 2000 elections, Tom came to the Young's camp at Bingwa ranch. Things were looking bad and Tom had plans to organize sandbags, bring all his rifles and fix up their camp as a military camp. He was going to fortify it for them and they were going to let the woman out of the country. Tom was not happy with the ruling party at the time, one reason being that as he was a non-party cardholder; he was not allowed to buy mealie meal, the staple food in the country. The government also began to target the white community in a big way. One of the ways they did this was to chase people off their farms

*War vet sign telling Mike Bramford to move out*

and take their personal possessions. Mike Bramford who worked on Matetsi River Ranch was an active and courageous MDC member, who Tom often helped. One day the war vets (political supporters of the ruling party and often violent) and the police arrived in a mob with the intention of taking over the ranch. Tom was babysitting the ranch house while Mike was away. The police and the war vets arrived at the security fence gate and Tom was there to meet them. They said to Tom in a threatening manner, "well what are you still doing here?" Tom replied, "Well what must I do? You can see I am old, you can see I am sick, I can't go anywhere, I can't do anything". They said, "Why are you sick?" He said, "Let me show you". Unbeknown to them, Tom had been bitten on the end of his manhood by a spider. It had now grown swollen, ugly and huge. To add emphasis to his story Tom wanted to show everyone the bite, as it was interesting what a spider bite looked like. Tom pulled down his pants to show them his swollen manhood. In horror they all took off and ran away. After that, they left him alone for a season. The police did harass Tom about his firearms and the much-persecuted Mike ended up in prison for a while on trumped up charges. The war vets had a real go at Mike and made a false coffin, which they placed at his gate. On it was the name and date of his death. One of the vets however stole some poison from the house and thought it was food. He cooked it with his sadza and eating it, killed himself and some of his chickens. The war vets came back early one morning with a message for Tom to pack up, move his kit before dark and go to his own house, otherwise they would not be responsible for any violence. "All whites must move out… the land belongs to them." They said they were tired of waiting and everyone had to leave. In the presence of the police, the war vets 'warned' Tom that he would be beaten on his buttocks if he did not listen. The police ignored this threat and the crime of a stolen weapon. Tom took the threats seriously and left the house for the war vets to take over Matetsi River Ranch and they closed the boom gate with barbed wire.

### *Gwaai*

It was the same all over the country with the land invasions. Some got it worse than others and at different times, with hundreds of thousands of black farm workers and their families made homeless, beaten up and some killed. In the Gwaai valley Buck de Vries had over 20 lions in captivity, a 50-bed Kumuna lodge, tame elephants and penned crocodiles. The government supporters raided the Gwaai farms and took them from the white farmers. Sport hunters shot Buck's crocs in the three pens as trophies. All the game on the ranch was slaughtered, with some being given to political trainees at Kamativi. The first time Buck returned to his farm after a month to see how things were, he found the lions were not fed in their cages and were half dead. The lions were let out the pens, but they had to be shot, as they tried to come back. The two tame elephant used to be chained up and would be taken by their handlers into the bush to feed. The handler was chased away leaving the elephants without food and water for about a week. Someone had to sneak back onto the farm at night to release them. Kamuna lodge had all its bedding, crockery, furniture etc stolen.

### *Home*

Tom loved Matetsi and would drive down the roads just to find out what was going on. This was the home of the "Poor old crippled hippo, lost in paradise," as he once noted about a resident hippo. As Tom got older, he like many older folk became more eccentric. He always had rules in his Matetsi railway house and especially in the bathroom. Here one would find written instructions on how much strips of toilet paper one could use and how to use the toilet properly. Sometimes he would even run the bath for the guests, so it was done properly. He got on well with his black neighbour, but would give the PTC telephone staff a hard time if the phone stopped working. They eventually got to know Tom and even did him a favour by helping dig his garden for him. Tom would give scarce fuel and other things to his friends even though he was quite often hard up. At the Matetsi siding houses, plenty of baboon caused havoc eating the maize, paw paws, bananas, mangoes and vegetables. To shoot them he would place mangoes out the back door and waited in ambush by hiding in the bathroom. After shooting one of the baboons that was troubling his black neighbour he cried, "Come and get your baboon and bury it or throw it away." He also told Kwanele his neighbour that it was a human being.

## *Daga Boy*

Tom was now a true 'Daga Boy'. Daga is a word for mud and this term refers to old buffalo bulls. These bulls are clever, independent, and defiant, have character, and are dangerous and unpredictable, just like Tom. Scott Bailey was told not to go and see old man Tom; otherwise, Tom might accuse him of poaching, as with Tom the law was the law. Scott went anyway out of curiosity to visit Tom at his old railway house. Tom would send the boy to open the gate for you if he felt you deserved to enter. When some strangers came to Tom's gate and he regarded them as poachers or bad guys, the response was, "what do you want?" and then, "f... off". He could be crude to those sorts of people. When Scott told Tom who he was working for, the response was, "Ahee working for crooks eh." He was referring to the same people who told Scott not to visit Tom. The two became good friends, with Scott helping Tom out with his shopping and in return, Scott was let in on all the secrets of firearms, hunting etc. The youngster would often get orders from Tom to go on antipoaching patrols, even though he was not working for Tom. Tom was well informed by his black friends about the activities of the poachers and the white operators. Tom tried his hand at training up an antipoaching team, which he wanted to operate in the district. He trained his men in a hard military style and they could be seen early in the morning at Matetsi siding. At his house, he would sit under his mango trees at his table with a cup of tea and drill them all day. They were taught a lot about rifles and when marching down the Pandamatenga road, he would give orders like a sergeant major. Down the road, they would go, in their heavy overalls and boots and as the morning progressed, they would sweat in the heat. The men sometimes laughed at his jokes so much that they would curl up with laughter. Others found it too tough and ran away. Doing antipoaching meant having to deal with the Forestry commission, which was a large landholder in the area. Tom was not always impressed with them. After visiting one of their managers he wrote in his diary, "Discuss liaison with patrols along our common boundary and hot pursuit. He is not very bright, squalid office, half eaten mealie cob on desk."

### *Dogs & Bats*

Tom's house at Matetsi siding was full of bats, squadrons of them. When Bryan slept there, he decided to sleep in the car rather than put up with the bats. The Young family paid Tom a visit for a few days and they brought their sausage dogs along. When night came the bats were everywhere, thousands of them, in the mosquito nets, the kitchen and even the bath in the morning. The bats also left a nauseating smell. Bobby Young's little sausage dogs were killing hundreds of them all over the place. The dogs were jumping and going mad as they caught them all night. Tom was not impressed, as Spotty his dog did not do things like that. Spotty only killed rats. When going to sleep Tom was not perturbed, as he had a mosi net over his bed, which protected him. All night the bats were flying around and everyone was exhausted in the morning. When tea was made early at daybreak, they said to Tom, "what is going on?" and he defended himself saying, "No these are my bats". After three to four nights, the Youngs had had enough. Tom was very attached to his dogs and would call them 'people dogs'. When the Youngs visited him on another occasion they came along with a tough Staffie Bull Terrier called Roxie. Roxie jumped out of their car while Tom's short legged, little Jack Russell was there. Tom shouted, "Get that dog back in the car quickly... quickly before my dog gets hold of it. I don't want your dog to get hurt". However Spotty was normally left in the vehicle while he was visiting, as Tom did not want him hurt by anything. Once at the Young's they were sitting and chatting and Tom's eyes went funny, as he had noticed Spotty happily playing outside with the sausage dogs. Spotty had somehow jumped out and was promptly placed back inside the Land Cruiser.

## *Bush Loneliness*

Keith, Bobby and Judy Young would visit Tom repeatedly in his last few years, the years when he was lonely. Tom would put some chairs on the lawn and they would sit and talk. If his white plastic mug was there he would say, "That's mine, don't touch," then he would get the drinks box out and give them tea. They were rationed to one sugar each and then he would stir it for you. The Marie biscuits would be brought out and he would give you two each, wrap up the packet and put it away. In the evenings, they would have sundowners and sit on camp chairs, which was signalled by a rattling of keys and out would come the brandy. Each person would get half a tot each and then he would close it up and lock it up. You could then add your coke or whatever and you had to sip it very slowly. Cooking a meal was always a palaver, as it had to be done in a certain way... his way. On his reciprocal visits, Tom would find unfixable vehicles for Bobby (a mechanic) to work on and would insist that his friend fix them. Tom would update them on the latest BBC news as he listened to it all the time. He often came across at lunch to see the Youngs at their abattoir. He would say he did not want any food, but he would load his plate and have his gin and tonic. He would visit them on weekends and on his birthday hoping to get a good reception, but he would not tell you it was his birthday. They knew though and Judy would make him a cake helping him with his loneliness. If the TV was on and he did not like what they were watching, he would get up, go and switch it off saying, "you can't watch that." Often he would get up abruptly and say, "I must go now" and he was off again back to the bush.

## *His account*

Tom was an incredible storyteller who could tell stories in a descriptive way, but could be controversial. Here is a little that he said at this time. "I am in what used to be Denda, which is unit 5. I have spent over a month here going down every by way and every path. My heart was filled with joy when I came here, because as I remembered in the past, when the Landreys were here, there were huge amounts of buffalo, waterbuck, zebra and lions roaring every night in every direction. Now the place is a faunal desert. Covering up to 30-40km a day very slowly, repairing roads, rebuilding drifts and walking around when I left the vehicle, all and every daylong, the amount of tracks I found is really negligible. The one great joy was finding black rhino middens at several points, which could be the

*Albert tries to get the land cruiser out of mud*

same animal moving around. There is also supposed to be a white rhino bull wandering around here and there is an old hippo ...I don't know its sex... that is crippled in croc pools. There are now huge areas over here that, due to uncontrolled fires, have turned into grasslands. These grasslands are mainly Heteropogon contortus and aristida and there is no life in these areas. There is very little bird life even along the rivers or streams. This area was taken over by the Forestry department as a hunting area in conjunction with the other areas. During this period of mismanagement and corruption and everything else, that went on, in conjunction with the assistance of the department of National Parks and mismanagement, large amounts of animals were removed from here. And even to this day the lessees of this area and now Roy Vincent, have (to put up with) hunting parties for relish for National Parks coming down, shooting buffalo and impala around where the Denda headquarters is. Local poachers coming in mainly around Hwange area through the Deka pool areas and Bumboosie have been highly active and sometime last year Roy Vincent recovered a fully maned lion, dead in a snare. He is given a quota of four lions, which he has to pay for up front and if he doesn't shoot them he loses the money. This is another part of the corruption of this organization. There used to be a system here some time ago, which was in my opinion an extremely fine method of insuring that only top quality lions were taken. I believe that the quota of 20 lions for the Matetsi safari area is far too high to produce sustainable big males. There are of course huge amounts of lionesses and hyenas around. In the past if you shot an inferior lion as compared to an A grade lion, you lost a lion off your quota for the following year. I have hunted on almost all the Matetsi safari areas in the years past and Denda and Unit One, which Piers Taylor once had, were the areas once noted for having large amounts of good maned lions. These areas you could hear the lions, I would say almost any night of the year and you know it was remarkable the amount of females they had around. The buffalo population has also in my opinion and other peoples' opinions in the Matetsi area …this is from the Zambezi to Robins area… been declining remarkably over the years. There aren't the huge numbers of buffalo herds. Now there was a researcher working here, an American woman called Cynthia Hunter. And she was working on the declining buffalo population of the national Matetsi herd. Cynthia used to (bravely …they wouldn't allow her to carry a weapon)… walk around following buffalo herds with a Kish hound, which had an American passport amongst other things. Taking notes and studying the buffalo population, she was of the opinion over the years that the buffalo population was declining in comparison to the burgeoning elephant population, because the elephants were actually keeping the young buffalo… the weaners and the long weaners away from the waterholes when the rains were bad. This caused massive die offs. She had 10 or 11 incidents with lions and considering all that she carried was a stick and her Kish hound with her and her GPS, made her a remarkable woman. In comparison, to all the other so called biologists who are actually ologists. I really have over the years lost my respect for most of the ologists, because all they were interested in was writing more papers for themselves to get higher degrees. The most noted examples were those that acquired the posthole diggers diploma. There were of course exceptions to the rule."

## *Speeding*

When Tom drove, he had a habit of drifting into the middle of the road and of going very, very slowly. Tom would panic if you went faster than 90 kilometres an hour. One day Keith Young met Tom in a Bulawayo bookshop. Tom was going back up to Matetsi, while Keith was going to Livingstone and he was fully loaded. Tom asked Keith where he was going and said, "well I am going up tomorrow, let's go together." So Keith agreed and they left next morning at about four in the morning for the Falls. They drove for about an hour and stopped to have a pee and a rest. Spotty was tied up, the table laid and then they had half an hour for breakfast. They continued in the convoy with Tom leading at 60-70 kilometres an hour. Tom was then stopping every few kilometres and Keith was getting irritated as he was in a hurry to get to Zambia. Tom would say, "Ah this is the place." They would lock up the vehicles and he would take Keith for a walk in the bush, where Tom would find various berries to eat. Another hundred kilometres and it was teatime and out would come the Walters Bakery rolls, with bits and pieces from Farm Fresh, as Keith got more frustrated. At lunchtime, they arrived at Half Way House (only about 220km). Later they got to Hwange as the sun was going down and had an ice cream at Coronation Motors. It was now too late for Keith to get to Zambia and they only reached Matetsi about 380 kilometres from Bulawayo that evening.

### *Eccentricity*

Bobby Young went to town with Tom, who took along his wildebeest tail. They went to the bank and were in the queue and some people started to press against Tom in the line. Tom started swishing the tail around and made a noise to frighten them. It worked as he got the space he wanted, but Bob found it embarrassing and avoided going to the bank again with Tom. Tom could also give them a good whack with his tail. Tom would also sit down and talk with the black folk for ages when in town. Nevertheless, Tom did not want to live in town, as there were no lions. Even when he was getting old and needed more financial attention from the family, he resisted it. He had his usual stop over places and friends to see in Bulawayo and he was feisty, loyal and ready for whatever came his way. On one occasion, he went to a Bulawayo garage where they worked on his cruiser. They used the wrong spanners on the sump plug, which was something Tom hated. He was furious that the edges of the plug were worn and undid it in the garage. Soon the whole garage was covered with oil. He was a bushman of note and hard as nails on 'Homo sapiens horribilius' as he liked to call certain people. If he did not like a woman, he would comment that she reminded him of a puff adder (snake). On one visit to Bulawayo, Tom popped around to pay for his cell phone at an office. Behind the counter was a big fat mama. The queue was long and everyone was getting nowhere. She then decided to eat her lunch and the queue came to a standstill. Tom complained and she told him she wanted to eat. She sat down to her full plate of rice and a whole chicken. Tom was furious and said; "you are fat like a hippo because you eat all our money." He then told everyone not to pay her. The manager then came and took Tom around, gave him a cup of tea and helped him out. In a restaurant once the service was terrible, so Tom just pulled the tablecloth and everything fell on the floor. Tommy came into Bulawayo to have his teeth removed and was staying with John Herbert for a few days, as his gums healed. Dot Herbert reduced Tom's food to a manageable 'puree' in a blender and Tom was religious about washing his mouth with salt water. When he returned to the dentist a week later the hygienist was amazed at how well healed Tommy's mouth was and asked what he had done in particular. "Well", Tommy said, "you know how... when you've been in the bush and you've got your legs all scratched up, so in the evening you sit in front of the fire and let your dog lick your legs to get the sores really clean? Well"...and the hygienist ran from the room.

### *Stroke*
One night Tom came and visited Bobby Young and he touched the electric fence, which hit him hard and his watch fell off. He then went to try and open the gate a second time, as he thought he had left his watch behind and got a second shock that knocked him again. He was also having black outs at this time, while working on his last job with Roy Vincent at Matetsi. Life went on as normal with Parks shooting a poacher near Pandamatenga on the border and the lions roaring nearby. He planted his spring onions and was enjoying the African nights. However, the pressures and stresses of life finally caught up about a week after the electric shocks. Age, having less security and the recent elections affected his heart. One day he collapsed with a stroke that nearly killed him and Mike Bramford, Howard Shackleton and others helped him. He was to recover a bit with most of his right side paralyzed, but was forced to abandon his beloved wilds.

### *Bedridden*
Tom was to be bedridden for two years, unable to even wash by himself. He was in a prison of sorts, his freedom stripped away and separated from the lions and elephants. He was like a caged lion and

Peter Goosen's opinion was that Tom was dying of a broken heart. He was so mortified at the devastation of the wild life in Zimbabwe and it was difficult for him being confined, especially when you think of the outside and independent life, he had lived. While recovering in the Edith Duly hospital, he became very grumpy, as he wanted his Jack Russell Spotty to be with him. Seeing Spotty cheered him up and the dog was a constant companion and support while he stayed in a Bulawayo cottage. At one time, Tom was taken on his final pilgrimage to Matetsi, to see his house and sort out his things. While stopping at the Hwange garage, Spotty bit a politically inclined youth who walked too close. Everyone had to make a quick departure before Spotty got them into trouble, as the young man went off looking to stir things up. Tom became so protective of Spotty that the dog was not allowed much exercise. The portly dog became like a sausage and would wheeze around the block if it got the rare walk. Tom still had his moments and was giving all and sundry away in his generosity. There was a cook on the property that had very sticky fingers and loved to sneak around. One day he was snooping around and pretended to work under Tom's window. Tom could see he was there and asked the nurse to throw a glass of water outside. She did it; not realizing the man was crouching there and covered him with water. One of Tom's nurses was Peter Chauke who came up to help Tom. Tom seemed to recover a bit with this, but Peter was to die on his off days, as he also had a heart problem. A young man named Bengani took over most of the nursing and later a fund was set up to help finish his schooling. Many helped Tom in his final days. Notable among these were his family, Sue Thomas and Bill Taylor who had the patience to spend hours with Tom when he was not at his best. These and others were worthy of medals in helping to alleviate his suffering.

## *Final Days*

Tom knew his time was up and he did not want to live any longer. In the weeks and days before he died, there were a few signs that he was on his way out. First, he gave his bible (which he couldn't read anymore) to Bengani. One morning he spoke about how in the night he saw this beautiful hyena with gorgeous brown eyes. Then there was the night he woke up to hear beautiful singing in both English and Ndebele. His health took a turn for the worse and he was taken to hospital. His land cruiser, which had been borrowed for two years, arrived back and was parked outside his cottage. Spotty saw the familiar vehicle with its smells and jumped in, sitting there for hours and waiting for Tom. His master was never to return and Tom died peacefully down the road that same day, at the age of 70.

## *The End*
We go to the Zambezi where he started his romantic career as a game ranger. The ashes sink in the swirling waters and sweep downriver, mixing into the wilderness that Tom loved so much, while some hippos watch nearby. I will leave you with some words from Tom's last diaries.

*Lord grant me a steady hand*
*And a watchful eye*
*That I hurt no man or beast*
*As I pass by*

*Father I abandon myself unto your hands.*
*Do with me what you will.*
*Let your will be done in me and in all your creatures.*
*I wish no more than this*
*O Lord! Into your hands I commend my soul!*